A SUMMER WORLD

A SUMMER WORLD

THE ATTEMPT TO BUILD A

JEWISH EDEN IN THE CATSKILLS,

FROM THE DAYS OF THE GHETTO

TO THE RISE AND DECLINE

OF THE BORSCHT BELT

STEFAN KANFER

FARRAR STRAUS GIROUX

NEW YORK

Library of Congress Cataloging-in-Publication Data.
Kanfer, Stefan.
A summer world : the attempt to build a Jewish Eden in the Catskills, from the days of
the ghetto to the rise and decline of the Borscht Belt / by Stefan Kanfer.
Bibliography: p.
Includes index.
1. Jews—New York (State)—Catskill Mountains Region—History.
2. Summer resorts—New York (State)—Catskill Mountains Region—
History.   3. Catskill Mountain Region (N.Y.)—Ethnic relations.
I. Title.
F127.C3K36   1989   974.7'38004924—dc20   89-11782

Excerpts from *Where Have I Been?* by Sid Caesar with Bill Davidson copyright © 1981 by Sid Caesar Productions Inc., reprinted by permission of Crown Publishers, Inc. Excerpt from Ellen Schiff, "Shylock's *Mishpocheh:* Anti-Semitism on the American Stage," in *Anti-Semitism in American History* edited by David A. Gerber © 1986 by the Board of Trustees of the University of Illinois, reprinted by permission of the University of Illinois Press. Excerpt from "Al Harei Catskill" by Maurice Samuel from *The Menorah Treasury*, used by permission of The Jewish Publication Society. Reprinted with permission of Atheneum Publishers, an imprint of Macmillan Publishing Company from *Jerry Lewis: In Person* by Jerry Lewis with Herb Gluck, copyright © 1982 by Jerry Lewis and Herb Gluck. Excerpts from *Jewish Times* by Howard Simons, copyright © 1988 by Howard Simons, reprinted by permission of Houghton Mifflin Company. Lyrics from: "The Ballad of a Social Director" and "Don Jose of Far Rockaway" (both Harold Rome) © 1952 by Harold Rome (renewed), all rights administered by CHAPPELL & CO., all rights reserved, used by permission; "They're Either Too Young or Too Old" (Arthur Schwartz—Frank Loesser) © 1943 Warner Bros. Inc., all rights reserved, used by permission. Excerpts from *This Laugh Is on Me* by Phil Silvers, used by permission of The Arthur Fine Association. Excerpt from "when muckers pimp and tratesmen" in *No Thanks* by E. E. Cummings, used by permission of The Liveright Publishing Corporation.

Photograph credits appear on page 333

Di velt iz a redl un es dreyt zikh

CONTENTS

An exhausted Hasid came running to his rebbe. "Rebbe, help. Take pity. My house is burning."

The rebbe calmed the Hasid. Then, fetching his stick from a corner of the room, he said, "Here, take my stick. Run back to your house. Draw circles around it with my stick, each circle some seven handbreadths from the other. At the seventh circle, step back seven handbreadths, then lay my stick down at the east end of the fire. God will help you."

The Hasid grabbed the stick and started off. "Listen," the rebbe called after him, "it wouldn't hurt also to pour water. Yes, in God's name, pour water. As much water as you can."

from Yiddish Folktales, *edited by Beatrice Silverman Weinreich*

A SUMMER WORLD

The Liberty-Jeffersonville State Road Passing Through White Sulphur Springs.
Where the Well Known Medicinal Springs are Located. Five Miles from Liberty.

In the time of the Indians, the region was called Ontiora—land in the sky. In the era of the colonial Dutch, the "Blue Mountains," first spied by Henry Hudson from the deck of the *Half Moon*, were called the Catskills, and so they have remained. The name derives from *kat kill—kat*, sloping walls of earth; *kill*, a creek. In the seventeenth century, the names Kaaterskill, Katskills, Caderskill, Kauterskill, Katzbergs, and others were scattered throughout the Mountains, and even today intonations of Holland can be heard in some villages.

But another group has exerted an even more pervasive influence in the Catskills, and it is their history that this book concerns. For more than two centuries, the Jews of New York, seeking livelihoods and vacations, changed and were changed by, those mountains. Of course the Catskills were not the only rural area to hear the pungent intonations of Yiddish. In the field of entertainment alone, the Adirondacks in upper New York State, the Pocono Mountains of Pennsylvania, and a number of New England lakesides were the starting points for hundreds of Jewish artists. But no other area has been as vital and influential as the Catskills; none has remained so forcefully in the public imagination.

Since this is a social history of the Jews in the Catskills, both those terms deserve an early definition. The first is elusive. The state of Israel itself has not found a satisfactory way to determine who is a Jew, and scholars are still wrangling about the true ethnicity of such figures as Job, Karl Marx, and Marcel Proust. Operating under these conditions, I have found Leo Rosten's *Treasury of Jewish Quotations* full of forbearance and wisdom:

Note. What is a Jew? Morris N. Kertzer's lucid answer, in a book bearing that question as its title, takes up 207 pages. One can list a bibliography of staggering length on the topic. A refreshing lucidity distinguishes the following passage from Dr. Morris Adler:

> Jews do not constitute a church but a people. One of the reasons the modern Jew finds it difficult to define his identity is that the English language offers no term to suggest the complex of ethnic, national, cultural and religious elements that constitute the collective life of the Jew. The irreligious Jew is not read out of the community. Affiliation . . . is not a matter of creed. The religion of the Jew embraces areas that modern man would call secular. There is no instance, in the Western world, of [another] ethnic group whose religion emerged out of its own history . . . the word church does not fit the Jewish situation.

On the easier subject of the Mountains, *Webster's Geographical Dictionary* is admirably concise: "Catskill Mountains. Group of the Appalachian system, SE New York, along W bank of Hudson chiefly in Greene, Ulster, and Delaware cos.; highest peak Slide Mt. 4204 ft.; heavily wooded; many resorts." But I prefer the definition of an old Catskill hand, because it could have been given to the immigrants two centuries ago. "You keep going," he said, "until you get to where there's two stones to every dirt. Then you're there."

CHAPTER 1

IMPLOSIONS

Picturesque Scene in Sullivan County, N. Y.

"I look at it with mixed emotions," Lou Goldstein was telling the audience, his vulpine face poised between wisecrack and regret. "It's like watching your mother-in-law drive over a cliff. In your new Cadillac."

Goldstein had been more than director of daytime social and athletic activities at Grossinger's Hotel and Country Club. He had become a fixture, like the indoor and outdoor swimming pools and the limitless kosher fare. For thirty-seven years, celebrities and guests had taken orders from him as he led his stand-up antic game of Simon Says, peppered with gags tested over decades ("Simon Says put up your hands. Look at that sky. You: Out! I didn't say Simon Says. Last year a lady stands right there and I say to her, 'What do you think of sex?' She says, 'Sex; it's a fine department store.' ")

And now the resort, owned by one family since Woodrow Wilson occupied the White House, was vanishing into the great corporate maw of Servico Inc. The new owners, exuberantly announcing plans to turn the place into a vacation center for young and upscale professionals, had invited the world to watch them "implode" the playhouse where innumerable comics, singers, and dancers once introduced and polished their routines. Dynamite would knock down the floors and ceilings, leaving only a gaunt wooden frame. Bulldozers would complete the demolition.

As they gazed at the trampled grass and unattended facilities, visitors found it difficult to believe that Grossinger's was once the epicenter of the Borscht Belt. In its day the term signified a loose confederation of some thousand Catskill Mountain resorts, named for the Eastern European Jewish clientele who filled the rooms with laughter and rumor, wandered the greenery, searched for mates, and consumed four Lucullan meals a day, including a midnight snack. In between, they cheered the *tummlers*, a Yiddish word for the manic, all-purpose entertainers who were the mainsprings of these resorts. The performers, like their audiences, formed a nation of immigrants: David Daniel Kaminsky, Aaron Chwatt, Jacob Pinkus Perelmuth, Morris Miller, Eugene Klass, Joseph Levitch, Milton Berlinger, Joseph Gottlieb. All were better known by their marquee names: Danny Kaye, Red Buttons, Jan Peerce, Robert Merrill, Gene Barry, Jerry Lewis, Milton Berle, Joey Bishop.

It had all begun decades ago, generations ago, even before Ellis Island teemed with immigrants. A few of the early families, unhappy with the urban struggle, had gone west of Manhattan to try farming on the Catskills' harsh soil. Vegetables would not grow in abundance, but debts and children did, and the farmers were obliged to take in boarders. In time, the old houses became inns, sometimes with names that reflected a yearning for assimilation. The vast and cryptically named Nevele was only eleven spelled backward, in honor of some early visitors. Ratner's old place had large *R*s in the wrought-iron fencing. The new owner called it the Raleigh.

But Grossinger's, like some of the other more confident resorts, clung to its identity. Before the Great War, the Galician émigrés Selig and Malke Grossinger had acquired their farm with a down payment of $450. The year they became innkeepers the annual gross was $81, barely above the poverty level even then. But between world wars the resort business suddenly grew robust. A growing number of Jewish immigrants, at once grateful and uneasy in their adopted land, wanted their families to enjoy some relief from the intense heat and jostle of New York City summers. At the same time, they wanted to be surrounded with familiar food and accents and styles—impossible requirements anywhere except in the Mountains. The Catskills provided it all.

Jennie, the Grossingers' gregarious daughter, acquired some adjacent property, and with an amalgam of public relations and philanthropy she became the lodestar of the Catskills. The plump blond hostess grew famous for knowing all her guests by name, and when they came home after the holidays, the customers spoke about her in the awed tones normally reserved for Eleanor Roosevelt. Politicians visited the arena they called the G in order to court the Jewish vote, athletes journeyed up from city gyms to train at the luxurious rings and courts and fields, and there was always a parade of entertainers anxious to try out new acts en route to Broadway or Hollywood.

Even rival resorts took delight in the Grossinger story. A neighboring entrepreneur saw it in the terms of a Polish proverb: "When the queen is in style, the peasants can smile." After all, not everyone could stay at the G, and the overflow filled many rooms in the surrounding hotels. In any entertainment business, profits as well as recessions are contagious.

During the good years, the walls of the playhouse were festooned with ecumenical snapshots: Jack Benny, Senator Robert Kennedy, Jackie Robinson, Terence Cardinal Cooke, Yogi Berra, Governor Nelson Rockefeller, U.N. Ambassador Ralph Bunche. Powerful friends in the federal government made the resort unique in the Catskills: it was granted its own post office, Grossinger, N.Y. Malke and Selig's little farmhouse grew to an 800-acre estate of 600 rooms, with a 1,700-seat dining area, two golf courses, and a $7 million annual gross. Its dancing masters, Tony and Lucille, introduced the mambo to the United States. Jennie appeared in prime time, on *This Is Your Life.*

Although no one could keep track of all the couples who had met and married at the G, everyone knew a salient reason for the seasonal romances: *The Tattler*, whose burbling editorial style made it the most frequently imitated house newspaper in the Catskills. When the Canadian novelist Mordecai Richler visited what he described as "Disneyland with knishes" he remembered how, thanks to the paper, the painfully shy old maid and the flat-chested girl and the good-natured lump were transformed into "sparkling, captivating" Barbara, Ida, the "fun-loving frolicker," and Miriam, a "charm-laden lass who makes a visit to table 20 F a must."

When Jennie died in 1972 there were the predictable utterances about the end of an era and the coming of new social arrangements. Few paid attention. A third generation of Grossingers was in charge, and if some of the smaller resorts had quietly gone out of business, if not so many of the old regulars were around anymore, there seemed little reason for concern. The small hotels were still turning a profit; owners of the great places were prospering. But so were their guests, and this was not only the handwriting, this was the wall itself. Potential customers could now afford to go to Miami or Las Vegas, to Europe or even Israel. A drive to a second home was very rapidly becoming the weekend of choice, and the city had hundreds of places catering to singles. Almost every month new diet books appeared on *The New York Times* best-seller list and none of them recommended heavy kosher meals.

And so in the fall of 1986, on a floor carpeted in bilious green, under a ceiling of dingy acoustical tile, a few score of Grossinger veterans and journalists gathered to witness the destruction of an old building and an invocation of Jennie's sacred memory. "I think she'd be delighted," said William Meyer, the confident young president of Servico. He went on to describe the changes planned for the coming year: the gourmet dining room, the spa, the whirlpool, the thermal wrap, the two-bedroom condominiums priced at $125,000, the 8,000-square-foot "ac-

tion lounge targeted to young people." The message was un-
ambiguous. History had to go; the Catskill Mountains were
under new management.

But a comedian named Mal Z. Lawrence, who had frequently played Grossinger's, did not find the occasion festive.
"If Jennie were here, she'd cry," he told a friend. His colleague
Mac Robbins, one of the fastest comedians in the Mountains,
was speaking andante today: "It's a sad, sad time. What can you
say? It's the passing of what used to be. The third generation
wanted out." So it seemed; none of Jennie's children or nephews
or cousins was in evidence. Of all the bygone headliners, Eddie
Fisher was the only one who accepted an invitation to the implosion. He had been discovered at the resort back in 1949, and
the story of his sudden ascent from the Mountains remained a
favorite show-business legend. But this afternoon, if he was recalled at all, it was because of the actresses who had married
him right here on the premises, Debbie Reynolds and Elizabeth
Taylor.

Fisher, with hair somewhat darker than one would have
expected on a man of fifty-eight, spoke solemnly about coming
up to Grossinger's as an untried tenor: "I was sent here to become
eighteen." As he reminisced, a young photographer arrived and,
setting up her equipment, asked a colleague to identify the
speaker, once the most popular singer in America. "Carrie Fisher's father," she was informed.

When the speeches were over and Jennie's name invoked
once more, but surely not for the last time, the small crowd filed
out to watch the widely advertised implosion. The dynamite
made a great roar, and smoke issued from the crumbling playhouse façade. The comedians turned away as bulldozers began
to crunch the walls. In profile, the yellow machines appeared to
grin, as barracudas do when they attack an obsolete old whale.

Driving through the Catskills that day, a visitor could have
found many parallels to the passage of Grossinger's. Small towns
that once seemed as Jewish as prewar Lublin, and as roiled and
noisy as Tel Aviv, were quiet and shrunken little hamlets with
shuttered stores and pensioners pushing aluminum walkers

down the undisturbed streets. Each place had the aura of a festival after the celebrants have gone and the lawn is scattered with rinds and empty glasses.

The thousand resorts now numbered less than one hundred, and only the largest were operating at capacity, many of them by offering large discounts, frantic promotions, and unprecedented ethnic events like Italian Nite. Nature was green in tooth and claw. Weeds grew out of the cracks in old swimming pools; moss covered the sides of old recreation halls; wisteria vines pulled down proud old hemlocks. The abandoned Laurel was rotting into Lake Kiamesha. White Roe, where Danny Kaye first capered, was gone. Scores of bungalow colonies awaited real-estate companies, predators as indigenous to the Mountains as sparrow hawks. One by one the old hostelries were being overtaken by shrewd new managers and refurbished with the image of youth, money, and ease. Brochures mailed to New York City extolled the good life less than two hours away and reminded readers that in the days of the Borscht Belt it took twice as long to get away from the pollution and the crowds. "Come to the Hills," said the billboards on Route 17. "Relive past traditions amid modern conveniences. See what brought generations to the Catskills."

In fact, the sight no longer existed. When those past generations arrived in the Mountains exhausted from the labors and the mephitic air of the Lower East Side, and further wearied from the trip across the Hudson and the voyage over miles of unimproved roads, they entered an entirely different province. Summers ago a whole world was here, a place of unparalleled vigor and humor—and sometimes of conspiracy and crime. There has never been a domain like it in America: with performers who shaped the taste of a nation, men and women who affected the operations of film studios and the commercial theater; hustlers and gangsters, basketball stars and basketball fixers; waiters and busboys who were later to run hospitals and serve on appellate courts; and audiences who saw it all from the beginning.

Just when was that beginning? The buyers of second homes, most of them in their thirties, tended to place it somewhere around the 1940s. But during World War II, curious hotel guests were reminded of the refugees who had fled the Holocaust early and come to the Catskills to wonder at the limitless fields and rooms and food. And those Europeans in their turn had been regaled with fabulous anecdotes of Yiddish theater barons in the early 1900s, imperious men with estates that dwarfed the holdings of the Rothschilds. And, as it happened, those tales were true.

Indeed, the impresarios were latecomers; in the epoch of czarist pogroms thousands had already arrived from the Pale. And even that period was late in the history of the Jewish Catskills. As long ago as 1880, the farmers and innkeepers and tourists considered themselves groundbreakers far more revolutionary than any of the eupeptic officials at Servico. And they were told about even earlier immigrants, Jews who had come to the hills long before the nation had a name.

CHAPTER 2

SHOLEM

Clements Lake Farm House,
Liberty, N. Y.

In a worn but carefully preserved account book of 1773, now in the archives of the New-York Historical Society, the Catskills' first Hebrew landowner can be run to earth. A plot near Livingston, New York, was registered to a man known only as "Jacob the Jew."

The distinction must have served to separate him from the region's other Jacobs, all Gentiles. There was, for example, Dr. Jacob Brink, Uncle Jacob to the English, "Oom Yakob" to the Dutch settlers. Germany, already acknowledged as "the classic land of witchcraft," supplied many of the first Catskill immigrants, along with Holland and England, each with its heritage of belief in the Devil and his handmaidens. Nights in the Mountains of eighteenth-century New York had a purity of darkness and a quantity of animal sounds that exceeded anything in the

Old World. It was the rationalist who was rare in those days.

Dr. Brink had the capacity to dispel witches and this made him a rare and cherished professional. Alf Evers, the reigning historian of Catskills past and present, notes that in the eighteenth century, "calling in the witch doctor was not as simple a procedure as it might seem. If a cow refused to give milk, if a previously vigorous man fell ill and seemed to be wasting away, if a child's growth became blocked, if money was lost, butter refused to form in the churn, if household objects took to flying through the air apparently under their own power—in such cases a pioneer would usually try a prayer or two. And if the prayer didn't work, the pioneer would conclude that his trouble was beyond the help of heavenly officialdom. His thoughts would then turn toward the possibility that he was the victim of witchcraft and he would place his faith in the skill of Dr. Brink." When the doctor was in top form, he could stanch the flow of blood from an open wound merely by chanting the phrase "Blood go, blood stay, blood abide as the body of Christ abideth with the truth," and he knew ways of persuading witches to change into cats.

Jacob Brink's energies were said to be at their zenith when he was in the company of another Jacob—Jacob Bonesteel, a seventh son and therefore the possessor of great and mysterious strength against the underworld. In the meantime, there were other Gentile Jacobs filling the land registries: Jacob Longyear, a weaver in his native Germany, became a Catskill tenant farmer. Jacob Chambers, a famous local guide and woodsman, liked to recall the time he tracked down an escaped slave who had fled to the Mountains. Jacob Middah, a Dutchman who sided with the British, was hanged for taking arms against Whig militiamen. Of all the Jacobs, Hardenbergh was surely the most significant. He was a member of the family who had bought the Mountains outright.

In the early eighteenth century, Johannis Hardenbergh had convinced the British governor of New York, Lord Cornbury, that he and seven partners required a "small tract" of land in the County of Ulster, New York. The place was unfamiliar to Cornbury, and evidence shows that geography was not a central concern. The lord's principal occupation seems to have been parading on the ramparts of Fort Anne, the most conspicuous spot in New York City, in women's clothing: he was partial to silk and lace, as befit a lady of his station. Cornbury readily granted Hardenbergh his petition, only to discover, after returning to England, that what was now called the Hardenbergh Patent stretched from the Kaaterskill Clove to the East Branch of the Delaware River, an empire of 1.5 million acres. They were almost all wild, thickly covered with red spruce and balsam, sugar maple and silver birch groves, beech and oak, hickory and chestnut. The Mountains reverberated to the calls and yawps of timber wolves, bear, moose, elk, and beaver, quarry of the Iroquois and Esopus and Mohican Indians. The tribesmen were fine hunters, but oddly trusting; Robert Juet, mate of Henry Hudson's *Half Moon*, wrote about the native Americans: "We came to other Mountaines which lie from the Rivers side. There we found very loving people and very old men; where we were well used." For their trust, the Indians would soon become an uprooted and wandering people, displaced by traders, lumbermen, fur trappers, and other colonists who looked upon the Catskills as a place of business.

For thirty years Hardenbergh attempted to defend his property in the courts against the claims of rival landowners—including the Indians. In the 1740s, his money and temper ran out. After a brief negotiation he and his partners sold much of their holdings to a wealthy New York businessman, Robert Livingstone, also connected to the British royal family. One of the Livingstone in-laws, William Alexander, Earl of Stirling, was a chronic debtor, and in 1772, he began the great tradition of Catskill gambling by holding a lottery for his acreage. A Colonel George Washington was one of the players; he bought half a dozen tickets by mail. At the drawing, two of the six proved to be winners, but before he could move to the Mountains, the lottery was declared null and void. The Revolutionary War had begun.

At its conclusion the country was suffused, as it has been after every victory since, with a sense of idealism and religious fraternity. When the new President took office, the Jews of Newport, Rhode Island, expressed delight to "behold a government which to bigotry gives no sanction, to persecution, no assistance, but generously [affords] to ALL liberty of conscience and immunities of citizenship—deeming everyone, of whatever nation, or language, equal parts in the great governmental machine."

In stately response, Washington declared: "It is now no more that toleration is spoken of, as if it was by the indulgence of one class of people that another enjoyed the exercise of their inherent natural rights. For happily the Government of the United States . . . requires only that they who live under its protection should demean themselves as good citizens . . . while everyone shall sit in safety under his own vine and fig tree, and there shall be none to make him afraid."

The President's reassurance traveled across temporal and physical borders, and it was no wonder that by 1820, at the consecration of a temple in Georgia, Dr. Jacob De La Motta could exclaim about America, "On what spot in this habitable Globe does an Israelite enjoy more blessings, more privileges?" In the north, Major Mordecai Noah provided more than mere praise. He decided to construct a Jewish utopia in his home state of New York.

Noah was not the kind of self-effacing worshipper to disappear into his services and his synagogue. A contemporary portrait by John Wesley Jarvis shows a man of lofty style, dressed expensively *à la mode* in high white scarf and black frock coat; the prominence of his ears and nose is alleviated by long sideburns and a serene brow. Matters have manifestly gone well for him, and his humorous eyes and round indulged chin indicate that since America has been so kind he intends to return the favor. The major was related by marriage or blood to most of the important Jews in North America. His mother's sister-in-law was a granddaughter of Haym Salomon, financier of the Continental Congress. His father's sister had married Ephraim Hart, one of the wealthiest Jews in New York. His grandfather had settled in Savannah; his father had been a soldier in the Revolution. Like many enterprising figures of the time, Noah essayed a series of careers: he was a carver in Philadelphia, the city of his birth, a peddler (like his father), a U.S. Treasury clerk, an editor of the *City Gazette* in Charleston, South Carolina, a vigorous worker for the new Democrats. It was on the hustings that he won his battlefield commission. In 1808, Noah settled in Philadelphia, just in time to write speeches for Simon Snyder, the Democratic candidate for governor. The victorious Snyder did not forget his aides. The following year, Mordecai Noah was appointed to a high post in the Pennsylvania militia. Forever after he billed himself as Major Noah.

The major fought duels and wrote pamphlets—including *Shakespeare Illustrated*, which sought to discredit the Bard by calling him a plagiarist and a purveyor of "indelicate and offensive" material. When Noah was not editing the pro-Snyder *Democratic Press* of Pennsylvania, he was attempting to persuade the governor and his own relatives to get him appointed consul to Tunis. To that end he wrote to President James Madison that he knew "of no measure which can so promptly lead members of the Hebrew Nation to emigrate to this country with their capitals, than to see one of their persuasion appointed to an honourable office attended with the confidence of the people."

In 1811, Madison responded. Noah was named first consul to Riga. War with England kept him from his post, and the restless major went south to Charleston, where he wrote pamphlets in defense of "Mr. Madison's War." At the time there were less than ten thousand Jews in all of the United States, and anti-Semitism was a rare occurrence. But Noah brought out the worst in his enemies, and one of them, a rival editor of the *Charleston Investigator*, wrote: "Your Red Whiskers and Hooked Nose tell me too plainly who you are." It did no harm; Noah was finally appointed consul to Tunis in 1814, and became briefly famous for ransoming two captives held by Barbary pirates. This seems to be the zenith of his achievement. Two years later he fetched up in New York City, where he was by turns a Tammany Hall sachem, journalist, sheriff, and leader of the Jewish community. In his *History of the Jews*, Paul Johnson calls Noah the first American Jew to emerge as "a larger-than-life figure," and asserts that a hundred years later Noah "would certainly have become a movie mogul." It seems more likely that the major, with his affection for power, fantasy, and journalism, would have been drawn to the role of Secretary of State.

Given the man's extraordinary *vita*, it is hardly surprising that in 1824 Noah became the first of his religion to be entertained at a resort in the Catskills. The hotel was called the House on the Pine Orchard, located near the Kaaterskill Falls. Its dramatic settings of rocks and timber had just been celebrated by James Fenimore Cooper in *The Pioneers*. Leatherstocking himself tells an acolyte,

"You know the Cattskills, lad, for you must have seen them on your left as you followed the river up from York, looking as blue as a piece of clear sky, and holding the clouds on their tops, as the smoke curls over the head of an Indian chief at the council fire."

"And what do you see when you get there?" the youth obligingly inquires.

"Creation!" claims Natty Bumppo, dropping the end of his rod into the water, and sweeping one hand all around him in a circle, "all creation, lad." The falls are "the best piece of work that I've met with in the woods; and none know how often the hand of God is seen in the wilderness but them that rove it for a man's life."

"What becomes of the water? Does the water run into the Delaware?"

"No, no, it's a drop for the old Hudson; and a merry time it has till it gets down off the mountain. I've set on the shelving rock many a long hour, boy, and watched the bubbles as they shot by me, and thought how long it would be before that very water, which seemed made for the wilderness, would be under the bottom of a vessel, and tossing in the salt sea. It is a spot to make a man solemnize. You can see right down into the valley that lies to the east of the High-Peak, where, in the fall of the year, thousands of acres of woods are afore your eyes, in the deep hollow; and along the side of the mountain, painted like ten thousand rainbows, by no hand of man, though not without the ordering of God's providence."

These hosannahs received national attention. It is reasonable to suppose that Noah knew of them, and of the suddenly famous tales of Washington Irving. The best of the stories, "Rip Van Winkle," had immediately attained the status of a classic, announcing to the country that it was now secure enough to laugh at its past. Rip, the Dutchman who slept for twenty years and awoke to a new American society, had taken his celebrated nap in the Catskills, that "dismembered branch of the great Appalachian family ... seen away to the west of the river swelling up to noble height and lording it over the surrounding country. Every change of season, every change of weather, indeed every hour of the day, produces some change in the magical hues and shapes of these mountains, and they are regarded by all the good wives far and near as perfect barometers. When the weather is fair and settled they are clothed in blue and purple, and print their bold outlines on the clear evening sky; but sometimes, when the rest of the landscape is cloudless, they will gather a hood of grey vapours about their summits, which, in the last rays of the setting sun, will glow and light up like a crown of glory."

Irving's radiant account might have persuaded the major to build his Jerusalem in the Mountains, only two days' ride from his home in New York City. But he was well informed about the drawbacks of the Catskills: the lawsuits over properties, the rural suspicion of new people, the infertile tracts. No doubt Noah also bore in mind the predicament of poor Rip, whose farm "was the most pestilent little piece of ground in the whole country; every thing about it went wrong and would go wrong in spite of him. His fences were continually falling to pieces; his cow would either go astray or get among the cabbages, weeds were sure to grow quicker in his fields than anywhere else; the rain always made a point of setting in just as he had some outdoor work to do. So that although his patrimonial estate had dwindled away under his management, acre by acre until there was little more than a mere patch of Indian corn and potatoes, yet it was the worst conditioned farm in the neighborhood."

So Noah looked upstate, where land was cheap and accessible. As W. H. Auden pointed out, our dream pictures of the Happy Place where suffering and evil are unknown are of two kinds: the Edens and the New Jerusalems. Eden is a past world in which the contradictions of the present world have not yet arisen; New Jerusalem is a future world in which they have at last been resolved. Noah, like so many American Jews who came after him, was a New Jerusalemite.

With several associates—most of them Christians—he acquired large portions of Grand Island in the Niagara River and in 1825 America's first Zionist published a proclamation:

In His name do I revive, renew and re-establish the government of the Jewish nation under the auspices and protection of the constitution and laws of the United States; conforming and perpetuating all our rights and privileges, our name, our rank, and our power among the nations of the earth as they existed and were recognized under the government of the Judges.

The colony would be called Ararat, commemorating the mountain where another Noah had brought his Ark to rest, and it would be supported by a tax equaling three silver shekels "upon each Jew throughout the world." The prominent were invited to visit there, among them the Chief Rabbis of France and Great Britain, European and American businessmen, and sympathetic political leaders. In early fall, a parade passed through the streets of Buffalo to the entrance of the Episcopal church, then the only house of worship in the city. The civic leaders in full Masonic and military dress, and the major in crimson judicial robes, paraded down the aisle to the music of the Grand March from Handel's *Judas Maccabeus*. They made their way to Grand Island, where, after a series of booming speeches, a cornerstone was laid. Its inscription read: "ARARAT, A City of Refuge for the Jews, Founded by Mordecai Manuel Noah in the Month of Tizri, Sept. 1825 & in the 50th year of American Independence."

That was the project's high point. European Jewry did not respond, nor did Indian tribesmen, whom Noah imagined were part of the lost tribes of Israel. Editorial comment was not indulgent. The *New York American* suggested that Noah look for "a convenient apartment in the lunatic asylum" and wondered if Ararat might be a device for swindling the wealthy Jews of Europe out of their money. *Niles Weekly Register*, an influential journal, labeled Ararat a "land jobbing business." The *New York Mirror* ran a mocking editorial: "Fall down! ye men of Israel, and worship this new Judge! Pay your capitation tax, and seven millions will forthwith enrich the treasure of your great Judge—Mordecai Manuel Noah."

Noah ignored the domestic criticism and optimistically turned to Europe. He found no warmer reception there. The Austrian Hebrew journal *Bikkurei Haittim* called Noah "a crazy man," the poet Heinrich Heine dismissed him as amusing, and the Chief Rabbi of Paris, Abraham de Cologna, judged Ararat "an act of high treason against the Divine Majesty."

Noah's grand vision ended as suddenly as it began, and all that remains of it is a three-hundred-pound cornerstone. In the late 1820s the rock was transported to the front lawn of an Albany estate. From there various historians moved it irresponsibly from place to place. It even spent a few months in an outhouse. The stone found what was called a "permanent home" in 1866, when it was transferred to the building of the Buffalo Historical Society. But in the 1930s, the international executive director of the B'nai B'rith Youth Organization found the "dirty, grimy, almost unreadable" antique in the basement of the Buffalo and Erie County Public Library. It was rescued and cleaned in 1958, and in 1965 found space in the Grand Island Town Hall. There it sits today, mounted on a pedestal and encased in glass, a heavy and all too obvious symbol of the Wandering Jew whose sufferings Noah sought to alleviate.

Yet the utopian dream would not die. In 1837 a group of German Jews led a movement to create agricultural settlements on the Great Plains, away from New York City's corrupting influences. They titled themselves the Society of Zeire Hazon, and it is not surprising to learn that they attracted few followers: a group known as the Tender Sheep is not likely to engender confidence. Nonetheless, the believers pushed on.

"Recent immigrants," they reported, "have endeavored to gain a livelihood by pursuing their different occupations, but owing to the difficulties with which they have to contend . . . [were] unable to lay up anything for their future support . . . [therefore] we have organized into an association, for the purpose of removing West, and settling on some part of the Public Lands, suitable for agricultural purposes."

Their aims were lofty, their timing catastrophic. Since the beginning of the Andrew Jackson Presidency in 1828, currency had been euphorically issued. Speculation was endemic; new towns and cities were constructed in months, and fortunes were created in weeks. And then, under President Martin Van Buren, came the new age of metal when gold and silver, current in Europe, were demanded by the holders of paper promises. The year of the Tender Sheep was also the year of the Panic. Not one of the flock became a Western farmer; most of them quietly abandoned the dream and returned to their jobs and stores in New York City.

But in 1837 another group of Jews were not so easily turned back. Certainly in their closed and anxious world—in the entire United States there were now only 15,000 Jews—they would have been aware of the Grand Island fiasco, and of the aborted voyage to the Plains. They had no wish to settle on an island or to make the long voyage West. If an idealistic colony was to be set up in the New World, why did it need to be so far away? Robert Carter had a solution.

Carter was a Polish Jew with a history of business failures in Eastern Europe and England. But in New York an immigrant's past was his own. It was his character, his business acumen that counted. In a few years Carter developed a reputation, according to a contemporary account, as "a man of plausible ways and engaging manners" who "had a constant eye to the shekels." Hanging about the waterfront as the arrivals were welcomed by relatives, he learned of a faction anxious to leave New York City.

Many of them were worshippers at the downtown temple of Anshe Chesed, and unlike so many other restless newcomers, they were people of some means. Carter had recently taken a four-year lease on a plot of several hundred Catskill acres in Wawarsing, Ulster County. He had paid $5 an acre; his asking price was $7.50 per. The New Yorkers opened negotiations with Carter and his partner, Edmund Bruyn, a Gentile with his own affection for coin. Bruyn was also a frequenter of the waterfront, principally the pier at Castle Garden, a point of disembarkation for immigrants. There he greeted newcomers from Europe with his own stories of a pleasant new life on Catskill land, available for one-third down. After short deliberation, the immigrants agreed to buy 489 acres on time, to be paid in full by 1842. The unsullied earth of the Mountains would serve as their retreat. They planned to call it Sholem—the Hebrew word for peace— and on that site, they said, a society would flourish, devoted to all that was best in Jewish life. In the spring of 1837, without having viewed their purchases, five families, led by Carter, packed up and headed across the Hudson to the future.

No portraits exist of the people of Sholem, but partial and fading records of their adventure reveal adults of goodwill and transcendent naïveté. None was very young; all were green. Some managed to be included in the census of 1840. Only one was then between the ages of twenty and thirty, and two were between seventy and eighty. Their backgrounds were disparate: Elias Rodman, a peddler, was born in Poland; his wife, Esther, in Germany. The furrier Charles Saroni came from Frankfurt. Moses Content's family originated in France. Joseph Davies and Marcus Van Gelderen came from Holland.

In the early nineteenth century travelers had only two routes to the Catskills. The colonists might have sailed up the Hudson to Rondout, then proceeded by way of a canal to Wawarsing, more than 100 hard miles from Manhattan, a journey that would consume at least three days. They would then transfer their belongings to horse-drawn lumber wagons before driving up a narrow rutted road to the site of Sholem. It is far more likely that they came all the way from Manhattan on wagons pulled by their own horses, purchased for the occasion and burdened with the heavy family cargoes of oil portraits and mahogany furniture.

Shortly after arrival, the travelers contracted with local builders. Accounts show that one, Wilbur Decker, received a dollar a day and a quart of rum as his wages. Two of his more experienced colleagues agreed to erect four very substantial houses for $436 each, and two less imposing structures for $275 per house. In addition, they built a synagogue, a store, and an art museum. Clearly this was no ordinary group setting out to learn the lessons of life from nature. That was its glory. That was also its tragedy.

Early in 1838 twelve more families joined the original five, even though it was already apparent that the soil was not going to yield a living. A later scholar, Rabbi H. David Rutman, believes that initial fears could have been mitigated by the biblical aura of their surroundings. "The pioneers," he theorizes, "may have likened their elevated plateau near the Shawangunk and Catskill Mountains to the mountains around Jerusalem." Still, even the figures of the Old Testament needed succor, and in April 1838, a letter from the colony's Committee on Arrangement was sent to the prosperous Congregation Shearith Israel in New York City, petitioning for financial aid. Minutes of the congregation meeting dryly note, "Consideration of the request was postponed."

While they waited, the Sholemites had to live, and there were no crops to feed them. The soil was stony and untillable. Bills were pressing. Children were hungry. It was increasingly evident to the most unrealistic settler that Sholem could not sustain itself with crops and livestock alone, that the colonists needed to look beyond their own rock-pile fences for work. Some of the men arranged to buy goose quills on consignment. Wagonloads of feathers began to arrive from the city. In one of the new buildings they were boiled in oil, scraped, split, and sharpened. The wagons then turned around and headed back to Manhattan with the latest in writing instruments, tied in bunches of a dozen with bright red ribbons. One of the men ran a small fur-cap factory, using local beaver and raccoon pelts as well as some imported sealskins. Others learned the cobbler's trade. A few joined Rodman to become peddlers, the classic Jewish profession. The men hawked used clothing purchased in the city by their wives, then mended for resale by John Kohlman, a Christian tailor who had come up to join them from Manhattan. Others worked in the local leather tannery owned by their landlord, Bruyn. Davies opened an inn and general store where, with an urban refinement previously unknown in the woods, he invited customers into a back room to join him for tea, cake, and conversation.

But economics and locale were against them all. For more than a year the nation had been in a recession, and now rural New York, once resistant to outside pressures, began to reflect the distress. There was no ready market for the goods, and distribution was difficult; the near settlements were miles away, inconvenient to reach in the best weather, and nearly impossible in the winter. Neither the caps nor the quills nor the clothing brought a profit. Even Bruyn was forced to shut down his tannery. Each month Sholem's debts grew more severe. It is a measure of the colony's dire condition that on one occasion the ritual slaughterer killed a day-old calf to provide some meals. An insignificant event in the lives of their neighbors, surely, but these were pious, observant souls and they would have been miserably aware that Jewish law prohibits the use of an animal for food before its eighth day.

By the fall of 1841 the Catskill town records start to show the melancholy downhill process of conveyance and foreclosure. In May of the following year, nine of the properties were put up for public sale. The highest bidder was Edmund Bruyn. The redemption price was $1 a lot. Slowly the colonists made the long trek back to the city, where the ideal of a righteous life in the American wilderness had been made only five years before. Their personal effects were sold at auction and the fine heavy furniture and large gilt mirrors found their way into homes several towns away. Some of the houses were removed to other sites, but the synagogue stayed where it was to become, in time, a dance hall. The last of the colonists bound his possessions to a wagon and drove east. But by the time he reached the town of Lackawack there was no cash left. He unloaded a carved bedstead, sold it on the spot, and bought two meals. One was for himself, the other for his horse.

All but one settler melted back into the life of the city. For Charles Saroni, an urban existence would no longer be sufficient, and his story provides a dark and appropriate finale for the colony of Peace. Shortly after his return, the furrier co-founded Saroni and Archer, Hat Manufacturers. But when the headlines of 1849 blared their news of gold strikes in California, he packed up once more and, as confident and airy as before, journeyed west.

He was not fortunate, and two years later he relinquished his gold-panning equipment in order to return to New York and begin again. He took the long way around by boat; in 1857 it was much cheaper than overland. Even then luck refused to run his way. Saroni's ship, *The Central American*, foundered in a gale. The first mate survived; all other hands were lost.

CHAPTER 3

EMIGRATION FEVER

KIAMESHA LAKE IN SULL. CO., N. Y.

As grass and wildflowers covered the ruins of Sholem, other Jews ventured to the Mountains. Most of them were born and educated in the country where Martin Luther had long ago advised that synagogues should be burned, Hebrew books confiscated, and prayers forbidden to these "children of the devil."

The first of the German wanderers left their homes in the 1830s, when a period of reaction overtook Europe. The principalities of Bavaria had been particularly vicious. Jews were held responsible for a list of national ills from the spreading potato famine to the forbidden literature of revolution. In a process that was to become more refined as the nation organized itself, selected homes were torched and shops looted. Authorities limited the number of Jewish marriages in an attempt to reduce the percentage of undesirable children. By midcentury, what the

Emigration Fever

Israelitsche Annalen called "emigration fever" had taken hold. "In nearly every community," the minority newspaper reported, "there are numerous individuals who are preparing to leave the fatherland . . . and seek their fortune on the other side of the ocean."

Almost half of them sought it with the *pak tsores*, Yiddish for "bag of troubles," as the peddlers named the hundred-pound luggage of wares they carried around on their backs. The New York City firm of Grossheim, Schreiber & Co. advertised to the trade that "German peddlers will find a complete and varied assortment of supplies at the undersigned." In the parlance of the day, German was understood to mean Jewish. The supplies were dry goods, hardware, costume jewelry—anything portable and easy to vend. Sometimes the merchandise was hawked to fellow immigrants in the city, customers afraid to deal with the bewildering American shopkeepers. But more and more business was done in rural areas where competition was less ferocious and prospects could literally be spotted a mile away.

Some great fortunes were built on the *pak tsores*: Adam Gimbel and Benjamin Bloomingdale from Bavaria went on to establish great department stores; the vastly successful financier Joseph Seligman, once of Baiersdorf, started his career by trading two yards of cotton print for a pair of robust hens and carrying them, wriggling and squawking, to a farm where poultry had been afflicted with disease.

But far more often the peddler was an obscure man who remained anonymous, anxious only to earn enough to nourish his family, to buy transportation for himself and his goods, and, if fortune was really generous, to open his own retail shop someday. His was never an easy living. In the backcountry he and his colleagues were subject to taunts, robbery, and, on occasion, murder. Farmers bought on the installment plan. If they defaulted, the sellers had no recourse. Every peddler was crucially dependent on whim and charity: one of them, Abraham Kohn, recalled the winter he and a companion "were forced to stop . . . because of the heavy snow. We sought to spend the night with . . . a Mr. Spaulding, but his wife did not wish to take us in. She was afraid of strangers, she might not sleep well, we should go on our way. And outside there raged the worst blizzard I have ever seen. Oh, God, I thought, is this the land of liberty and hospitality and tolerance? Why have I been led here? After we had talked to this woman for half an hour, after repeatedly pointing out that to turn us both into the blizzard would be sinful, we were allowed to stay."

In the worst instances, the itinerant was called a Christ killer and a usurer, and even in lighter times he was likely to be dogged by a chant born on city streets and reprinted in country journals:

> *On ev'ry path, by almost every tune*
> *Industrious Israelites a living "earn"*
> *By selling colored specs to screen the eyes,*
> *Which would not serve an idiot in disguise,*
> *Purchase by all means—yellow, green or blue—*
> *You will aid one member of a useful crew;*
> *He will not work; he neither starves, nor begs*
> *But peddles healing salve for wooden legs.*

Throughout the Mountains, peddlers became the standard butt of yokel comedy, usually in the ancient role of seducer. Many a traveling-salesman story was born in his wake; Benjamin Franklin had printed a legend that was being modernized and retold in the Catskills more than a hundred years later:

"A Jew pedlar went to a house where he offered his goods for sale, but the good man being out, and all his family, except his wife . . . the pedlar . . . offered to make her a present of a piece of calicoe upon condition of her giving up her charms to him. . . . After taking a repast in the banquet of love, he went about his business, but . . . met with her husband, and having some knowledge of him, said: 'Sir, I have sold your wife a very cheap piece of calicoe, and on six months' credit.' With that the poor man stood amazed and said: 'I wonder at my wife's ill conduct in running me in debt, when she knows that I have a considerable sum of money to pay in a few months' time.' He then persuaded the pedlar to go back. . . . When they came to the house, he ordered his wife to give the pedlar his calicoe again, which she did, after privately concealing a coal of fire in it.

"The pedlar took the calicoe and put it up in his pack, which was a wallet slung across his shoulders, and so marched off, pleased with the thoughts of his success. But for his sweet meat he soon found sour sauce. He, not suspecting the cheat, jogged along till he met with a countryman, who, seeing his pack on fire and just ready to blaze, cryed: 'Hey, friend, from whence came you?' 'From Hell,' replied the pedlar. 'So I perceive,' says the countryman, 'by the flames at your back.' The pedlar then looked behind him, and to his great surprize found all his goods on fire, which made him stamp and rave like a mad man and curse his folly in cuckolding the poor man."

These anecdotes were written from the outside looking down. The most revealing stories were passed about on a lower level. They were brutal farces, in Freud's term, comic biographies told by Jews *about* Jews. This sort of humor always serves two purposes: it uses self-ridicule to anticipate and disarm critics; and it expresses a resentment of those who step away from tradition and start acting like *goyim*.

In 1858, a German-born satirist named Theodor Griesinger offered a case in point with the adventures of Sam Ferkelche, a man who runs around "with his store on his back." Sam finds that the farmers are delighted to see him, but he is "still happier, since he sells at 200 percent profit. . . . His business is no longer in drawers and handkerchiefs and socks and suspenders; he needs also buttons and needles and thread and yarn and lace and braids, and sponges and combs and steel penpoints and pencils, and thimbles and silk ribbon; he needs everything and he has everything." Once he masters the knack of bargaining in English, Sam stops dealing with his fellow immigrants altogether, and concentrates on an "American" clientele. He has only one major affliction now—dogs. "It is peculiar," the author notes, "but there is on American soil no dog that does not bark and bite whenever a Jewish peddler comes. Sam would therefore rather not be taken for a Jew, and he forbids his German countrymen to greet him as such." To the American farmer he poses as a Canadian Frenchman, but "the accursed dogs do not believe it; it is not the odor of a Canadian Frenchman!"

Sam does well enough to purchase a little wagon and horses, and soon he augments his store with cigars and goldware, he claims, from Paris. Griesinger remarks, "God knows that this tobacco was not grown in Havana, but in the Palatinate, and Sam knows it, too, but the farmers and their farmhands don't know it. God knows that Sam's Parisian watch chains, his brooches, his lockets, his watches, his earrings, have never seen Paris, but come from the famous city of Providence . . . God knows it, and Sam knows it, too, but the farmer's wives don't know it and the young fellows, who are glad to leave 'mementoes' to the girls, do not know it either."

The rise of the peddler cannot continue unabated: "Sam dare not show himself himself twice in the same place. Such Parisian gold turns gray and smudgy all too soon, and not everybody wants to puff at his cigars let alone suffer their odor." Fearful of a future on the road, Sam makes acts decisively, forsakes peddling, settles down, and marries his beloved Rebeksche.

"Sam," says his biographer, "is now a made man. He speaks nothing but English, because he has completely unlearned German. His sign does not read 'Sam Ferkelche,' God forbid; it says 'Simmy Fairchild.' Sam has become Americanized."

Professional Catskill comedy begins with this sketch. From here on, the stories will gain in velocity and the punchlines in zest. They will be spoken by men and women with fast tongues and resourceful minds; they will form the bases for songs and an unending parade of sketches, Broadway musicals, films, and situation comedies. But the elements will remain: the striving for acceptance even at the cost of identity; the account of dizzying ascent coupled with a mockery of the climber.

Peddlers could never afford to be still. Contemplation of chimney smoke at sunset had to be done in transit, between calls on customers, riding or hiking from one cluster of dwellings to another. Aesthetics were left to men who could sometimes be seen on the peaks of hills, poking about the vegetation and setting up tripods.

Those Catskill artists had been working with oils and watercolors since the early nineteenth century. At an address before the American Academy of Fine Arts in 1825, Richard Ray, an academy leader, appealed to the painter of landscapes: "No matter what species of scenery is best suited to his taste: if vastness and grandeur fill his mind—if he can command the rich and golden hues of colouring, let the new Titian touch his pencil on the Catskill Mount." Thomas Cole accepted the invitation at once. The painter embraced all the arts. He could render a waterfall with three-point perspective; he was also a natural philosopher, a diarist, a lyric poet. The Catskills, he believed, "though not the loftiest that begirt the land . . . yet sublimely rise." Frederic Edwin Church, Jasper Cropsey, and others of the Hudson River School came to regard the Mountains with the same pantheistic spirit familiar to readers of Wordsworth.

In the painters' arrangement of color and composition, farmers go about their tasks as they have for five thousand years, subordinate to nature, part—and by no means the most important part—of God's radiant works. Cropsey's entirely typical *American Harvesting, 1851* grants trees and mountains major roles. The harvesters are minuscule figures seen as if from the wrong end of a spyglass. But the garden is about to undergo a dreadful transformation; in the foreground a series of stumps appear. The foresters have begun their work.

Depredation was characteristic of the Catskill tanneries. The leather factories expanded in the Mexican War of 1846, and again fifteen years later in the Civil War, with its voracious demand for boots and saddles and outerwear. It is axiomatic that leather must be tanned with heat and smoke, and the fires were fed with the bark of oak and hemlock. More ugliness was on the way. A rudimentary railroad system began to push its way across Sullivan County, promoted by wealthy tanners anxious to finish off the remaining groves of virgin hemlocks. *Lippincott's* magazine vainly pleaded, "Let not the Catskills be made more accessible; they are accessible enough. We want no more railroads, no improved means of transportation to transform pleasure paths and byways into highways. The old lumbering stagecoach was the vehicle best suited to mountain roads." In the meantime, groves and woods were felled to provide homes for a growing population. Grim bluestone quarries unearthed paving material for the new city sidewalks of Albany, Boston, Philadelphia, Baltimore, and Charleston. Cole looked around, and in his 1840 poem, "The Complaint of the Forest," he wrote:

> All then was harmony and peace—but man
> Arose—he who now vaunts antiquity—
> He the destroyer—amid the shades
> Of oriental realms, destruction's work began . . .
> And dissonant—the axe—the unrestraining axe
> Incessant smote our venerable ranks. . . .

The noise of progress, the stench of drying hides, and, worst of all, the presence of people, all filled the once tranquil valleys, destroying what Cooper had called "the holy calm of nature" and creating the Higher Malaise. Despite the lyricism of the Hudson River School of artists, this was not an entirely authentic feeling. Barbara Novak comments in *Nature and Culture*: "Much of their mortal nostalgia seems to have been . . . part of the age's emotional equipment. Nostalgia, which like sentimentality has been called 'unearned emotion,' side-tracked the troubling moral issues raised by progress into comfortable meditations on time's passage."

Authentic or not, the sense of a corrupted Eden pervaded the Catskills. It was emphasized by those unpicturesque individuals who were as out of place on an idealized landscape as a menorah at a church picnic. The immigrants were beginning to come in great numbers.

Between 1840 and 1880 two hundred thousand German Jews settled in America. Most were quiet and anxious to conform to the new rules; they embraced a Reform Judaism that allowed them to be less caricaturable, less reminiscent of the bearded, cringing residents of Europe's Jew Streets. They assimilated rapidly, and one or two enjoyed sudden wealth, bringing a new ostentation to the Mountains. In the early eighties Charles F. Fleischmann, the millionaire Ohio senator of Hungarian Jewish origins, came to the Catskills via the new railway. This part of New York had the elevations and sweeping vistas that his home state lacked. Enchanted, he bought sixty acres near the Ulster and Delaware station called Griffin's Corners and saw to it that the town signs were changed to read FLEISCHMANN's. The alterations acknowledged the family name, promoted the yeast and distilleries that had founded his fortune, and infuriated some local citizens.

"If, as I suspect," one carefully editorialized in a newspaper, "the purchase of a few acres of land followed by a little clever wirepulling can secure ambitious persons as an advertisement of this sort, some steps should be taken to discourage the practice. Tannersville, Pine Hill and Big Indian are designations that may or may not appeal to the poet; but Minzesheimer [and] Hommersloeb . . . will go no further toward making the bard tune up his lyre."

Such objections only served as a goad. Over the course of five years, from 1883 to 1887, the imperious Fleischmann family built itself an elaborate summer compound. It abounded in turreted and terraced buildings painted in what were described at the time as "tasty colors." The senator introduced a deer park, a riding academy, an outdoor heated "swimming bath," and a baseball field complete with professional players. All this was for the amusement of a few dozen relatives and friends. As conspicuously indulgent as the Fleischmanns were, they were outshone by the only other great landholder of the region, Jay Gould. On the thousand acres of his neighboring estate, Gould had installed a game preserve for deer and elk brought illegally from the West, kennels for Russian wolfhounds, and breeding pens for pheasants. The industrialist and descendant of a colonist named Nathan Gold was so mysterious about his personal life and so obsessed with power and property that assumptions were immediately made about his ancestry. "Gould," wrote Henry Adams, "was small and slight in person, dark, sallow, reticent, and stealthy, with a trace of Jewish origin"; and the Catskill naturalist John Burroughs went on about Gould's "Jewish look." The fact that the robber baron came from an old, modestly distinguished English family was irrelevant. He was avaricious and secretive. In the Mountains those attributes were the unmistakable signs of a Shylock.

The natives, mostly workers in the local tanneries and quarries, could hardly be blamed for gossiping about the owners of the Fleischmann and Gould estates. Within five years the plutocrats came to represent the only prosperity for one hundred miles. Fashion styles—loose-cut woolen suits, flowing skirts tinted with newfangled analine dyes—suddenly gave leather an unwanted military look. Tanneries began to sell off their equipment and shut down for good. The quarries had no future either. They were doomed the day that a cheap and durable material called Portland cement was invented. In the Age of Progress it swiftly replaced bluestone as the material of choice for city buildings and pavements.

This decline had its beneficent side. It meant that forests would not be totally destroyed, and that streams could run clean again. Once more the region was advertised as a great nature preserve, and the New York, Oswego, and Midland Railroad began to bring hundreds of visitors through a new tunnel under the Shawangunk Mountains. There were two views of this latest invasion. It might lead the way to financial recovery or it could also bring a fresh wave of plunder. Catskill property holders, torn between nostalgia and anticipation, between suspicion of newcomers and a need for their custom, warily examined passengers as they stepped from the trains onto platforms of the new stations. As closely as the onlookers stared, they could not have seen that the next wave of immigrants was one day to make the Catskills a trove, a sanctuary, and a joke.

In 1881 the new Czar of Russia, Alexander III, resolved to find a solution for the Jewish Problem that had confounded his predecessors. Previous Romanovs had sought to impose Christianity on the Jews, to integrate them into agricultural programs, to force them into army service at the age of twelve, to segregate them in the Pale. They remained obdurate, insular, resistant to any changes imposed from above. To official Russia, the religious Jews seemed to be growing more fanatic, while their secular brothers embraced socialism or Zionism, mysteriously communicating with each other in *zhargon*—the contemptuous Russian term for Yiddish.

Emigration Fever

East of Germany the fate of the Jews was an old story. The city of Vilna had been created in the fourteenth century when Gedymin, ruler of the Grand Duchy, ventured out on a hunt for game. He slept where one of his arrows fell, and dreamed of a big wolf wearing an iron shield and howling as loudly as a pack of a hundred wolves. Awakening in fright, he asked the chief of his priests for an interpretation. The holy man told him that the wolf represented an important place that would rise where he stood, and that the roar indicated its future reputation. Gedymin was pleased with the prediction; he built a city on the site and named it Vilna for the river Vilia flowing through it. Anxious for a population to fill his new streets, he welcomed all newcomers regardless of their religion, and Jews made their first appearance in this part of the world. Some of their families were to endure for six hundred years, through attacks and wars and pogroms, as well as through strangely benign periods of tolerance. But, as always in Eastern Europe, they were subject to the arbitrary logic of someone else's dream. In nineteenth-century Russia a vision of racial purity came to the Czar, and the lethal interpretations were dispensed by his religious adviser.

Konstantin Pobiedonostev, Procurator of the Holy Synod, was put in charge of the Jewish Problem and ruthlessly offered a three-pronged solution: "one-third conversion, one-third emigration, and one-third starvation." So began a virulent series of expulsions and pogroms, culminating in the May Laws of 1882, which restricted Jews from owning land, practicing a profession or craft, and attending schools and universities. These decrees immediately altered the villages and cities of Imperial Russia; anti-Semitism had been granted official sanction and "spontaneous" riots broke in carefully selected cities. One of the sufferers later remembered the thousands of Jewish left homeless. "Of still greater moment," he felt, "was the moral effect which the atrocities produced on the whole Jewish population of Russia. Over five million people were suddenly made to realize that their birthplace was not their home. . . . Then it was that the cry 'To America!' was raised. It spread like wild-fire, even over those parts of the Pale of Jewish Settlement which lay outside the riot zone. This was the beginning of the great New Exodus that had been in progress for decades."

The journey of Eastern European Jewry is an epic told with most eloquent detail in Irving Howe's *World of Our Fathers*. Yet at least the lineaments bear retracing, for the destiny of the Catskills begins in the steerages of ships bound for America. In 1881, 3,125 Jews made their way out of Russia, parting with loved ones, clinging to possessions and customs, traveling by foot, coach, or train to the tumultuous port cities of Hamburg or Bremen. For thirty-four dollars (twenty-five if they could board at Liverpool) they bought steerage tickets to New York. On board, in fetid air and crowded conditions that barely supported human life, they adhered to their kosher diets and subsisted on black bread, tea, and the occasional herring for as long as three weeks. The following year, 10,489 made their way out of the Pale. By the end of 1886, another 38,751 had come to the port of New York City. The immigrants were processed through, first at Castle Garden, then at the Barge Office at the Battery, and finally at the new center on Ellis Island. Some went west and south; the great majority settled in a place where the stores displayed familiar Yiddish signs and the air was filled with the cries and aromas of Eastern Europe: the Lower East Side.

Anything was better than living under the Czar, but hell could still be a place very much like New York. The tenements were filling up and every ship seemed to bring new claimants for space, until the Lower East Side averaged 700 people per acre, more than the slums of Bombay. A *New York Times* correspondent called it "the eyesore of New York and perhaps the filthiest place on the western continent." He thought it "impossible for a Christian to live there because he will be driven out, either by blows or the dirt and stench. Cleanliness is an unknown quantity to these people. They cannot be lifted up to a higher plane because they do not want to be." When the immigrants got work it was usually in a sweatshop, characterized by Morris Rosenfeld, a poet who supported himself for many years as a tailor in clothing factories:

Emigration Fever

Corner of Pain and Anguish, there's a worn old house,
tavern on the street floor, Bible room upstairs.
Scoundrels sit below, and all day long they souse.
On the floor above them, Jews sob out their prayers.

Higher, on the third floor, there's another room,
not a single window welcomes in the sun.
Seldom does it know the blessing of a broom.
Rottenness and filth are blended into one.

Toiling without letup in that sunless den:
nimble-fingered and (or so it seems) content,
sit some thirty blighted women, blighted men,
with their spirits broken, and their bodies spent.

Scurf-head struts among them: always with a frown,
acting like His Royal Highness in a play;
for the shop is his, and here he wears the crown,
and they must obey him, silently obey.

Wanderers who expected aid from their American brethren were swiftly disabused. Of the 10,000 German Jews who had arrived in the United States between 1850 and 1880, almost all had prospered. By 1890, 1,000 of the 10,000 employed three or more servants, 2,000 had two, and 4,000 had one. Half the immigrants were in business. One out of every twenty was in a profession; one out of every eight was engaged in such occupations as tailor, jeweler, cigar maker. Fewer than 1 percent were farmers, common laborers, or domestics. Only one in a hundred was still a peddler. The German Jews, together with the Sephardim who had come from Spain and Portugal two centuries before, constituted something of an elite. When they gazed at the influx of peasant Russians, Poles, and Rumanians they were appalled. These new people seemed to bear a Talmud in one hand and *Das Kapital* in the other. The established groups, as Leo Rosten observes, had turned themselves into cosmopolites, pleased to remember that their ancestors once served as advisers to bishops and kings. To them the Eastern Europeans were nobodies—peasants, proletarians, fundamentalist in faith, steeped in poverty, bound to Orthodoxy and fervent Messianic dreams. The long-settled Jews, noting how many of the green-horns' names ended in *ky* or *ki*, invented a derisive title. They called their co-religionists "kikes."

In Rochester, New York, the United Hebrew Charities, whose members were almost all of German derivation, labeled the newcomers "a bane to the country." The Jews (by which was meant the Western Europeans), they asserted, "have earned an enviable reputation in the United States. . . . This has been undermined by the influx of thousands who are not ripe for the enjoyment of liberty and equal rights, and all who mean well for the Jewish name should prevent them as much as possible from coming here. . . . It is no relief to the Jews of Russia, Poland, etc. and it jeopardizes the well-being of American Jews."

But the tide would not be halted, by Congress, by Christians, or by the Germans. After a series of private debates, the Jewish Alliance of America desperately offered its Plan of Action . . . with Regard to Russian Immigration: "The gravest of evils," said the official Alliance paper, "may be traced to the massing of the newcomers in the great centers of population. . . . The immediate purpose to be kept in view is the settlement of small Jewish communities in the towns and villages of the interior."

In Europe, the great philanthropist Baron Maurice de Hirsch backed these sentiments with grants in order "to give a portion of my companions in faith the possibility of finding a new existence, primarily as farmers, and also as handicraftsmen, in those lands where the laws and religious tolerance permit them to carry on the struggle for existence as noble and re-sponsible subjects of a humane government." This warm state-ment was tinctured with more pragmatic considerations. "All our misfortunes come from the fact that the Jews want to climb too high," the baron confided privately. "We have too much brains. My intention is to restrain the Jews from pushing ahead. They shouldn't make such great progress. All the hatred against us stems from this."

A farm: what better way to provide a fresh start—and a

guarantee that the recipients would remain out of sight? It did not require much effort to convince the Lower East Side Jews. No one had to tell them about the asphalt streets, the suffocating tenements and sweatshops. When they thought of the shtetl these days, their memories were suffused with a golden light. Still, the dreamers were not so foolish as to forget the May Laws, the murderous pogroms and decrees. Going back was out of the question. Instead, they began to explore the possibilities of rural life.

The Catskills had never been more accessible. Every day ferries left from the edge of Forty-second Street and took passengers across the Hudson River to Weehauken, New Jersey, near the depot of the Ontario and Western Railroad. The large, anthracite-burning locomotives that promised no soot or cinders, and sometimes kept the promise, journeyed north and west to New York State towns with the reassuring names of Liberty, New Berlin, and Smyrna. Tannersville grew so popular that a guidebook to the Catskills remarked that it "has become the resort of a very mixed and rapidly moving summer population, and is a great resort, in particular of our Israelitish brethren who love to gather where they can be together." Seekers of fresh air for a few hours could browse through *Summer Homes*, a promotional booklet published by the O. & W. extolling "the peaceful and fertile slopes of the valleys through which we pass . . . almost over the spot where Alexander Hamilton and Aaron Burr fought their famous duel," then travel near the road that "skirts the base of the low hill upon the summit of which . . . Major André was executed as a spy."

Of far greater interest to passengers were the hotel advertisements. In previous decades German Jews were seldom barred, even from the tonier establishments. Eastern Europeans were another matter. A few places now dared to warn—or assure—readers of *Summer Homes* that there would be "No Hebrews" accepted.

The protest was immediate. A writer to the Liberty, New York, *Register* demanded to be addressed in a proper manner. "The word Hebrew," he pointed out, "now has but one meaning, and that is a dead language. . . . We are Jews, not Hebrews or

Israelites." Very well, responded the owners and operators; their establishments would not only bar Hebrews, they would bar Jews.

Until the summer of 1877 only a handful of hotels went public with their policies. That season Joseph Seligman, former peddler, now prominent New York City banker, took his family up to a prominent Saratoga hotel. At the desk of the Grand Union he was informed that whatever policy had applied in the past, "Israelites" were no longer accepted. Seligman, who understood the value of publicity, wrote a furious letter to Judge Henry Hilton, manager of the Grand Union, and sent copies to selected newspapers. They responded on cue with banner headlines: SENSATION AT SARATOGA. NEW RULES FOR THE GRAND UNION. NO JEWS TO BE ADMITTED. MR. SELIGMAN, THE BANKER, AND HIS FAMILY SENT AWAY. AN INDIGNATION MEETING TO BE HELD.

The men had clashed before over political and business matters, but this affair was more of a war than a dispute. Judge Hilton's return letter clarified his views: "The law yet merits a man to use his property as he pleases; and I propose exercising that blessed privilege, notwithstanding Moses and all his descendants may object. . . . I don't like this class as a general thing." Then he added the line that was to travel to the Catskills and beyond: "I believe we lose much more than we gain by their custom."

Hilton's statement persuaded some and provoked others. Several prominent Americans spoke out against the new anti-Semitism, among them the celebrated Reverend Henry Ward Beecher, who dedicated a sermon to the controversy titled "Gentile and Jew": "When I heard of the unnecessary offense that has been cast upon Mr. Seligman, I felt that no other person could have been singled out that would have brought home to me the injustice more sensibly than he." Bret Harte, the grandson of a Jewish merchant, contributed some not quite nonsense verse:

> You may give to John Morrisey supper and wine
> and Madame N.N. to your care I resign,

Emigration Fever

You will see that those Jenkins from Missouri Flat
Are properly cared for but recollect that
Never a Jew
Who's not a 'Ebrew
Shall take up his lodgings
Here at the Grand U.

Mark Twain held his tongue for a while, then responded, "If the statistics are right, the Jews constitute but one per cent of the human race. It suggests a nebulous dim puff of star dust lost in the blaze of the Milky Way. Properly the Jew ought hardly to be heard of; but he is heard of, has always been heard of. . . . He has made a marvelous fight in this world, in all the ages, and he has done it with his hands tied behind him."

Echoes of this concern sounded deep in the Mountains. *The Catskill Examiner* testified for the defense in its editorial of August 11, 1877: "In the limits of our village we have a number of these descendants of Solomon and if we have observed rightly a better class could not be desired."

Like most high-minded editorials, it had little effect on readers. The most dependable feature of anti-Semitism is contagiousness. It may lie dormant for generations, whispered about but unexpressed in actions or laws. But once it erupts, it assumes an independent career. Alf Evers has noted that the Catskill Mountain natives were predominantly old-school Baptists and Methodists. Their preachers had long denounced the keeping of summer boarders as "a snare of the devil." The hotels were equally damned; how could good Christians enjoy an "an ethical vacation" when, everywhere they looked, visitors desecrated the Sunday Sabbath—though they may have kept their own on Saturday—played pinochle openly, often for money, and showed no interest in attending services?

Encouraged by Judge Hilton, upstate New York resorts in the Adirondacks advertised for the first time that "Hebrews need not apply" and "Hebrews will knock vainly for admission." At the Lake Placid Club it was announced that, henceforth, "no one will be received as member or guest against whom there is physical, moral, social, or race objection. . . . It is found impracticable to make exceptions to Jews or others exluded, even when of unusual personal qualifications."

On Coney Island, the railroad magnate Austin Corbin, who hoped to develop a fashionable summer resort, was prepared to use the monosyllable. He assured prospective guests, "We do not like the Jews as a class. There are some well behaved people among them, but as a rule they make themselves offensive. . . . I am satisfied we should be better off without than with their custom."

Now the enlarging village of Pine Hill in the Catskills felt secure enough to open its Anti-Hebrew Crusade. In the local *Sentinel*, readers were informed of twenty local boardinghouses that had "entered into an agreement not to take a Hebrew as their guest for the coming season." The one luxurious hotel, the Grand, added a "Special Notice" to its circular: "In order to exclude the mixed and undesirable element . . . it is our intention to be very strict in making engagements. Each applicant will be required if not personally known to give references."

The situation could not long escape national notice, and as the Crusade continued, *The Forum* weighed in. This was a liberal journal concerned with social issues of the day. Its plain cover was patterned after the Boston-based *Atlantic Monthly* and its tone echoed the sober prose of *The American Scholar*. In the fall of 1877, *The Forum* published, along with articles on "The Infliction of the Death Penalty" and "Dangers of Unrestricted Immigration," Alice H. Rhine's "Race Prejudice at Summer Resorts." She reported in some detail that "in the Catskills especially, more than half the Jewish applicants for board are refused accommodation." Owners spoke out as never before: "It is found that the Gentiles charge the Hebrews with being 'too numerous'; 'they swarm everywhere' and, like the Egyptian locusts, eat up the produce of the land. More specifically, it is alleged that 'the Jews as a race lack social refinement.' "

Nor was that all: "It is said of them that their ill-breeding shows itself in an ignorance of the canons of good taste in dress, which causes them to affect 'patent leather boots, showy trousers, and conspicuous and vulgar jewelry.' "

There were further impeachments: " 'They display a disregard of table etiquette, and ignorance of the courtesies of the drawing-room'; also . . . they show a marked disrespect for the Christian Sabbath, by playing cards in their rooms with doors ajar, so that the passing boarders may see." Finally, there was the accusation received intact from Europe: "As soon as a Jew can afford it he will try to get into society that is above him, rather than remain where he is best fitted by education to stay."

Rhine did her best to refute the charges: she thought it "hyperbolical," for example, "to affirm that 'Jews swarm every-where'" when the country contained, by her reckoning, "two hundred Christians to one Jew." As for the accusation of pervasive vulgarity, "it portrays the characteristics of the great Snob family, that family whose branches ramify through all nations."

But, possibly because the subject was distasteful to readers, "Race Prejudice at Summer Resorts" avoided the most active cause of anti-Semitism in the Catskills: crime. The upstate farmers and innkeepers seldom journeyed to the city, but they knew about it. Their newspapers and magazines told them of the corrupt scene: "No dumping ground," said *Leslie's Weekly*, "no sewer, no vault contains more filth or in greater variety than [does] the air in certain parts of [New York] city. . . . No barrier can shut it out, no social distinction can save us from it; no domestic cleanliness, no private sanitary measures can substitute a pure atmosphere for a foul one." To those who woke up to the aroma of pines and the sound of mourning doves it was no wonder that, given its foul air, the city brimmed with violence. *Wood's Illustrated Handbook* warned visitors to beware of all "who accost you in the street." The rule was to avoid walking late at night anywhere "except in the busiest thoroughfares." A threatened strike of gas workers underlined the urban hazards. "Even with the streets lighted, assaults and robberies are frequent," wrote *Harper's Weekly*. "In total darkness crime would hold high carnival. . . . Every dwelling house would have to be converted into a fortress."

The outsiders' terror of New York was further deepened by three reformers. Each of them perceived city life as a lurid restaging of *Pilgrim's Progress*, complete with Delectable Mountains and the Slough of Despond. Every summer in the late 1880s

Dr. Howard Crosby spent his vacations breathing the pure mountain air of Pine Hill. Every fall he returned to direct the New York Society for the Prevention of Crime. He had a particular distaste for the Eleventh Precinct in Manhattan, a gerrymandered place beyond the law, known as the Lower East Side. There were enough Jewish criminals here to fill the docket every day. Mother Mandelbaum, a 250-pound woman, was the journalists' favorite fence. She, her husband, Wolfe, and their three children lived at 79 Clinton Street in a duplex elegantly furnished with furniture and draperies stolen from the homes of uptown aristocrats. Mother was supplied by a series of colorful burglars, among them Mark Shinburn, who invested his profits in foreign money orders payable to relatives in Prussia, and then retired to Europe to become Baron Shindell of Monaco.

All this was of some amusement in the ghetto, where the right kind of outlaw could assume heroic proportions. Dr. Crosby was of another mind. He found criminal and Jew nearly synonymous, and he regarded the notion of wild beasts escaping from the corral and heading for the hills as a very real threat. So did his successor, the Reverend Charles Parkhurst, and their colleague and counselor for the society, Frank Moss. Neither of the directors had a flair for writing; Moss did. In his influential three-volume exposé, *The Great Metropolis*, published in 1887, a chapter was devoted to "New Israel: A Modern School of Crime." Here was all the evidence Anti-Hebrew Crusaders required.

Moss begins sympathetically, describing the sweatshops "where men and women labor far into the night, without holidays or vacations, at the lowest possible wages, barely sustaining life with the utmost expenditure of force and the most unremitting application." He examines the reason why these unfortunates cannot extricate themselves and concludes that it is nothing more than "a stubborn refusal to yield to American ideas, religious habits and requirements, clannishness, and hatred and distrust for the Christians."

He goes on to find that the colony had its origin in a "willingness to pander to vice and crime." The strong racial traits were used, "not for godly, moral or humanitarian purposes, but for the making of money out of wicked practices."

Few readers could stop after that enticement. Moss goes on to describe schools for thieves that rival Fagin's, "though in them the tutor's name generally ends with 'ski.' " And this is the least of it. The dwellers in Moss's New Israel are "addicted to vice, and very many of their women have no other occupation than prostitution." In this they are aided by "a fraternity of male vermin (nearly all of them being Russian or Polish Jews) who are unmatchable for impudence, and bestiality, and who reek with all unmanly and vicious humors. They are called 'pimps.' "

Strangely enough, Moss has little of the anti-Negro bias of his contemporaries. The Jews are his main concern, and he recalls that "the colored people who once lived in Baxter Street were a decent population and were zealous in church going and other religious duties. They moved away, and the people who took their places were of such abandoned character that Baxter Street became the vilest and most dangerous of all the streets."

As appalled as he is at the sight of debased Jewry, the author, an otherwise grim and humorless figure, finds dialect jokes irresistible, especially if they show Hebrews to be craven or money-hungry. In one: "A thief tried on a coat . . . then suddenly broke away and sped down the street with the new coat on his back. The clerk of the store . . . leaped through the doorway after the thief with his pistol leveled for a good shot. The [owner] stumbled to the doorway, saw the vanishing procession, and then recovered himself sufficiently to bawl out, 'Jakey! Jakey! Shoot him in de leg, don't spoil de coat!' "

In another he tells of a moneylender who charged 9 percent. His client objected: " 'Vhy, Israel, dat is usury. You vould not ask usury from von uf your own beoples!' Then a bright thought struck him and he said, 'Israel, Fader Abraham vill look down from Heaven und he vill see dat nine per cent, und vhat do you tink he vill say!' Israel quickly responded, 'He vill say nuddings. Vhen he looks down on dat nine it vill be upside down, und he vill see only a six.' "

Moss's favorite story dredges up the reliable Satan. An ailing

Irishman begs a priest to bury him among the Hebrews. "Father," he confesses, "I've been a pretty wild lad and I'm thinking that the devil would never be looking for an Irishman in a Jews' cemetery."

But in the end, the author resumes his straight face and gets to the point: "I have made many inquiries . . . among intelligent Hebrews of the district, and uniformly they recognize the unpleasant traits of their people and the danger which they have brought to us but they say that the conditions will improve, because immigration is falling off." Even so, says Moss, "the danger of giving these ignorant and illiterate people the ballot as we do is one that cannot be lightly considered."

The volley of social and moral critiques had a lasting effect. It was not merely that the words were mean-spirited and snickering; they also contained some embarrassing truths. Like all slums, the Lower East Side did breed criminals; like many recent immigrants, the Eastern Europeans had clung to their Old Country habits, with little regard for the Gentile niceties of the spas and resorts. Jewish visitors to the Catskills may have been fleeing the very crime that the reformers clucked about, and they may have responded to a waterfall with the same awe as a Christian. But the critics had spoken, the lines had been sharply drawn, and, as both sides now saw it, there was only one reasonable response to the problem: segregation. The Pine Hill hoteliers heightened their requirements for entry and in the process encouraged a few local vigilantes. A group calling themselves the Yellowstone Cowboys responded. Armed with bowie knives, revolvers, and horse pistols, they entered a kosher boardinghouse run by Simon Epstein, brandished their weapons, and demanded supper. Some sixty terrified boarders fled.

In these weeks of sporadic violence many opportunists appeared, eager to exploit the crusade for their own purposes. In the process they threw it into ludicrous perspective. "Jews or Gentiles?" demands a provocative insertion in the local paper, followed by the anticlimactic "No matter which, they will appreciate it more than a little to find that instrument in order when they arrive. James Warswick, the piano tuner from New

York, who tuned with such remarkable success in the place last season, will be in Pine Hill next week."

Their backs up, the undesirables let it be known that they, too, could employ code words, as they have ever since. From here on, for example, Dietary Laws Observed would be the standard way of signaling the presence of *landsmen*. Still, the Jewish proprietors organized no meetings about restrictions and wrote no more defensive letters to the paper. They could afford to be sanguine. Any weekend rider knew that half the passengers on the Ulster and Delaware Line were Jewish. The travelers had to stay somewhere. Simon Epstein ignored the unpleasantness of the past, moved his boardinghouse farther north to Hunter, and operated the Grandview House. Other hoteliers swiftly followed him.

In the last year of the century, two men testified to the changes in population and style. Albert Nichols, eighty-nine-year-old surveyor for the Ulster and Delaware Turnpike, revisited the places of his Catskill youth. With uncommon eloquence he predicted that the coming decades of the 1900s would see some dramatic alterations. "I am quite seriously impressed that on these hills the Jerusalem of America is to be built," Nichols told a newspaper reporter in 1899. "That ancient people who in the reign of Solomon were the greatest people on earth, now humbled and wandering over the world and whose heart and love are bound up in love of ancient Jerusalem . . . seem to be drawing, providentially or otherwise, to this locality."

And in the same season, in *Summer Homes*—the same *Summer Homes* that had carried hotel ads prohibiting Hebrews—John Gerson boldly published an insert:

> CENTERVILLE STATION—Glen Wild Post Office Rock Hill Jewish Boarding House. 5 miles; accommodates 40; adults $6, children $3, transients $1; discount to season guests; transportation free; new house, newly furnished; prepare our own meats; raise our own vegetables; scenery unsurpassed. Jewish faith and customs

throughout; ¼ mile from Post Office; good road
to station; fine shade; good airy rooms.

This was the first listing of a Jewish resort in the Catskills.
Of making many ads there is no end.

The first decade of the twentieth century had a greater effect on Jewish history—and subsequently on world history—than any previous time since the Spanish Inquisition. Like the Inquisition it started with the murder and exile of a people, and ended with cultural agitations whose tremors can still be felt. The drama that began in the shtetls of Russia unfolded in the Lower East Side and spilled out into the Catskill Mountains of New York State.

On April 24, 1903, *The New York Times* reported the "Massacre of Jews in Russia" with 25 killed and 275 wounded, "many of them mortally, in the anti-Semitic riots at Kishinev, capital of Bessarabia . . . when a number of workmen organized an attack on the Jewish inhabitants." From reliable sources in Russia *The Yiddish Daily News* found that the riots were "worse than the censor will permit to publish." The final count was 120 dead, 500 severely injured, and over 100,000 left homeless. *The American Hebrew* reported "popular belief among the . . . peasants that the Czar decreed the slaughtering of the Jews."

Massacres went on, convulsing the Pale. Revolutionary activities gave the government new pretexts for barbarous repressions. Between 1901 and 1903, of 7,791 political prisoners, 2,269 were Jews. From March 1903 to November 1904, 54 percent of those sentenced for political transgressions were Jews and more than 64 percent of the women who received such sentences were Jewish. In 1904, of an estimated 30,000 organized Jewish workers, 4,476 were imprisoned or exiled to Siberia.

In her autobiography, an exile remembered the main topic of conversation among persecuted Russian Jews. "America was in everybody's mouth. Businessmen talked it over their accounts; the market women made up their quarrels that they might discuss it from stall to stall; people who had relatives in the famous land went around reading letters for the enlightenment of less fortunate folks, the letter-carrier informed the public how many letters arrived from America, and who were the recipients; children played at emigrating. . . . All talked of it, but scarcely anybody knew one true fact about this magic land."

Ignorant, possessed, they fled to New York by the thousands and then the hundreds of thousands. Like their immediate predecessors the Jews arrived at Ellis Island and poured into the Lower East Side, hungry for social justice. Most of them found shelter in what the Yiddish writer Leon Kobrin called "a gray stone world of tall tenements, where even on the livliest spring day there was not a blade of grass. . . . The air itself seems to have absorbed the unique Jewish sorrow and pain, an emanation of its thousands of years of exile. The sun, gray and depressed; the men and women clustered around the pushcarts; the gray walls of the tenements—all look sad."

They were soon to grow more dispiriting. Early in the new century, *The Jewish Daily Forward* received a letter. "I am one of those unfortunates who for many years have suffered from the worker's disease," it said. "Every time I kiss [my] child I feel my wife's eyes on me, as if she wanted to shout 'Murderer!' but she doesn't utter a word—only her face reddens. . . . What can I do when I cannot control myself? I beg you to advise me how to act."

The Forward could only reply, "It's heartbreaking for us to have to tell this unhappy father: 'Control yourself and do not kiss your dear child' . . . with good treatment he might yet live to have a lot of pleasure from his little daughter."

Lower East Siders did not have to ask the medical name of the "worker's disease." Everyone knew it was tuberculosis, the White Plague of the Promised City. The open sewers and over-crowded tenements of the Lower East Side provided laboratory conditions for the breeding of bacilli. Long working hours, crowded apartments, and feverish indoor lives produced the victims. There seemed no way out. Official aid came late, and when offered it was seldom accepted; too many sufferers remembered the abattoirs that passed for infirmaries in Russia. The social reformer and journalist Jacob Riis found that Jewish parents actually hid their sick children from medical inspectors because "they firmly believed" the authorities would carry the young "off to the hospital to be slaughtered." Even so, Riis reported, "officers are on constant and sharp lookout for hidden fever nests."

With good reason. Dr. George Price, sanitary inspector for lower Manhattan, determined that "these buildings in which the Jews lived were crowded, damp, without elementary sanitary facilities, half in ruins. . . . The flats were dark, dank, emitting an unbearable stench, particularly those flats which also served as shops. The inhabitants were in a poor state of health. Children died like flies during the frequent epidemics. . . . Parents were forced to have their children help them in tobacco or tailoring work, or else send them—at the age of six or seven—to work in a shop, which meant physical, psychological and moral deterioration. . . . Not infrequently, we came across buildings housing one hundred families with eight persons (in each room)."

A Board of Health report confirmed his findings: "As many as 119 Jewish families have lived in one tenement house on Lewis Street within the past five years." Hundreds of flats had been occupied by fifteen families within a brief period, and "Many of these houses are known to be hotbeds of the disease, the very walls reeking with it."

Everyone in the ghetto knew the universal symptoms of racking cough and bloodstained spittle. The shiny eyes and febrile, neurasthenic personality of the sufferer were commonplace. Ernest Poole, an investigator, continually heard the cry of the tormented, "*Luft, gibt mir luft*—Air, give me air." It was not something that could be dispensed. As the editor of the *Forward*'s collected letters recalls, "A . . . doctor would call on the sick man and look around his house of three children and his pregnant wife and what could he tell him? Could he tell the workingman to go to Colorado? With what money? So the best he could do was prescribe some cough medicine and tell the man to rest as much as possible. One doctor used to write on the prescription slip, 'Join the Cloakmakers Union.' "

But it was many years before pure air became a part of union demands. In the early 1900s it was an ideal as remote as the Rocky Mountains, an elixir reserved for legends and dreams. And then, quite slowly at first, reports came drifting back from round-trip passengers to the Catskills. In Liberty, on the highest elevation between New York City and Lake Erie, lay the new Loomis sanitarium. It had been built in 1896 with funds from J. P. Morgan, whose first wife had died of tuberculosis. According to Loomis spokesmen, 90 percent of the early patients had shown improvement and 10 percent no longer had any detectable tuberculosis bacilli. Some had actually been discharged. Word spread to sufferers on the Lower East Side. It was not to be expected that they would be admitted to Loomis. However, this was a free country; where was it written that Jews could not inhale the Catskill air?

A Yiddish poet named Joseph Rolnik was one of the first to benefit from this argument. A group of friends saved enough to grant him ten weeks in Liberty, New York. The hotel, he told them gratefully, "stood on a high hill. I slept in a tiny room on the third floor. It was the first time in my life that I was so close to hills and clouds. . . . Room and food cost eight dollars a week. . . .

"We ate at two long tables. There was ample and delicious food. We had meat twice a day. Big pitchers of milk stood on the table at all three meals. The guests ate and drank more than they needed, because we all believed that the more we ate, the sooner we would get well. In ten weeks I gained thirty-eight pounds."

Before the decade was out, an unassuming New York City businessman who signed his name J. Weinberg had arranged to buy a farm near the place where Rolnik was recuperating. Joseph Weinberg was the president of the *Arbeiter Ring*—Workmen's Circle—a benevolent and fraternal society of trade unionists. At one meeting it adopted the slogan "Fight Against Sickness, Premature Death, and Capitalism," and at all meetings it stressed the need for self-respect through self-help; i.e., no handouts from above, and, where possible, independent health care. That was the reason for J. Weinberg's journey to the Catskills. He did not want it known that the Workmen's Circle was planning to build its own sanitarium—the price would surely have risen if the seller had known the buyer's identity. Once the deed was safely tucked in his pocket, he returned to Manhattan to transfer ownership to the circle.

In February 1910, with impressive ceremonies and one patient, the sanitarium opened. Two days later a second patient was admitted, and before the year was up, 130 were sheltered there, every one of them guaranteed a free six-month stay. "Nor is it only their bodies that are ministered to," the official circle historian later wrote. "There are frequent lectures and entertainments by lecturers and stage artists brought from New York."

Even those who had no disease—except the grating combination of weariness and rage that came with living in New York City—started to take interest. The welfare societies and the unions experimentally sent members to some dozen kosher boardinghouses establishing themselves in the Catskills. Very quickly the demand for rooms exceeded the supply. The land rush was on.

Before long, natives of the Catskills were on the defensive once again. It was not enough that the town of Liberty had been invaded by hundreds of emaciated tubercular visitors hacking into their sputum flasks. Miles from the sanitarium New Yorkers in good condition, not to say rude health, were spoiling the atmosphere. As they crowded into a new kind of summer hotel, according to *The Ellenville Journal*, the nearby trout streams turned into "mere sewage channels." This renewed concern for ecology was "given added muscle," says Alf Evers, "by the hostility of many of the older valley people to the proliferation of Jewish boarding houses which brought with them a way of life conspicuously different."

No matter what or who was in the running waters, wholesome environment remained the region's great selling point. "DOCTORS SAY Go to the Mountains," trumpeted a New York, Ontario & Western Railway insert back in 1901. There one could find a "region of Absolute Health at Moderate Cost, 2,000 Feet Above the Sea with PURE AIR. PURE WATER. PURE MILK." Essentially, this represented truth in advertising. There were indeed instances of improper drainage, and places where the presence of hotels had discouraged wildlife. But they were far less damaging than the predatory work of the old tanneries and quarries. Besides, there were compensations for the sudden influx of visitors.

A survey begun in 1909 found that, for the last ten years, more than a thousand farms had been sold to Jews, most of them in a ten-mile strip near Ellenville. The *Journal* began to change its editorial tone. "Nearly every one of the purchased farm houses is used as a summer boarding house," it noticed, "and much of the produce of the land is consumed on the place by the boarders." Old suspicions and resentments had hardly vanished, but the Anti-Hebrew Crusade would find no support here. The once-hostile paper concluded that the new owners had "not come to spy out the land and see if it flows with milk and honey. They know it does and they have come to stay and bear their share in the payment of taxes. They are as a rule law abiding people and will make good citizens. . . . At the present time their methods are much criticized but every year there will be an improvement in this regard."

Was this welcoming policy a reflection of the new democratic ideal, a Catskill version of Ellis Island? Or was it simply a pragmatic view of rural economics? The *Journal*'s reassurances offer a hint: "Presence of Jews does much to put money in circulation . . . and keeps up the price of poultry, eggs and vegetables. Their coming has enabled many a poor farmer to get rid of land from which he could not get a living."

The lessons of Catskill history were lost on some Jewish landowners. Others took the trouble to hear or read their neighbors' history of hard soil, difficult winters, and vigorous competition from more successful farmers in New Jersey, New England, and the South. The shrewdest ones took appropriate measures. A headline from the *Hurleyville Journal* indicated the new movement: HEBREWS BUY SMITH FARM; PAY THIRTY-SIX THOUSAND. The story added piquant details: "It is thought that the new owners, instead of farming it on the scale the farm is capable of (at one time more than eighty cows) they [sic] will keep summer boarders." One entrepreneur obtained a low-cost loan from the Jewish Agricultural Society. He and his family, he assured the lenders, would dedicate the land to raising animals and produce. "Actually," he admitted later, "we used it to put up a resort."

In the summer of 1905, a time when so many farms were changing over to hotels and boardinghouses, a famous expatriate stepped gingerly into the world of New York Jewry. The writer had returned to America the previous year after an absence of twenty years, thereby acting out his own version of "Rip Van Winkle." Henry James had crossed the Atlantic on the *Kaiser Wilhelm II*, a steamship of the North German Lloyd line. Although he was celebrated for his searching curiosity, James never seemed to notice the passengers beneath him in steerage. Another, less celebrated figure did.

Professor Edward A. Steiner, a Grinnell College professor, ventured belowdecks to see that "the 900 steerage passengers crowded into the hold of so elegant and roomy a steamer as the *Kaiser Wilhelm II* . . . are positively packed like cattle, making a walk on deck when the weather is good, absolutely impossible, while to breathe clean air below in rough weather, when the hatches are down, is an equal impossibility." On high, Steiner discovered, "the food is excellent, it is partaken of in a luxuriantly appointed dining-room, is well cooked and well served; while in steerage the unsavory rations are not served, but doled out, with less courtesy than one would find in a charity soup kitchen." He was certain that "steerage ought to be and could be abolished by law. It is true that the . . . peasant may not be accustomed to better things at home and might not be happier in better sur-roundings or know how to use them; but it is a bad introduction to our way of life to treat him like an animal when he is coming to us. . . . Every cabin passenger who has seen and smelt the steerage from afar, knows that it is often indecent and inhuman."

James wandered for months in his native land before he could bring himself to consider these peasants by peering at "the hard glitter of Israel" in New York. He did it one June evening the following year, in the company of another writer. The two men formed what must have been the most unlikely literary couple in the history of the city. The younger man, Jacob Gordin, was the Yiddish theater's first great realist and a dominating presence on the Lower East Side. He talked frequently of his eight children, his adaptations of Shakespeare, his interpreta-tions of Tolstoy's thought. He cultivated a modern Russian man-ner, very evident in Jacob Epstein's charcoal portrait and in contemporary studio photographs, complete with black curly beard and deep-set, glowering stare. His companion was a ded-icated novelist, a master of nuance, a lifelong bachelor, bald, clean-shaven in recent years, tentative in style and speech, as Gentile in his way as the other was Jewish. The playwright pointed the way and chattered on; Henry James did the listening.

What he apprehended was not encouraging. His most thor-ough and sympathetic biographer, Leon Edel, acknowledges that James's "view of Jews in the mass had always been distant; he had repeated the clichés by which their national distinctness was marked in the English novel, very much as Dickens had depicted them in *Oliver Twist*." New York City ratified all of the Master's notions and fears. For one thing, he remarked later, these people bred like animals: "There is no swarming like that of Israel when once Israel has got a start, and the scene here bristled, at every step, with the signs and sounds, immitigable, unmistakable, of a Jewry that had burst all bounds." It was an elegantly expressed variation of Henry Adam's letter to his brother: "God tried drowning out the world once, but it did no kind of good, and there are said to be four-hundred-and-fifty thousand Jews now doing Kosher in New York alone. God himself owned failure."

In the benign greenery of Central Park it was possible for James to unbend, to regard the unbounded with the eye of a painter. There "the polyglot Hebraic crowd of pedestrians" had "none but the mildest action on the nerves. The nerves are too grateful, the intention of beauty everywhere too insistent; it 'places' the superfluous figures with an art of its own, even when placing them in heavy masses."

Downtown the superfluous figures were something else again. All around James was the pulse of cultural life, the voracious appetite for scientific knowledge and dramatic art—the very art that he had found so compelling and at which he had failed so publicly in London. But the great observer had no true understanding of what lay before him. His visual, aural, and olfactory senses were besieged and affronted. The fire escapes that ran down every tenement were reminiscent of "a little world of bars and perches and swings for human squirrels and monkeys." On other occasions he was put in mind of "some vast sallow aquarium in which innumerable fish, of over-developed proboscis, were to bump together, for ever, amid heaped spoils of the sea." In the Royale and other cafés, actors held forth on their work, but he heard only the accented and ungrammatical English that turned restaurants into "torture-rooms of the living idiom." The "Hebrew conquest of New York," he was certain, would permanently maim the language. In the future, "whatever we shall know it for, certainly, we shall not know it for English." The Yiddish theater, to which he was politely escorted, was equally cringe-making. He exited after the first act of a comedy, not because it was incomprehensible, but because its audience offended. Those around him, it seemed, emanated "a scent, literally, not further to be followed."

Others had less affected sensibilities. Shortly before James held the Lower East Side at fastidious arm's length, another

Gentile made New York Jewry the subject of a searching and astonished book. Hutchins Hapgood had all the credentials for snobbism: his family had settled in Massachusetts in 1656, he had graduated magna cum laude at Harvard, and he considered himself a Victorian in the modern world. Yet he was possessed by a wistful curiosity and a total lack of ostentation. Hapgood refused an academic career in order to work for Lincoln Steffens on the muckraking *Commercial Advertiser.*

At the time Steffens was, by his own account, "almost a Jew." He had become as infatuated with the ghetto as Eastern boys were with the Wild West, and nailed a mezuzah on his office door; Steffens went to the synagogue on all the great Jewish holy days, and on Yom Kippur spent the whole twenty-four hours fasting and going from one synagogue to another.

Hutchins experienced the same heady and romantic fascination with a people outside his experience. In *The Spirit of the Ghetto*, published in 1902, he celebrated the immigrants whom Adams and James would not recognize. "The public schools," he found, were "filled with little Jews; the night schools of the East Side are used by practically no other race. . . . Altogether there is an excitement in ideas and an enthusiastic energy for acquiring knowledge which has interesting analogy to the hopefulness and acquisitive desire of the early Renaissance." Hapgood believed it a "mistake to think that the young Hebrew turns naturally to trade. He turns his energy to whatever offers the best opportunities for broader life and success. Other things besides business are open to him in this country."

One of the most significant of those things was the stage. Hapgood did not exit from the Yiddish productions at intermission. The young journalist stayed to observe an unrestricted, awed audience, most of whom had never before seen a drama or comedy of any kind. The theaters themselves were smaller versions of the ones uptown, with chandeliers and balconies and flies for the scenery. They were located on or close to Second Avenue, the main artery of the Lower East Side, where everyone could gaze at the marquee and feel the proximity of culture and pure entertainment. The audiences at these houses could be as boisterous as a crowd at the Elizabethan Globe or as rapt as children at a pantomime. An entire population was in attendance at both the serious plays and at the *shund*—the blatantly commercial fare that told stories of wayward wives, drunken husbands, cruel landlords, and children who married "no-goods." Hapgood observed "the sweat-shop woman with her baby, the day-laborer, the small Hester Street shopkeeper, the Russian-Jewish anarchist and socialist, the Ghetto rabbi and scholar, the poet, the journalist." He wrote without mockery about "sincere laughter and tears [accompanying] the sincere acting on the stage," and delightedly watched "pedlars of soda-water, candy, of fantastic gewgaws of many kinds," as they mixed freely with the audience between the acts. "Conversation during the play is received with strenuous hisses, but the falling of the curtain is the signal for groups of friends to get together and gossip about the play or the affairs of the week."

Given these wide-eyed ticket holders, it was natural that the leading actors were considered demigods. Jacob Adler was recognizable from the rooftops. He had the profile of an eagle and the manner of an Oriental prince, and he strutted down the populous sidewalks of Second Avenue with a black cloak wrapped around his shoulders and a disdain worthy of a silent-film star. Two women left their husbands for him, and he enjoyed innumerable, widely publicized liaisons. David Kessler was famous for his great peasant strength and animal magnetism. Sigmund Mogulescu was the theater's greatest clown and, in Hapgood's eyes, "a natural genius." But it was Boris Thomashevsky who caused the deepest sighs and most uninhibited applause. He billed himself as "America's Darling," and a Yiddish poem dedicated to him (which he reprinted in his theatrical programs) included the lines "Thomashevsky! Artist great! No praise is good enough for you. . . . You remain the king of the stage; Everything falls at your feet."

Among the objects that fell were a parish of enraptured women. Hapgood considered the actor-producer "a rather listless barnstormer," but he may not have been the most reliable critic. More than seventy years later, Boris's sons Harry and Teddy Thomas found fault with *The Spirit of the Ghetto*. The night the writer went to see Thomashevsky, according to Harry, "there was a lot of conversation in the orchestra seats. Father was sick for that performance and his understudy was going on." There was another reason for the commotion. As the cast peeked out between the curtains, they heard low mumbles reporting a unique event: "A goy is in the audience."

The understudy was a phlegmatic performer named Nathanson. The goy, of course, was Hapgood. He was delighted with the play, but marked down the leading man as a "fat, effeminate actor." Harry remembers that "at this time in his life Father was very proud of his figure, and if there was one thing the ladies could testify to it was that he was not effeminate. But in Hapgood's book Nathanson is standing in for Boris Thomashevsky, forever." The evidence seems to support the son's claim. The real Thomashevsky thrived on presents and flowers presented to him almost every night by admirers. Women were known to faint when he made his mesomorphic entrances, barechested and in flesh-colored tights, barely acknowledging the audible swoons. When he played Solomon, the Second Avenue wags said that the only difference between Thomashevsky and the biblical king was that Solomon had to support his harem, whereas Boris's harem supported him.

The other items that fell at Thomashevsky's feet were coins, and he spent them all. In his self-celebrating but strangely revealing biography he remembers that "if Kessler wore a big hat with a long feather . . . Adler wore a bigger hat with three feathers and a gold scarf. . . . I piled on colored stockings, coats, crowns, swords, shields, bracelets, earrings, turbans. Next to me they looked like common soldiers. . . . If they rode in on a real horse, I had a golden chariot drawn by two horses. If they killed an enemy, I killed an army." His dressing room at the People's Theater on the Bowery was filled with tapestries, gilded mirrors, and lamps arranged to cast a seductive light. But this was not enough; a Yiddish matinee idol needed a dacha, a country estate. Others found theirs in the far reaches of countrified Brooklyn or Long Island. Thomashevsky went to the Catskills.

He built his version of a palace in Hunter, high in Ulster County, and on the twenty-acre estate he produced the first Yiddish plays anyone had ever seen in the Mountains. Joseph

Schildkraut, the son of Vienna's most famous actor and later an Academy Award winner himself, was invited to Hunter on his first visit to America in 1905. To the adolescent, it appeared to be "the domain of a millionaire. Even the great director [Max] Reinhardt had not yet achieved this style of living." There were newfangled automobiles, horses, and, best of all, "a part of the spacious grounds had been set aside for an open-air theater. . . . During the summer Father starred here in a one-act play that Thomashevsky staged just for the entertainment of his friends and colleagues."

Thomashevsky's sons never forgot the 800-seat outdoor auditorium their father called Paradise Gardens, and the indoor theater that seated 500 worshipful and loquacious patrons behaving much the same way they did back on Second Avenue. "Originally," Teddy told an interviewer more than seventy years later, "the family went to Carlsbad. Then we summered in Far Rockaway, and finally the Catskills, where there was a substantial Jewish population. Every summer, after a strenuous 38-week season, Father took us up past Tarrytown by carriage and then across the Hudson on the Kingston ferry. And by carriage again to Paradise. And there he was, onstage again."

Paradise included vaudeville—Boris initiated the Catskill convention of nonstop entertainment when he brought professional entertainers to the Mountains. When the curtain rang down, there were poker games that continued through the night. The next day guests could hear brass bands playing on the lawn. On gray afternoons when no live plays were scheduled, silent films unreeled on an outdoor screen. It was during one showing that Thomashevsky started another hallowed Mountain custom of heckling the performer—in this case Boris himself. Harry Thomas recalled that "Father showed a picture he had starred in. He hated his work in the movie. It was shown on an outdoor screen, there were plenty of rocks on the ground and he pelted his image with stones. Then he had it run again and threw more things until the screen was in shreds. Back in New York City, people thought he was smitten with himself, and perhaps he was. But in the Catskills people will do surprising things."

* * *

The presence of Thomashevsky and his friends and colleagues helped to lend Sullivan and Ulster Counties a new cachet
on the Lower East Side. The Mountains were no longer simply
a refuge for the diseased or work-weary, they were becoming
playgrounds of the privileged. *The Jewish Daily Forward* took
notice with a column headed "In the Catskills." The writer, Z.
Libin, describes an encounter with an impoverished old friend:
" 'Do you know a good place to spend the hot summer months
in?' I glanced at him, expecting him to shrug his shoulders and
answer: 'I have no idea, how do you expect me to know about
those things?' But that was not what I saw.

"His face became serious and he answered in a most busi-
nesslike manner, 'If you're doing OK and you can afford to go
to the country, you have to go to the Catskills . . . only the
Catskills. . . .'

" 'It's nice there?' I asked.

" 'And then some . . . the air there is as sweet as honey.
. . . You can have as much fresh milk, right from the cow, as
you like, as many fresh eggs as you want. And the mountains,
the woods—pine trees—high up, just below the sky. . . . You can
pick berries, sorrel leaves, flowers. A stay there does wonders
for your well-being.' "

Libin listens, enthralled. A pants maker with leisure and
money enough to spend his summers in the Mountains. . . .
"And when were you there last?" he inquires.

" 'Me? Me in the Catskills? Are you kidding?'

" 'What did you expect me to think?'

" 'With the kind of living I make? If I can afford one rent
payment on Clinton Street it makes my day. How could you
think such a thing?' "

Yes, Liblin reflects, "he's right, how could I have thought
such a thing? He breaks the silence: " 'Well, how is it that you
know so much about the Catskills?'

" 'My boss sends his family for the summer. . . . His wife
writes him from there and he reads us the letters at work.' "

The Mountains held a special interest for Abraham Cahan,
editor of *The Jewish Daily Forward*. He had arrived in America
in 1882, a twenty-two-year-old firebrand from czarist Russia.

Five years later, he helped to found the paper which he edited from 1907 until his death in 1951. He was the one, Lincoln Steffens later acknowledged, "who brought the spirit of the East Side into our shop [the *Commercial Advertiser*] . . . took us, as he got to us, one by one or in groups, in the cafés and Jewish theaters."

Readers of *The Forward* were for the most part refugees who shared Cahan's background and outlook. What they lacked was a real understanding of cause and country. These he attempted to supply in every issue. The paper once awarded a gold fountain pen to the workman who best defined a strikebreaker: "God . . . took the legs of a horse, the head of an ass, the face of a dog, the hair from a hog, the heart of a hare, combined them and out came a scab." Simultaneously it advertised a ten-cent Yiddish translation of the Constitution as "the little Torah and "the highroad to citizenship, employment, and success." Cahan had visited the Catskills at the turn of the century, appreciated the locale, and, naturally, disapproved of the parvenu visitors. He saw to it that the resort scene was properly—and often wryly—covered by reporters and feature writers.

One series on the Mountains, begun in 1904, describes a pattern of life and leisure that remained valid for more than half a century: "The boarders don't take advantage of the fresh air. They sit either on the porch or under a tree nearby. When the husband of one of the women does come for a few days, she is very proud—and besides, it makes the other women jealous. They in turn can't stand it and send for their husbands. The visiting husbands set up pinochle games and play all day, forgetting their wives."

The unmarried enjoyed their own rites: "The girls are bored and try to find boys; when a young man wanders onto a farm they do their utmost to hold him there. Life in the Catskills is free; ceremonies are ignored, although the girls remain honorable. If a boy doesn't come along, the girls go to look for one, ostensibly paying a visit to another farm."

They could scarcely be blamed; according to *The Forward*'s statistics, in the Mountains there were twelve Jewish girls to every eligible boy. That accounted for a new, Americanized way of spending the weekends: "Some of the hotels have dances. They are free and people come from miles around. There are Chinese lanterns strung up half a mile from the hotel. The crowd in the dance hall is really happy, more than if it were a wedding.

"On hayrides, which are very popular, the noise becomes deafening. . . . There are no seats on a hayride; the girls and women and few boys are tangled up and every few minutes a girl 'loses a leg.' "

Hard as the paper was on hoteliers, it was harder still on insensitive city folk. One column mocked the housewife who preferred her apartment to a farmhouse. When fashion forced her to spend some time in the Catskills, she sulked indoors, waiting for the day she could go home. Then, "the Thursday before the awaited Sunday, she looked in the mirror and noticed that she didn't even have a tan. How could she show her face in New York City? No one would believe she'd been away on vacation. She spent the next three days outside. When she came home, her face was good and tanned, but now it's peeling and looks awful. She's got half a drugstore's worth of things now for her sunburn."

Irving Howe feels that this unresponsiveness to landscape is a result of grinding ghetto life: The people "were tired; they had worked hard all year; they possessed no articulate tradition of nature romanticism; and a plenitude of food was still, in their eyes, a cause of wonder. Many of the men preferred to play pinochle, and many of the women to sit around gossiping, rather than commune with the famous beauties of nature; but it cannot be excluded that some Jewish vacationers did take walks in the woods. A few Yiddish-speaking boarders may even have stumbled upon words of praise for the countryside's 'sweet air.' "

It is true that fatigue and ignorance kept visitors from admiring the sublime. But there was also a subtle religious factor. Observant Jews looked far off to the hills of Jerusalem rather than at the accessible ranges of New York State. One of the great Yiddish writers, Mendele Mocher Sforim, describes the education of a shtetl boy: "Little Shlomo had accumulated before his bar mitzvah as much experience as if he were a Methuselah. Where hadn't he been and what hadn't he seen! Mesopotamia, the Tigris and Euphrates rivers, Persia . . . Egypt and the Nile, the deserts and the mountains. It was an experience which the children of no other people ever knew. . . . He could not tell you a thing about Russia, about Poland, about Lithuania, and their peoples, laws, kings, politicians. . . . But you just ask him about Og, King of Bashan. . . . He knew the people who lived in tents and spoke Hebrew or Aramaic; the people who rode on mules or camels and drank water out of pitchers. . . . He knew nothing concerning the fields about him, about rye, wheat, potatoes, and where his bread came from; didn't know of the existence of such things as oak, pine and fir trees; but he knew about vineyards, date palms, pomegranates, locust trees. . . . He knew about the dragon and the leopard, about the turtledove and the hart that panteth after the living waters: he lived in another world."

Shlomos could not last long in the new world. They looked around with nervous, eager eyes and learned to dress in a different way, to modify their accents, to polish their manners. Cahan instructed them in American behavior in the pages of *The Forward*, sometimes against reader resistance. When he suggested that mothers supply their children with handkerchiefs, he received letters asking what this guidance could possibly have to do with socialism. Cahan's answer: "And since when has socialism been opposed to clean noses?" Then he went to work on table manners. "Not all rules are silly," he reminded his readers. "You would not like my sleeve to dip into your soup as I reach over your plate to get the salt; it is more reasonable for me to ask you to 'pass the salt, please.' " And his newspaper regularly ran stories in English, accompanied by Yiddish translations, so that assimilation could be accelerated. Once the immigrants had a grasp of the new tongue, they rapidly discovered how their fellow citizens conducted themselves, uptown and outside the city limits.

They heard reports from neighbors and bosses and they read about it in *The New York Times*: at the restricted Hotel Kaaterskill "near the clouds," the paper elaborated breathlessly, some three hundred guests, "among them many beautiful and charming women," whirled around a magnificent ballroom. "Before the trumpet call announced the beginning of the ball, the rotunda of the hotel was thronged with them, and their jewels and smiles made the scene a delightful one. . . . There are few summer resorts that surpass the famous Kaaterskill in the splendor of its hills, and the opening festivities of this year has been one of the greatest social achievements in the history of the hotel."

With this description as a model, the larger Jewish establishments attempted to provide a similar grandeur. They raised their prices, hired bands, and advertised for a rich clientele. Sweatshop owners, real-estate speculators, successful merchants, and their wives were delighted to provide their own versions of social achievement.

The Rise of David Levinsky, Abraham Cahan's observant autobiographical novel, describes the mimicry of the Jewish arrivistes at a fictional Catskill resort. At the Rigi Kulm, "the bulk of the boarders [circa 1910] . . . were made up families of cloak-manufacturers, cigar manufacturers, clothiers, furriers, jewelers, leather goods men, real estate men, physicians, dentists, lawyers, in most cases people who had blossomed into nabobs in the course of the last few years. The crowd was ablaze with diamonds . . . and bright colored silks. It was a babel of blatant self-consciousness, a miniature of the parvenu smugness that had spread . . . over the country after a period of need and low spirits." Some families are in attendance for the whole season, but "the hotel contained a considerable number of single young people of both sexes—salesmen, stenographers, bookkeepers, librarians—who came for a fortnight. . . . These were known as 'two-weekers.' "

Saturday-night dinner, in Cahan's account, is not merely a meal. It is, "in addition, or chiefly, a great social function and a gown contest. . . . As each matron or girl made her appearance in the vast dining-room the female boarders already seated would look her over with feverish interest, comparing her gown and diamonds with their own. It was as though it were especially for this parade of dresses and finery that the band was playing. As the women came trooping in, arrayed for the exhibition, some timid, others brazenly self-confident, they seemed to be marching in time to the music, like so many chorus-girls tripping before a theater audience, or like a procession of model-girls at a style-display in a big department store." The socialist is immediately offended by the women who strut "affectedly, with 'refined' mien. Indeed, I knew that most of them had a feeling as though wearing a hundred-and-fifty-dollar dress was in itself culture and education."

The Rigi Kulm is overrun by lonely wives until the arrival of the "husband train." The narrator watches from the platform as males, travel-worn, begrimed, their eyes searching the throng, slowly emerge from the cars. "Men in livery caps were chanting the names of their respective boarding houses. Passengers were shouting the pet names of their wives or children; women and children were calling to their newly arrived husbands and fathers, some gaily, others shrieking as though the train were on fire. There were a large number of handsome, well-groomed women in expensive dresses and diamonds, and some of these were being kissed by puny, but successful-looking men. 'They married them for their money,' I said to myself."

A detested shirtwaist manufacturer, "a man with the face of a squirrel, swooped down upon a large young matron of dazzling animal beauty who had come in an automobile. He introduced me to her, with a beaming air of triumph. 'I can afford a machine and a beautiful wife,' his radiant squirrel-face seemed to say. He was parading the fact that this tempting female had married him in spite of his ugliness. He was mutely boasting as much of his own homeliness as of her coarse beauty. . . . I thought of Lenox Avenue, a great, broad thoroughfare up-town that had almost suddenly begun to swarm with good-looking and flashily gowned brides of Ghetto upstarts, like a meadow bursting into bloom in spring."

Nothing like this had ever occurred in Eastern Europe. These isolated women and the husband trains were uniquely American, and so were the attempts to divert guests with food and music. But they could not yet expunge the memories of the Other Side. Levinsky describes one epochal evening when the diners are being entertained after a monumental meal: "The conductor, who played the first violin, was a fiery little fellow with a high crown of black hair. He was working every muscle and nerve in his body. He played selections from *Aida*, the favorite opera of the Ghetto; he played the popular American songs of the day, he played celebrated 'hits' of the Yiddish stage."

The melodies can barely be heard over a cacophony of gossip and laughter. Furious, the conductor strikes up "The Star-Spangled Banner." "The effect was overwhelming. The few hundred diners rose like one man, applauding. . . . There was the jingle of newly-acquired dollars in our applause. But there was something else in it as well. Many of those now paying tribute to the Stars and Stripes were listening to the tune with grave, solemn mien. It was as if they were saying: 'We are not persecuted under this flag. At last we have found a home.' " With it, they had found a new idea. There was no proper equivalent for it in Yiddish or Hebrew; "vacation" was an unaccustomed word. There was no point in looking it up; for a definition you had to go to the Mountains.

CHAPTER 5

THE LESSON OF WINDY

The Catskills never failed to provide a backdrop for Jewish criticism of Jewish behavior. In 1911, *The Forward* sent a reporter up to the Mountains. He started making notes on the train: "The conductor announced, 'Liberty! Liberty!' When I looked up, I saw that nobody had been idle on the way. They had rehearsed like crazy. It looked as if a hurricane had hit the car. Bones, pieces of meat, egg shells, banana peels, orange peel, peanut shells, onion skin . . . cookies and empty paper boxes. And in the middle, a lonely diaper that some baby had left behind.

"The conductor himself helped me carry my light suitcase off the train and I left amazed at the appetite the Exile had produced."

Sexual appetites were also recorded. In a subsequent article entitled "Country Cousins," a writer named Morris Rosenfeld admitted to the time "I made a fool of myself, and who put me up to it? Some woman in the Catskills whose name I don't even know."

They had gone for an innocent walk in the woods, claimed the author, and he inquired, "Your husband sends you money here in the Catskills?"

"She became annoyed: 'Hey, don't torture me with questions like that! Look around, it's beautiful here, the leaves are speaking of love, the birds are singing of love, the whole forest is full of love . . . take advantage . . . I'm yours!'

" 'But your husband thinks that you're *his*, that you love only him,' I answered sternly.

" 'He's an idiot if he thinks that,' she said, 'I love him too. How do I know that he loves only me?'

" 'Madam, let's go back—it's getting late,' I said.

" 'My love!' she pressed me against her.

" 'It's cramped out here in the woods, I can't breathe,' I shouted in pain. 'Let's get out of here!'

" 'You bastard!'

" 'Come on, madam, let's go home.'

" 'You're a coward!' "

Rosenfeld has the unanswerable repartee: "You're a woman!"

To further amuse readers of *The Forward*, the humorist B. Kovner invented a shrew named Yente, given the gift of a few weeks in the Mountains. She shows her ingratitude with a series of letters to her citybound husband, Mendl. Kovner knew the Catskills well. His pieces are exaggerations, but there is a hard undercurrent of truth to Yente's "Letters from the Country." She begins, "It would have been much better if both you and I had two broken legs, so that I wouldn't have to go to the Mountains." As soon as she and the children got off the train they were besieged by Jewish farmers. "One shouted, 'Lady, stay at my farm. You eat till you're stuffed. . . .' Another farmer, holding a whip under his arm, shouted: 'Lady, don't trust that guy. Come stay at my farm. I have lots of cattle.' A third one ranted: 'Lady, don't pay any attention to him, I have more cattle than any of them. . . . I have a big hotel with 16 bedrooms.' 'Lady, stay at my place,' roared a farmer who was blind in one eye. 'At Yokl's farm you'll be devoured. . . . Last year the mosquitoes at his place ate four babies: three little girls and one little boy.' "

Yente is one of thousands who could not afford to stay at hotels like the Rigi Kulm. She vacationed at a new kind of establishment, the *kuchaleyn*. These "cook-alones" were improperly named. The patrons slept in separate rooms of a large house but shared the overpopulated communal kitchen. There the heat, combined with the squalling children underfoot, the closeness of bodies, and the absence of men during the week led to desperate cooperation and violent arguments.

In a staccato onslaught, Joey Adams recalled the days before he became a comedian, when his name was Abramowitz and his mother fought with other guests "to establish a beachhead at one of the two sinks. Armed with . . . scouring power, each lived by the motto: *'Take the sink—and hold it!'* Even the two ovens and the bread box became battle grounds. Everybody fought for the best spot in the icebox too. The status symbol was the two cubic inches assigned to you, and the top shelf on the front was equivalent to a triple A rating in Dun and Bradstreet.

"Every jar of goodies had a label. The little lump of farmer cheese . . . was tagged 'H. Potkin.' The pickled lox in the wax paper said 'J. Traum.' One always heard such anguished cries as 'Somebody's been at my stewed prunes'—'Who spilled and left the shelf so dirty?'—'All right, so it was a little yellow, but did I give you permission to throw out my farmer cheese?' "

Bungalow colonies were a step up from the *kuchaleyns*: wooden shacks clustered behind the main farmhouse. Both were considered the slums of the Jewish Catskills, but both allowed the poorest Lower East Sider to get some fresh food and air. And both provided *Forward* readers with some badly needed subjects for comic elaboration.

"Here's some news," Yente writes in midsummer. "The farmer's horse just died. The farmer skinned it and arranged to have it gotten rid of. But so far no one's come to pick it up. So the skinned carcass has been lying in front of the house and getting a good suntan. . . . So you can imagine, dear Mendl, what the air is like! The farmer says that it won't lie there forever.

Another day, another week. Eventually it'll have to be removed. If not, he says, the flies and mosquitoes will definitely eat it. Dear Mendl! I hope you enjoy city life as much as I enjoy the country!"

Kovner published his columns in book form in 1914, and soon Yente became the favorite of every literate Lower East Sider. One of the most celebrated pieces described some lonely wives out to seduce a Catskill guest named Khone, who "struts around, as proud as a peacock."

"But when Sunday arrives, Khone is in big trouble!

"That's because on Sunday every woman has her husband around, and ignores Khone—doesn't speak to him, look at him, as if she didn't know him.

"He's all alone. Poor Khone!

"However, last Monday, when all the men left on the 'Husband Express,' and the women had come back from the station, they began to start up with Khone again—but he went on strike!

" 'I don't want to have anything to do with you!' he said sternly. 'I don't want to kiss you, or caress you, walk arm-in-arm with you, hold you on my lap, go berry-picking with you or tell you stories! If I'm good enough for you all week, I'm good enough for you on Sunday too!'

"The strike lasted from Monday morning until Tuesday at dinner time, and Khone won.

"The first woman to give up was a brunette, about twenty-two or twenty-three, nice looking with dark eyes.

"She walked up to Khone, took hold of his chin, and said: 'Mr. Khone, please, don't be angry.'

"Khone grinned and stroked her right cheek, and she sat down on his lap.

"When the other women saw the brunette sitting on his lap and him hugging her in a very 'friendly' way, they called a meeting next to the stable and decided to give in to Khone's demands.

"And that's how the strike was settled."

On less frivolous occasions *The Forward* reminded its readers that life in the Catskills was not always a subject fit for satire.

The Lesson of Windy

According to the paper anti-Semitism was still alive in rural New York State; some farmers were calling the Catskills the Sheeny Mountains. In August 1911, five men disembarked at Falls-burgh, boisterously threatening the local Jews and pummeling a Jewish grocer as he entered the railroad station to pick up tickets. A friend rushed to help him, several passersby joined in, and a fray began. As a contemporary report had it, "The station agent . . . drew a gun and threatened to shoot if it were not stopped. He called a constable . . . who, after a heroic effort, arrested [the men]. Joe Cathcart, who was one of the trouble-makers, raced out while the hearing was going on and, when hurriedly boarding a New York-bound train, was overheard to say 'never again—in Fallsburgh.' "

Hotel signs advertising Jewish boardinghouses were painted over or vandalized, fights broke out in other railroad stations, and it became known that the English aesthete Ralph White-head, searching for a place to found his art colony, was so re-pelled by what he had seen and heard about the influx of foreigners that he told his associates, "I won't go to the Catskills. They are full of Jews." Whitehead later decided on Woodstock only because, alone of the important Mountain towns, it was completely free of Hebrew landowners and hotelkeepers.

The best regional travel guide of the early twentieth century confirmed the uneasy relations of Jew and Gentile. In the opinion of its author, T. Morris Longstreth, the subject was "a bull that I must take by the horns, and that I think I can gently lead away and yet stay honest. Let me repeat two remarks: One of my friends exclaimed, when I mentioned my trip, 'Didn't you find [Sullivan County] overrun with Jews?' And one day, while walk-ing through Fleischmann's I overheard this: 'Wouldn't there be too many Gentiles in Hunter?' 'Oh! Not enough to hurt.'

"So long as there are so many inconsiderate Jews, so many non-practising Christians, it will be easier for both to keep clan-nishly apart. In the Catskills there are certain sections visited exclusively by Jews and others exclusively by Gentiles. One race likes one thing and the other another. It seems infinitely petty to me for either to sacrifice the charms and satisfactions of a beautiful region because he might be disturbed by the other.' "

Max Lerner's family was one of the last to attempt a purely agricultural life in the "beautiful region," and its story is instructive. In about 1910, his parents spent their life savings to move from a New Jersey flat to a thirty-room farmhouse in Woodridge, N.Y., hoping to live off the soil, just as the Sholemites had done some eighty years before. The acres, he remembers, overflowed with rocks, and it was impossible to coax a living from a dozen cows, some poultry, and a truck garden.

Increasingly aware that they had bought disaster, the Lerners blamed an uncle who had sold them the property in much the same way the innocent Sholemites had bought their land, sight unseen. Many afternoons, young Max watched his father lifting boulders onto a horse-drawn sledge, hoping to clear the field for agriculture. The main result was a hernia.

A disabled farmer and obstinate fields might have meant ruin, but Lerner's mother had a plan: the farmhouse would become a boardinghouse. City-bred visitors from New York would be grateful for local produce and home-cooked Jewish meals. Alas, Woodridge was far from the successful new resorts of Monticello and Liberty and there was no great rush of boarders. Then in the second winter in the Mountains, Max's frail brother Hyman came down with pneumonia and died in the big old house. The family buried him in the rain in a sad little cemetery nearby.

Hyman's death was also the death of a dream. The elder Lerners waited until the end of the summer and then fled the harsh winters that had killed their little boy. The livestock was auctioned off along with some household goods, and the family left for the more benign climate of New Haven, Connecticut. Decades later, the columnist found himself in the Catskills, lecturing to audiences at Grossinger's. He drove back to Woodridge and attempted to locate Hyman's grave. Not a trace was left. It had been covered over by the indifferent land.

The Lerners and many others departed in the first dozen years of the new century, undone by personal tragedy or victimized by climate and economy. But in the next dozen, boardinghouses enjoyed a new prosperity. In Fallsburgh the haughty old Flagler House ("lawn tennis, croquet; first class in every respect.

References exchanged") was taken over by Asias Fleisher and Phillip Morganstern and made into a very different establishment ("Strictly Kosher; special rates for families for the season. Ask for booklet"). And in 1913, the Galician refugees Selig and Malke Grossinger, encouraged by the Jewish Agricultural Society, made their way from New York City to Ferndale in the Catskills. They were restaurateurs back in Manhattan, and they actually seemed to enjoy waiting on their guests. It did not take long for their reputation to spread. In retrospect, the Grossingers' triumph seems inevitable—they began accepting guests the first year the number of automobiles registered in the United States rose past the million mark and created a new economy.

But Selig and Malke had not reckoned on the desperation of one visitor, and she nearly destroyed the business before it began. In the hotel's second season a rachitic woman made the trip from Brooklyn to Ferndale to stay at an inexpensive place where she could rest and rid herself of a nagging cough. Or so she said. The Grossingers' young daughter, Jennie, was pleased to help. She encouraged the guest to nap in her room instead of standing in line, as the other guests did, for the five o'clock milking of the Grossinger cow. As a special favor Jennie brought a cup to the woman's bedside.

The sufferer was almost forgotten in the sudden prosperity of summer. The Grossingers had done so well that they hired a combination of chambermaid and practical nurse named Mary. As Selig put it, "If someone should get sick, she'll be here already. It's like buying a new suit—it's better with two pairs of pants." Mary took her nursing degree seriously. She had scarcely begun her work week when she listened to the coughing and realized that the guest was hiding symptoms of tuberculosis.

Jennie was puzzled. "And what is tuberculosis?"

"Consumption," she was informed, and this Jennie understood. When the woman was confronted, she swore, "on the memory of my sacred parents, and on the lives of my darling children," that she did not have TB, and Jennie decided not to make an issue of the cough. Still, there was no point in taking extra chances. After much palaver about the unavailability of regular rooms in the main house, the guest was given a private tent and separate dishes, to be soaked in a separate pail of boiling water after each meal. Late at night some two weeks later, Jennie was awakened by sounds of distress coming from the direction of the tent. As she approached she saw the woman standing in the moonlight, racked by uncontrollable spasms, spilling blood into a basin held beneath her chin.

Like hundreds of others she had been drawn to the Catskills too late. Selig was informed; he hitched up a wagon and went in search of the local physician, more than an hour's ride away. Jennie and Mary helped the ailing guest into her tent and onto a cot. The nurse held a kerosene lamp and shook her head. The woman seemed to be drowning in her own blood. By the time the doctor arrived, he could only make out a death certificate. After he rode off, Selig and his daughter conferred. "All our hard work," Jennie told her father, "and now we could be ruined if somebody found out one of our boarders died of a terrible disease."

"But don't we have to tell them?" Selig asked her. "Everybody here should be examined by a doctor, so if they have caught it, they can do something about it in time."

Jennie was adamant. "We took every precaution. There's very little chance anybody could have caught it . . . I can't ruin the business now, just when it's getting good. I can't do it."

The argument was persuasive. Selig, crying as he loaded the body onto his wagon, agreed to take it to an undertaker in Liberty. In the dark, Jennie and Mary burned the tent and everything in it. The next morning, when boarders inquired about the sick lady who coughed so much, Jennie had her cover story ready: "She took a turn for the worse. She left during the night."

None of that summer's guests ever learned the truth. For years afterward, Jennie followed their fortunes, fearful that someday one of them would exhibit the fatal symptoms. Through the early years, if any of those boarders failed to return, she made a point of paying a home visit the following fall, chatting with elaborate nonchalance as she listened to their breathing. The news was always reassuring; no Grossinger guest ever reported symptoms of TB. For some, the Mountains would always be a sign of luck.

The Lesson of Windy

The rise of the Grossingers reflected the total shift of the Jewish population in New York. The comfortable German Jews had once dominated the Catskills; now it was the turn of the *folksmasn*, the common people of Galicia, Poland, Russia, Lithuania, to take command. The rich still went their way in Fleischmanns. The poor were taking control of Monticello, Fallsburgh, Liberty. *The Forward* called the Mountains "a continuation of Hester Street," the marketplace of the Lower East Side. The Jews, it maintained, at last "had their revenge on the Gentiles who didn't want to accept them. Their gardens now have grown *peyes* [unshorn sideburns, a mark of the Orthodox] and their trees have been circumsized."

The Jewish Agricultural Society welcomed these new *landsmen*. At last the caricatures of Shylock and Fagin could be replaced by portraits of the poor and honest plowman. From 1909 to 1920 the society's annual reports insisted that the way of Catskill survival lay in the soil and not in the resorts or boardinghouses. One report warned that "those who neglected their farms for boarders came to grief," and another insisted that "many of our farmers who came to these counties with the sole intention of conducting summer boarding establishments eventually graduate into good farmers. In consequence each year sees more actual farming done than the one preceding."

These were statistics adulterated with wishes. A new group of Jewish farmers *had* appeared in the Mountains, but the number of Jewish boardinghouses was increasing at a far more rapid rate. By the end of World War I, the society could no longer deny the evidence before its eyes, and the annual report admitted that Sullivan and Ulster Counties were "but ill adapted to farming. The soil, save in spots, is stony, the growing season short, and the precipitation is unevenly distributed."

It went on to recognize the towns and villages as "small and few, the roads bad, and the markets in consequence . . . poor. The farmers have therefore not only figuratively but literally a steep uphill road to travel, and as a means of augmenting their incomes, combine boardinghouse keeping with farming. As the boardinghouse business prospered, it gradually developed into a thriving industry, all the more so because of the difficulty to make farming profitable."

By the early twenties thousands of poor Jews were spending their weekends in the Catskills. A survey in the *American Hebrew* found that "the room renters are the families of the men who work at the machines in [New York City]. They rent a room in which live a mother and two or three children. . . . The children are always in the fresh air. They obtain for them milk, in many cases from T.B. tested cows; eggs which they themselves can go out and gather in the chicken coops; vegetables which are pulled up right from the ground. . . . They spend a day and a half in the open. . . . These masses of the metropolitan district are just as satisfied with their lot in the boarding and rooming-houses in the Catskills as are the people in the 'country club.' "

Joey Adams recalled the sacrifices made for that time in the country: "You had to take everything with you, from pillows, mattresses, heavy quilts and linen to pots, pans, dishes, silverware, hammocks and toilet paper. The kuchaleyn guaranteed you unsurpassed outdoor facilities such as sun, air and trees. Nothing that cost money. But they were not heavy on indoor facilities; in fact they offered nothing but a roof and the use of the kitchen and tables."

It was not quite so Spartan as all that. Refrigeration, for example, was free to the patrons because it was free to the proprietors. Every winter they and their hired hands would venture out onto the frozen lakes to saw 3 x 3 foot chunks of ice. "The water was clean and clear in those days," says one of the helpers. "No acid rain, no motorboats. When the January thaw came we dug a canal and floated the ice to the nearest barn. And then with tongs and tools and a lot of sweating and grunting we would stack those enormous ice cubes between layers of sawdust. Sometimes the ice would rise up three stories high. And in that house people could store their meat and vegetables all summer long, or they would have chunks broken off for the boxes in their kitchens. The sun brought people to Sullivan County, but it was ice that kept them here."

The county could be reached in a number of tortuous ways. By rented or borrowed car, says Adams, "the hundred-mile trip took about twelve hours because the only throughways were cow paths through the center of every hamlet. Route 17 started at the George Washington Bridge and whether you were headed for Ferndale, Livingston Manor, Hurleyville, Woodbourne, Greenfield Park or Kiamesha, you somehow still had to go through every wood and glen on the map."

The weekend appearances of city folk gave small-town sheriffs a fresh source of revenue: "After a short stretch of open road, they'd suddenly hit you with a four-mile-an-hour speed limit. Tickets were handed out for offenses like 'driving dangerously near the white line' . . . or even going too slow."

Other visitors chose to travel by "omnibus" or train. The bus trip consumed a full day, because "these smelly, gassy, creaking vehicles had to detour hours out of their way. At the midpoint of the trip, when everybody was thoroughly carsick and nauseous enough to die, the belching bus lurched to a stop and it was 'everybody out.' There, at the . . . restaurants, the rest rooms and the lunchroom usually looked like the battle scene in *Quo Vadis*. It appeared that every other coach in the country . . . was in drydock at the same time, with hundreds of milling passengers rushing, pulling, eating and throwing up."

The train offered matching discomforts. Passengers boarded a trolley from Brooklyn across the bridge to Forty-second Street. There they transferred to a crosstown bus which took them to the edge of the Hudson River. Then, says Adams, "we grabbed the Weehawken Ferry, which joyous trip blackened your face and nostrils. . . . Next came the New York, Ontario and Western. This was a long caterpillar made up of a dozen railroad cars, and it was a good quarter-mile hike to the behind end of the track because that was invariably the position assigned to the 'Ellenville' car. . . . The trip never took under six hours, and there was that change-over in Summitville where we had to drag all our stuff off again and wait for a through train."

This traffic persuaded the Jewish Agricultural Society to make a historic concession. It not only recognized the dominance of boardinghouses, it mounted a campaign to improve their sanitation. Other philanthropic organizations entered the territory. The Jewish Working Girls Vacation Society granted free vacations to some 150 young workingwomen at its house in Margaretville. The WGVS attended to the spirit first and the body second. An appeal went out to its benefactors for indoor games and volumes for the library: "Can one fail to sympathize with the girls whose holiday of a week or less in a year is half full of days of gloom or wet weather? We must be prepared to meet such disappointments, however, by giving some compensating pleasures. Books of short stories, by standard authors, help to pass time most pleasantly and profitably, and add to the gentle refining influence which it is our aim to spread."

The *Arbeiter Ring* was no longer satisfied simply to have a sanitarium. "We will have a camp," it decided, "where the future heirs of the Workmen's Circle will be educated to love and appreciate the socialistic and labor ideals for which their parents fought all their lives."

And on June 8, 1917, *The Message*, official magazine of the Ladies Waist and Dressmakers' Union, Local 25, International Ladies Garment Workers Union, had a glorious announcement. "Preparations are almost complete for Unity House," it said. "The new furniture has been bought, rugs, cots, lamps and even a piano. . . . The apple trees in our orchard are all in bloom, and the mountains have put on a new suit of spring green in preparation for us."

The house was near Tannersville, surrounded by five hundred acres, "in which we can roam as on our own estate." The predominantly Jewish membership had gathered great moral and financial force since the days of the Triangle Fire in 1911, when on March 25 a conflagration broke out at a nonunion shop. Some 850 workers, most of them women, most of them Jewish, had been trapped on the top three floors of a ten-story building near Washington Square. Some made their escape down a small elevator, but those who tried the stairway exit were doomed: management had locked the doors to prevent seamstresses from leaving early. After hours spent battling the flames, the fire chief worked his way upstairs to the factory. There he found blackened skeletons at the locked doors and bent over the sewing machines. That was a professional's view. The public had witnessed worse: ladders that could not reach high enough, and girls, some as young as thirteen, leaping from window ledges to their deaths. "They hit the pavement just like hail," an onlooker said. "We could hear the thuds faster than we could see the bodies fall."

The funeral service became a union rally. Some 50,000 angry mourners marched through the rainy streets of the Lower East Side. Uptown at the Metropolitan Opera House, Rabbi Stephen Wise, calling "the life of the lowliest worker . . . sacred and inviolable," asked for immediate action to prevent sweatshop tragedies. In the rabbi's Free Synagogue, its vice president made certain that the message was clear: "The so-called unavoidable unpreventable accidents which, it has been said, were once believed to be the result of the inscrutable decrees of Divine Providence, are now seen to be the result in many cases of unscrupulous greed or human improvidence."

A commission was formed, and out of its investigation into working hours, safety, and working conditions came recommendations that were enacted into law. The unions would never again be pusillanimous, and the garment workers would no longer suffer the old indignities and humiliations. When Samuel Gompers addressed the United Hebrew Trades, his argument was gaudy but irrefutable: "The changes that have been wrought in these Hebrew trade unions have transformed to a great degree not only the outward lives but the character of the workers. Many of them came to our city, outcasts . . . helpless, wounded in body, mind, and soul; hopeless, they accepted that there would be nothing better for them except the great beyond. They have been turned toward hope in the present."

Unity House was a manifestation of that hope—a declaration of labor made in the city and erected in the Mountains. The unionists saw oil paintings on the walls and heard lectures and concerts on the lawn. There were some grim references to the sadness of the past, to the brutal indifference of the bosses and the difficult war overseas. But there were also glasses and fists raised to the workers' future, and on certain golden evenings, laughter was permitted. Some amusement came from reading *The Forward* aloud: one wry article claimed that even the horses of Sullivan County were Jews: "Quite often they stop short at the foot of a hill and refuse to go on . . . Jewish horses—Jewish strikes."

Some nights the guests were treated to live entertainment, and during one of these an epochal performance took place. An eyewitness gave his account: "All form a large circle and make a big fire in the center. Our jolly comrade, Windy, sits down on the ground and calls for volunteers, and almost every girl steps out and tries her best to amuse the crowd. Some sing Russian, English, Jewish songs, some recite, and the entire crowd insists that Windy should give us some of his amusing Jewish songs and recitations."

At the conclusion of the evening everyone sang:

> For we are comrades, one and all,
> One and all in Jolly Unity.
> Hurrah for Unity, hurrah for Unity!
> This is glory, this is might.

The writer remembered that he "absolutely felt at home. How I hated to go away!" So did everyone else. Yet none of them knew the importance of the man who had made the days at Unity House so memorable, who had coaxed performances out of even the shiest of them, and who had then gone on to divert them with his own manic routines. Windy, the Mountains' first *tummler*, had unobtrusively entered history.

It was Windy's fate to be forgotten, and in that he was not alone. The Jewish jester is such a central figure in American entertainment that his work is often assumed to be a native art form, like jazz or the Broadway musical. But he is not the result of spontaneous combustion or the sudden release of ghetto energies; his genealogy is as long and eccentric as his routines.

In the Eastern European past, marriage ceremonies provided the only opportunities for comic celebration. The jester (*badkhn* in Yiddish) first appears in the Middle Ages, amusing the guests and annoying the Jewish leaders with his impudent diversions. A sixteenth-century poem speaks of a king who "danced so merrily/with the beautiful maiden/that he became thirsty/he forgot all his cares/to the jesters he nodded/that they stop not too soon." The regulations of Hesse in 1690 prohibit "the custom in vogue to date of riding to meet the bridegroom" except for "waiters and jesters." The method of compensation never varied: in a wedding song of the eighteenth century the merrymaker pleads, "Give also gifts today to the clowns and to the musicians."

A scholar of the Jewish past has noted certain modern parallels: "The merrymaker did not occupy a prominent social position. He was feared on account of the rhymes which he freely utilized to his own purposes and frequently caused embarrassment. People exploited his friendship for their personal advantage, they were amused by his apt parables, paraphrases and merry songs and then proceeded to censure him as a sinner."

In his memoirs of nineteenth-century Vilna, Jacob Zizmor recalls a *badkhn* known as Sanye of Bialystok: "He possessed great gifts of mimicry and comedy . . . he could invent impersonations, such as 'The Stingy Bachelor,' 'The Small-Town Cantor,' 'The Deserted Wife Looks for Her Husband,' and 'From the Cradle to the Grave' (the various periods in man's life). He carried with him a suitcase with false beards, various costumes, even women's costumes, and portrayed every role with mimicry and comic gesture like a true artist." Alas, comments Zizmor, by the end of the century the Enlightenment, combined with a liberalized faith and the new delights of the burgeoning Yiddish theater, had undone the *badkhn*. "The people had become accustomed to operas, operettas, the ballet. . . . Once, early in the morning on a summer day I met [a jester] coming from weddings. He complained to me: 'Brother, things are bad. If the best people, the cream of the public, leave me on the platform and retire to play cards, there is no longer any room for me here.' Six months later he left for America."

Those who doubt Philip Johnson's dictum—that architecture is the art of how to waste space—have only to look at photographs of the first great Catskill reconstruction. The old Flagler House, like many of the traditional hotels, was made of unobtrusive white clapboard. When Fleisher and Morganstern opened their New Flagler in 1920, visitors knew they were in the presence of a Statement. It was being made with a profound, almost religious trust in the Catskill future. Hundreds of thousands of dollars had been invested in this great structure, and behind it was faith of another kind: in the young men who had come back from the Great War.

A local plumber named Joseph Gold had been a corporal in France when, like many of his fellow enlisted men, he became obsessed with thoughts of his own death at the Somme. What would happen to his family if he died with debts outstanding? Didn't the Book of Proverbs warn that the borrower is the servant of the lender? Gold had run up a bill of four hundred dollars at a supply house in New York City. Now, from his personal and military savings, he extracted the full amount, mailed off the check, and prepared to die with an easy conscience. To the soldier's astonishment, he survived, full of shrapnel but fit for his old trade. Back in Fallsburgh, he was hired to install plumbing at the New Flagler. It was an immense job, and he had no cash to pay subcontractors or helpers. Joseph Gold journeyed to the city to ask if he might be advanced a few hundred dollars' worth of equipment. The executives hid their smiles and soberly conducted him past the reception room into the offices. There he saw his check framed and hanging on the wall. It had never been cashed. "Any soldier who believes in paying a debt all the way from France deserves a break in civilian life," they told him, and, after some investigation, advanced the enormous sum of $50,000.

Gold worked on a place where the exterior walls were made of pink-tinted stucco, topped by parapets and false gables in homage to Florida-Spanish baroque. Sunlight streamed into the public rooms from arched French windows, copies of those in Louis XIV's palace at Versailles. This was the beginning, says Alf Evers, of the Mountains' "period of furious stuccomania. . . . Owners of elderly Sullivan hotels often masked them with stucco, which had the advantage of giving a deceptively 'fireproof' as well as an elegant look at moderate cost. Some hotels turned 'Tudor'—Grossinger's adopted a cream and mock half-timbered dress."

The Lesson of Windy

This display of postwar opulence was all very well, but it fell short of the customers' expectations. "In more innocent earlier days, Sullivan's summer hotels had relied upon plenty of good food and the opportunity for young women and men to meet on a less constricted basis than that which prevailed at home. They drew social climbers who knew that it was easier to make contact with the upper levels of their society at summer resorts than anywhere else. They appealed to tired and ailing people eager for fresh clean air and sunshine. But as the New Flagler first shone in its stucco glory, all this was no longer enough."

The lesson of Windy had spread through the hills, and now, in the period of expansion and affluence, guests—particularly young ones—demanded more than big buildings, more than hayrides and fresh eggs. And that, says Adams, was how the owners of large hotels and modest resorts, *kuchaleyns* and rooming houses were forced into show business. "Each had to get a specialist to calm his nervous customers. As the owners burrowed deeper into their kitchens . . . the Social Director, better known as 'The Toomler' came into his own."

The tummler was bitterly resented by owners who could not understand why city people were no longer happy to line up for mugs of warm milk from a real cow. "The owner hated to board these 'free eaters,' let alone pay them," Adams recalls, "but it was better than checkouts. He figured if the Social Director could create enough of a divertissement to laugh Mr. Marcus off his lumpy mattress then it was worth it. A tummler was cheaper than a new box spring.

"If Mrs. Rappaport complained about not getting her third portion of blueberries or Mrs. Davidoff was scrounging fruitlessly for a dancing partner or Mr. Spiegel wanted a gin game, it was the Toomler to the rescue. . . . His job it was to keep the guests from getting bored with their card playing, dieting or viewing nature. . . . The Social Director took over all of the activities, day out and night in. He had to sing, dance, tell stories, arrange parlor games, plan hikes, organize the community sings at the campfire, kibitz with the fat old women and entertain in the dining room during meals."

In the early twenties, comedy was as rudimentary as the clientele: borrowed songs and sketches from vaudeville, ascerbic remarks about the weather, inoffensive topical humor. Social directors could never be certain about the politics of their employers, much less the guests, and they shied away from the headlines and the market. Only one national subject was considered safe, and that was because of the validity of an old country proverb: *Der goy is a shicker*—the Gentile is the one who gets drunk. After the Nineteenth Amendment became law in 1920, speakeasies appeared in the Catskill towns, but not in the resorts. There, social directors circulated an exchange between two women. In his classic compendium, *The Joys of Yiddish*, Leo Rosten places the dialogue "in the lounge of a Catskill resort, an hour before the dinner hour . . .

How about a cocktail before dinner?
No, thanks. I never drink.
No? Why not?
Well, in front of my children, I don't believe in taking a drink. And when I'm away from my children, who *needs* it?

Despite the frequency with which those fictional ladies were quoted on the subject of drinking, it was two Jewish men who inspired most of the early twenties jokes about alcohol, and the anecdotes that concerned them were not apocryphal. When the country first went dry, Isidor Einstein was a forty-year-old postal clerk with a salary of $40 a week. As soon as the federal government announced a new position of Prohibition Agent at $1,680 per annum, Einstein applied for the job and became one of 1,526 appointees hired to enforce the Volstead Act. He seemed a strange choice at first: balding, fat, short of breath, the antithesis of the alert and well-conditioned federal hound. In fact, he was an ideal agent. Einstein was of Austrian origin, and he spoke fluent German, Hungarian, Polish, and Yiddish and got along in Russian, Spanish, French, and Italian. He could even parrot one or two phrases in Chinese. He skillfully assumed disguises, imitated accents, played the harmonica, the trombone, and the violin. "I ain't no Heifetz," he liked to say, "but I could earn a living."

He performed alone until 1921, when he persuaded his equally unprepossessing friend Moses Smith, the owner of a cigar store, to join him in the service. Together, Izzy and Moe, as the newspapers delightedly called them, enjoyed a series of highly publicized triumphs. In their search for stills and bars they impersonated cattle ranchers, hod-carrying longshoremen, gas-meter inspectors, musicians, tourists. They went to Harlem in blackface and to Sheepshead Bay in fishermen's boots and overalls. And in the winter of 1922, they crossed the river to appear in Liberty. The town was proud of its dryness; when Prohibition came in, the local paper praised the "beneficent law of the people by the people and for the people," and hundreds of teetotalers staged a torchlight parade and a march to the Presbyterian church for services. It was not a likely place to find liquor, and that was why the agents searched it out: Izzy and Moe always welcomed a challenge. They ingratiated themselves with the local farmers, and, complaining of an overpowering thirst, asked where they might buy a drink or two. Helpful retailers took them to Monticello, where they hired a wagon and rode out to Bethel. In a barn at the edge of the town cemetery the visitors were shown a ten-gallon still. When they seemed disappointed, farmers showed them another one three times the size.

THEY LOOKED LIKE 'RUBES'; THEY WERE "DRY" AGENTS read the headline the next day. Izzy and Moe were admiring the liquor-manufacturing equipment when a wagon drove up with a load of prunes and raisins. The agents flashed the inconspicuous little shields on their suspenders. The arrests took only a few minutes. There was no violence this time, but the peace and laughter of Sullivan County would not endure for long. Nor would the careers of Izzy and Moe. One of his superiors complained to Izzy, "You get your name in the newspapers all the time, whereas mine hardly ever gets mentioned. I must ask you to remember that you are merely a subordinate—not the whole show." Neither man could keep that in mind, and they were given notice shortly afterward. A bureau spokesman intoned:

"The service must be dignified. Izzy and Moe belong on the vaudeville stage." Indeed, after their dismissal the men were offered $100,000 to make a nationwide theatrical tour, but they decided to become insurance men instead. From then on, when they went to resort country they left the entertaining to professionals.

CHAPTER 6

SHARPENING THE

ENEMY'S DAGGER

LIBERTY MOTORIZED FIRE DEPARTMENT, LIBERTY, N. Y.
IN THE BACKGROUND MAY BE SEEN ONE OF LIBERTY'S
MANY MODERN BUSINESS STRUCTURES.

The Catskills' oldest tale was refurbished in 1920, when *The Liberty Register* presented its readers with a short story entitled "A Modern Rip Van Winkle." An old Dutchman, Hezekiah, awoke from a twenty-year slumber to find that "many of the names on the store windows were strange and the letters . . . Hezekiah was unable to read. Droves of children were on the streets and followed him as he went. 'Oi, oi,' they yelled, 'oi, oi.' "

Hezekiah called out for his old associates, but none answered. "Instead, people came running from all directions, attracted by the crowd and his hollering. " 'Vell, vat you vant?' demanded a short, stout, black-haired man, rubbing his hands as he came out of what used to be the Old Central House. 'I vill sell you somedings cheap.'

(89)

"Hezekiah learned that the immigrants had taken posses-
sion of the region and that the native residents, all but a few
who wished to live and die on the grounds of their fathers, had
emigrated to other parts."

In its social notes, the *Register* further amused itself with an
account of insatiable Jewish appetite: In the village of Arden a
man named Mirsky was "not afraid he won't get his money's
worth, but you oughta see him getting it. He thinks he is sick
because he is not hungry after eating 18 pancakes, 4 eggs and
6 glasses of milk."

Deeper into the twenties this kind of satire suddenly disappeared from the local papers. Front pages began to report
unbiased news of the immigrants: that a Dr. Simon Volet was
inducted as president of the local B'nai B'rith, for example, or
that Jewish farmers were gathering to celebrate the holiday of
Succoth. The reason for the altering policy could be found in
the telephone book, in store fronts, and, inevitably, in advertisements. The Jews were on their way to becoming the majority.
B. Lubin informed readers of the Ellenville daily paper that he
handled Real Estate and Insurance, and bought, sold, or exchanged farms. K. Goldman was a whiskey retailer. N. Leopold
& Son promised, "We'll sell you a suit or an overcoat here at
the right price." Moses Wolf offered horses, wagons, and har-
nesses. Jakowitz & Karelity, butchers, did a large non-kosher
business and guaranteed "cash paid for Beef Cattle, Milk Cows,
Hogs, Sheep, Calves, Lambs, Poultry. &c." Reminiscing two
generations later, New York State Senator Daniel G. Albert recalled the members of one of the first synagogues in the lower
Catskills. There were, he said, "besides my father, Adolph (flour
and grain); Mr. Affron (apparel and furnishings); Mr. Hersh-
kowitz (handkerchief factory); Mr. Aronowitz (grocer); Mr.
Goldman (grocer and baker) . . . Mr. Joseph Slutsky (farmer);
Mr. Charles Slutsky (farmer); Mr. Levitt (grocer); later joined
by Mr. Glusker (confectionery) and Mr. Rosenberg (confectionery)."

The prevalence of Jewish merchants was to be expected;
not every failed farmer chose to become a professional host.
What surprised many natives was the energy and cohesion these

newcomers brought to the Mountains. When major insurance companies refused to write policies for the Jewish farmers, no complaints were registered. They simply banded together and insured themselves.

Faded minutes of those early days enumerate the first principles of the Co-operative Fire Insurance Company. First was "to provide the best fire protection at the lowest possible cost. Second to support activities of benefit to the community. Third to educate constantly against fire hazards." These were not merely sonorous goals to be boomed at monthly meetings. Bulletins were printed, in facing pages of English and Yiddish, informing farmers about the hazards of electricity, lightning, and kerosene stoves. The directors and builders of the co-op seldom restricted their activities to the Fire Insurance Company. I. D. Wolf, a director, was typical. He was responsible for the incorporation of the village of Woodridge, helped bring water, power, and light facilities to his community, and organized the First National Bank.

The co-op began in one room above a drugstore in Woodridge. It was heated by a coal stove, furnished with a kitchen table and wooden chairs, and staffed by one woman. Rose Hecht served as office manager, janitor, and, most significantly, as interpreter for those who could not speak English. In its first year, 1913, the co-op paid one of its farmers $200 after a fire, but the company survived: it had assets of $911. They were never to dip so low again.

As new resorts began to rise, coverage offered by the co-op was deemed inadequate, and a second company, the American Co-operative Fire Insurance Company, was created in 1920. When that proved insufficient, a Third Co-operative Company was formed, then a fourth, the Mountain Co-operative, and in 1926 a Fifth Co-operative began signing up clients. Years later, an executive would recall that the phenomenal success of the co-op omitted a few "black pages." There were, she admitted, opportunists "who tried to use their position for selfish purposes . . . There were directors who sought gain for settling a loss or writing a policy, but in every single case offenders were discovered and expelled, and the fireworks took place at that wonderful annual meeting . . . lots of rhetoric, lots of emotion . . . and the color was such that Metropolitan or Travelers or Mass. Mutual will never know. I'll always remember Louis Rosenblatt getting up at an annual meeting and assuring his audience, 'Ich vill reden in English'—and not an English word followed." One saleslady especially savored the day when she visited with a bartender in Narrowsburg: " 'How much you Jews going to charge me this year?' said he. 'Emil,' said I, 'see a stock company, I don't think we want your business.' 'Just kidding,' says he, seeing the low rate flying out the window. 'Can't you take a little joke?' " By the time the large insurance companies roamed the Catskills searching for business, they were no longer needed. The farmers had finally had their dish of revenge, and just as the proverb had promised, it was best eaten cold.

The unimpeded spirit of the Jazz Age took a long time to reach the Catskills. Women who came visiting from the city sometimes assumed flapper styles, but in other ways they remained as unworldly as before. Wives and children still arrived for the summer, setting up their domestic lives in the *kuchaleyns*; the men still journeyed up to see them on what were now called "bull trains," except that they came for shorter times than ever before. That was not their intention. Family feelings were unaltered; it was the character of work that was different. Self-employed retailers and manufacturers were being replaced by wage earners in the city's retail stores and garment industries. Those establishments had no intention of ceding anything to labor, especially time.

The vice president of the IRT subway represented most of his fellow employers when he remarked that "the value of a vacation depends upon how far you go down the line. I am a great believer in vacations and very liberal ones for men who work under mental strain. But it is different with the man whose work is merely physical." Another railroad executive saw it as an intractable social problem: "The laboring man seems to be in a class by himself, so far as vacations are concerned. . . . Many corporations now hire this force under hourly wage agreements and it is rare that a man has a full year's work. The result is that the time 'off,' owning to changing conditions, takes the place of a vacation, but of course at their own expense."

Supreme Court Justice Henry Bischoff conceded that "the laboring man ought to get a vacation," but noticed that "unfortunately he cannot unless he takes it—and then it is without pay which means a lot to him, you know."

Through the twenties less than 15 percent of the work force ever enjoyed as much as two weeks of paid summer vacation. Hired laborers could get some respite only on the weekend— half of Saturday and all of Sunday. Limitations of time ruled out any trip longer than 100 miles, and brought the Catskills more popularity and custom. The columnists and reporters kept writing about crowded railroad cars, cacophonous boarding-houses, pretentious resorts and playgrounds. The guests read the criticism and kept coming anyway. One of the guests told an owner, "Let *The Forward* whine and *kvetch*. All week our lives are lived from the tenement to the factory." He waved at the green hills. "To us it's paradise."

The Catskill Gentiles looked at these grateful laborers, first with dismay, then with amusement, and finally with a measure of respect. Dave Levenson, whose father founded Tamarack Lodge in 1903, recalled his twenties childhood in Liberty: "My father, who was Orthodox, wanted me to learn Hebrew. There were no other Jewish kids in the immediate area, and I didn't want to get taught all by myself. So my father paid my Christian friends, the Townsends and the Newkirks and the Fitzgeralds, to take lessons with me. Years later I would run into one of them and he would tell me, 'Look, I still remember how to write Jewish.' "

The Wawarsing town historian described the early days of Spring Glen, where "Jews and Gentiles became friends more quickly than elsewhere." Assimilation provided the benign climate: "For many years, Jews joined worshippers in events at the Methodist church; some of the Jewish children took part in the Methodist exercises at Christmas and other times; many Jewish ladies attended meetings of the Methodist Ladies Aid.

"At first, Jews met in each other's homes . . . for religious services . . . and they held a sacred service for dedicating the

Scrolls. . . . There was a great parade to the property . . . where the dedication ceremony was to take place. Just as it was starting, two Christians arrived—Wells C. Smith [the stationmaster] and John Thornton [the postmaster]. They had raised money to buy the Jews a Bible. Mr. Smith presented it, and made a warm speech in which he expressed the hope that a synagogue would be built soon which would honor the entire community."

While this glow warmed the lower Catskills, the northern regions maintained an air of suspicion and distrust. Much of it could be traced to the harangues of Henry Ford. The genius of the assembly line, whose inventions had made the Mountains accessible to the immigrant poor, had adopted a new career of anti-Semitism. "International financiers are behind all war," he told an interviewer for the *New York World*. "They are what is called the international Jew: German Jews, French Jews, English Jews, American Jews. I believe that in all those countries except our own the Jewish financier is supreme . . . here the Jew is a threat."

In his private newspaper, *The Dearborn Independent*, Ford printed sections of the Protocols of the Elders of Zion. The notorious pamphlet, purportedly written by Jews for Jews, described a secret Zionist plan for world domination: "Note the successes of Darwinism, Marxism, and Nietzscheism, engineered by us. The demoralizing effects of these doctrines upon the minds of the Goys should already be obvious." After a lengthy investigation in 1921, *The* (London) *Times* had exposed the Protocols as a concoction by the Russian secret police. But Ford had no interest in the work of British scribblers. His excerpts carried assurances that "the statements offered in this series are never made without the strictest and fullest proof."

At times the automobile maker's rantings made the men around him exchange private glances. He once bit into a candy bar and said the brand had lost its savor because "the Jews have taken hold of it. They've cheapened it to make more money." Somehow he came to regard brass as a "Jew metal" and all traces of it in his factory were painted over in black. Ford saw instances of the international Jewish conspiracy at every turn, and the Protocols offered him the documentary "proof" he needed. "People of all opinions and all doctrines are at our service," it read, "restorers of monarchy, demagogues, Socialists, Communists and other Utopians. We have put them all to work. Every one of them from his point of view is undermining the last remnant of authority, is trying to overthrow all existing order. All the governments have been tormented by these actions. But we will not give them peace until they recognize our supergovernment."

This screed was gospel to Ford; it showed how pervasive the Jew really was. It was he who had created godless amusement parks like Coney Island, "centers of nervous thrills and looseness." In an article entitled "Jewish Jazz Becomes Our National Music," the *Independent* assailed "the moron music of the Yiddish Trust" and linked it with a degeneration of motion pictures, now in the hands of the Jews. "The reels are reeking of filth. They are slimy with sex plays. They are overlapping each other with crime." In the staves of popular music, "the mush, the slush, the sly suggestion, the abandoned sensuous notes, are of Jewish origin," a reference to Irving Berlin, George Gershwin, Jerome Kern, Sigmund Romberg, and other highly visible songwriters.

Links between Dearborn, Michigan, and the Catskills of New York State were not as remote as they seemed. Ford's good friend was the naturalist John Burroughs, and the two had once set up camp in Roxbury. The *Independent*, as Alf Evers records, "had many readers among the Catskills, and did much to excite mountain people."

The place of greatest excitement was the neighborhood of Woodstock. This was the home of Ralph Whitehead, who, it will be remembered, chose the locale because it was free of Jewish merchants and guests. Whitehead, another friend of Burroughs, was made uneasy by the appearance of a hotel owner. His name was Morris Newgold, and he came from New York City, where he had made a specialty of buying unprofitable hotels and turning them around. Newgold confirmed the worst suspicions of the Woodstock natives by leasing the once restricted Overlook Hotel to the Unity Club, a recreational division of the International Ladies Garment Workers Union. In the summer, hundreds of the club members, all young women, walked along

Woodstock's main street dressed in uniform white blouses and dark bloomers and talking of factories and strikes. It was a situation calculated to bring trouble, and in the early twenties, the Ku Klux Klan began to recruit new members in the Mountains. Late one September evening in 1922, Whitehead's son, Ralph Jr., imbibed too much prohibition gin and joined two drunken friends in an assault on Newgold's hotel. They woke the sleeping guests, and when the owner ordered the men to leave, they assaulted him, causing injuries to his head and ribs. The trio was arrested, Newgold sued, and before an out-of-court settlement could be arranged, the town was aroused by inflammatory testimonies. Chief among them was Mrs. Whitehead's defense of her son in the local *Freeman*: "The men in my family never lose their heads when they drink, and [Ralph Jr.] wouldn't touch a Jew with a ten foot pole." Whitehead's friend Hervey White circulated a long narrative poem, "Tinker Tom," which referred to

> . . . *the invasion of Belgium by the Germans; us, by Jews,*
> *Which is the worse, I leave you free to choose.*

The Klan needed no further encouragement. A recruiting agent signed up some local businessmen and issued them white robes. A resident remembered the evening he biked to a pasture, hid in the shadows, and watched a scene more appropriate to Reconstruction Mississippi. "Men in white gowns began to arrive, several to a car," wrote Charlie Crist some fifty years later. "Some walked to the farm, having parked their cars on side roads, so they might not be recognized.

"Flashlights flickered across the thorn bushes. The beams penetrated the stillness, searching through the limbs of the big elm tree near where the cross was to be burned.

"There had been a rumor someone was spying on the gathering and he had hidden in the tree. Some men climbed the tree. There was no spy.

"The white clad men gathered in a close circle. They held their secret meeting and the torch was touched to the rough wooden cross, wrapped in burlap and saturated with kerosene.

The glow died down and the men disappeared. They would appear another night on someone else's property."

In case any residents remained ignorant of the Klan's history and purpose, the Woodstock Weekly *Hue and Cry* enlightened them. The burning crosses, it said, were "due no doubt to the influx of undesirable aliens." Ultimately, of course, it was the aliens who stayed and the Klan that went. In part that was because its organizer vanished with the initiation fees, in part because most residents were repelled by the notion of hooded *agents provocateurs* in their quiet little village. A printed sheet, circulated soon after the cross-burning, expressed the popular sentiment: "There occurred a meeting in our town of Woodstock professing to uphold the ideals of Americanism which at the same time spread insidious propaganda contrary to the ideals of our forefathers. We, the people of Woodstock, who live in peace and harmony in a well governed community, resent all such outside interference."

The Klan and the Bolsheviks represented opposing terminals of the American experience. Yet they felt a common attraction to the Mountains. Years after his appointment as head of the Federal Bureau of Investigation, J. Edgar Hoover noted that "in May 1921, after another year of bickering, the United Communist Party and the remainder of the Communist Party formed the Communist Party of America, Section of the Communist International at a secret two-week convention at Woodstock, N.Y." Beneath the noses of the suspicious and resentful townspeople, the radicals, many of them of Russian Jewish origin, agreed that the "Party would work for violent revolution, preparing the worker for armed insurrection as the only means of overthrowing the capitalist state. The convention officially accepted the twenty-one points for admission to the Comintern. The Communist Party was now a complete prisoner of Moscow."

All this had occurred in plain sight, as *The Communist* recorded in its July 1921 issue. The Unity Convention, it said, "was called to order in the open air, the delegates seated in a semi-circle, the U.C.P. delegates on the right and the C.P. delegates on the left, in a natural amphi-theatre with a boulder for the chairman's desk." Some of the subversives had been living at the Overlook house for days, whispering in foreign tongues. They were the hotel's last paying guests—Morris Newgold was never able to obtain a return on his venture, and he closed the hotel shortly after the meeting in order to make improvements. They were still in the planning stage when the Overlook burned down three years later.

The American Communist Party was founded in the Catskills without infiltration of any kind. The anti-radical raids of Attorney General Mitchell A. Palmer had brought deportation proceedings against hundreds of foreign-born residents, and anyone suspected of subversion was run to earth. But the key members of the Party were untouched. As Alf Evers notes with bemusement, "Neither Hoover nor anyone else has ever given the public an explanation of just why the convention managed to be held in such complete secrecy. All other Communist gatherings of the period were infiltrated by federal agents." In the Mountains there was never a shortage of wonders.

Oddly enough, the closer the Catskill villages were to New York City, the less influence politics seemed to play in their everyday affairs. One or two children's camps tried to indoctrinate the young: a counselor from the old days remembered when Camp Kindering (socialist) and Camp Kinderland (Communist) established bases on opposite sides of Sylvan Lake. Although their parents refused to speak to each other, the boys and girls managed to socialize by shouting messages to each other from canoes in the middle of the lake.

But most resorts and camps and *kuchaleyns* were apolitical. Their only interest was in banishing the pressures and demands of daily life. It was no easy task; visitors seemed to bring the agitations with them, and so did the people who provided the amusements. Irving Howe describes the way "a long-contained vulgarity, which had already come to form a vital portion of Yiddish culture in eastern Europe as a challenge to rabbinic denial and shtetl smugness . . . broke through the skin of immigrant life. It was a vulgarity in both senses: as the urgent, juicy thrust of desire, intent upon seizing life by the throat, and as the cheap, corner-of-the-mouth retailing of Yiddish obscenities. It may be easy to separate these kinds of vulgarity when talking about them, but in life it was not. The budding comics and entertainers, eager to make 'the big time' and impatient with customary refinements of taste, were ready to employ either kind of vulgarity—since they were themselves a compound of both—in order to hold an audience."

The demands of that audience were ferocious; its members were in the Mountains to be ceaselessly amused and their memories were short. Last night's entertainment was all very well, but tonight they wanted new reasons for laughter and applause. Hotel owners knew that the only good business was repeat business, and that a customer who failed to return had vanished into the arms of a competitor. They outdid each other with plans for ceaseless diversion.

The social directors who executed those plans were on duty every day for two months. The Catskill week became as rigid and uninviting as a school calendar. On Saturdays, in addition to informal amusement of the guests, the entertainment staff rehearsed the evening show. Sometimes it was a musical with local references woven into the script. On other occasions, audiences saw a comedy like *The Show-Off*, whose brash hero reminded some onlookers of themselves. "The part of Aubrey is very difficult," players were advised, "because his character is nearly obnoxious yet the audience must like him." A few days later, the cast would be memorizing their lines for the *The Trial of Mary Dugan*, with its Yiddish theater overtones of the Wrong Woman vindicated.

Moss Hart served a bitter apprenticeship in the Catskills, overseeing everything and forgiving nothing. When the social director was not supervising productions, he was expected to perform monologues ("Mrs. Cohen at the Beach" was his dialect specialty) and sing in the boy-and-girl numbers of musicals. Every hour contained some new demand: "Up at nine and the daytime activities until the dress rehearsal at four . . . fulminating pandemonium was the rule. These weekly musicals—stolen, slapdash and amateur though they were—were elaborate and difficult in terms of light cues, props and quick changes of costume and scenery. Since the general level of weariness and irritability was pretty high by Saturday afternoon, the dress rehearsals of the musicals were major horrors that went on until we could see the audience coming down the hill to the social hall. Then we drew the curtains and prayed for the best, the hammering and setting up of the scenery sometimes drowning out the overture being played by the six-piece orchestra."

At checkout time on Sunday afternoon the social staff was expected to fill the air with camp songs and parodies of popular hits, interspersed with guests' names and family jokes, until the cars and buses arrived. Sunday was Introduction Night, with efforts, recalls Joey Adams, "pointed toward girl-meets-boy. We tried to balance each table so there was an equal amount of single girls and an equal amount of any kind of men. If we were short of men, and there was never a time we were not, we drafted the boat boy . . . and any other men we could find lying around. These were ordered into their Sunday-go-to-meeting clothes and stationed around the dining hall. The girls never knew who was a rich guest and who was a peasant."

Monday was campfire night. The evenings were calculated down to the number of logs to be placed on the campfire: large blazes for comic recitations, low flames for dramatic readings. After the guests were arranged in cozy proximity, the program opened with a community sing. This was often accompanied by heckling, Hart bitterly wrote. It began "as I stood up in front of the fire to start the singing off, and it had to be answered with equally good-natured banter in return on my part. It was a rare campfire night that I did not devoutly wish that I could disappear into the air or sink into the earth." This agony was followed by poetry recitations, ranging from humorous light verse to dramatic narratives like "The Raven" or a soliloquy from *Macbeth* or *Hamlet*. As the flames ebbed the evening chill began. It was the hour for ghost stories.

Tuesday was Costume or Dress-Up Night. Female guests customarily arrived with a costume; most of the men carried no more than the requisite summer evening wardrobe of white flannel trousers and blue sport jacket. For the inevitable emergencies, every social director kept a trunkful of policemen's uniforms, maids' outfits, old fashioned two-piece male bathing suits, and an assortment of bowler hats and false mustaches. Perennial themes characterized these Tuesday evenings, among them Hillbilly Time, A Night in Old Japan, and A Night in Old Montmartre, marked by Apaches, gypsy women, and, the next day, a shortage of catsup because so much of it was used for blood in the Grand Guignol sketches.

On Wednesdays, Amateur Night, the one evening when guests were permitted center stage, alternated with Games Night. On that occasion racers with potatoes, peanuts, and sacks competed for prizes. In theory, since staff members were not allowed to enter any contests, they were superfluous. Actually, they were required to be out on the dance floor for each game, says Hart, "seeing to it that the shy or unattractive girls in particular were included in at least one game during the evening." Human sympathy was hard to find. "It is not easy to feel the proper compassion for a shy girl or an ugly duckling when you are tied into a sack with her and are hobbling down the social hall to the finish line. On the contrary, rolling a peanut along the floor side by side with a bad complexioned girl with thick glasses and unfortunate front teeth does nothing to kindle the fires of pity within you, but instead makes you want to kick her right in her unfortunate teeth."

Thursday was Nightclub Night, a time for what Adams calls "our 'intimate night club revue'—a dreary phrase for a quickie, cheapie, throw-away show designed simply to hold the guests until the weekend." Three- or four-piece bands played requests and the male staff members threaded their way through the audience, asking guests to dance. Early on, the owners realized that there would always be a disproportionate number of single women and they hit upon a solution. They stopped hiring professional waiters, who tended to be middle-aged, with sore feet and sour outlooks, and replaced them with college men, preferably those studying for careers in medicine and law. These students were an employer's ideal: they were attractive to the girls and, more importantly, to the parents; they elevated the tone of the hotels; and they were content to work for minuscule salaries, augmented by tips from customers. The duties were onerous and complicated. Waiters and busboys were expected to pay flattering attention to the "pots" or "dogs"—the most unattractive females. Every summer a few employees would prove insubordinate and fall in love with a beautiful guest. The unwritten law had been transgressed. They were swiftly and ostentatiously sent home as an example to the others, who then meekly returned to the task of steering lonely partners around the dance floor. "I am certain," the acrimonious Hart says, that "those camp years ruined the pleasure of dancing for me forever. It is seldom now that I will venture out onto a dance floor. For six whole years I danced with nothing but 'the pots,' and that was enough to make me welcome the glorious choice of sitting down for the rest of my life."

On Nightclub Night the tummler held center stage. His routines were infallible: they were lifted in their entirety from Broadway or vaudeville. At White Roe the owner's son, Julius Weiner, hired a stenographer to attend stage hits and transcribe comic patter and song lyrics. Within a week they would surface in the Catskills. So would the acts of such headliners as Eddie Cantor, Willie Howard, Al Jolson, Harry Richman, and Smith and Dale. In all resorts tummlers plundered shamelessly, reshaping the sketches to fit their audiences.

Early in their careers, the performers learned to deal with chivvying from the onlookers. They returned insults ("You want to match wits?" "Sorry, I never attack an unarmed man") or, diplomatically, they tried to involve the guests in the comedy by teaching them a few lines and casting them in the part of hecklers:

GUEST (*acting drunk*): What's going on behind that curtain?
M.C.: There's nothing going on behind that curtain.
GUEST: There must be—there's nothing going on in front of it.
M.C.: That must be one of your father's jokes.
GUEST: What are you, one of your mother's?
M.C.: How did you get in here?
GUEST: It's raining outside.
M.C.: How long can a man live without brains?
GUEST: I don't know. How old are you?

Sharpening the Enemy's Dagger

Friday night was Basketball Night. In the twenties the game was played by waiters who still retained enough energy to run up and down the court to the amusement of the crowd. When interest flagged, the owners arranged for one set of waiters to play another. No one took the home games or the away games very seriously. There were no leagues, no standings, no individual statistics. Admission was free, but the players soon devised a method of increasing their summer incomes. A hatful of papers was passed around the stands, and guests could buy one for a dollar. On it was written a number, and if the total points of the final score matched the sum, a cash prize was awarded, to be split with the players. One of them later recalled that he would "pocket an extra ten or fifteen dollars every time we played." And there was another hidden reward. "If the chef had number sixty-four, we'd sometimes make sure that was all the points we'd score. Then we'd eat like kings for a week." Harmless enough in the beginning, but it was here on the Mountain courts that athletes learned to shave points and rig games. What began as a private joke among summer sportsmen was to end as one of the greatest scandals in the history of American amateur sports.

But that was a generation away from the time when the Mountains seemed as young as the resorts. In the early twenties, crime was something that brought a smile, because it usually concerned the stills that brewed liquor under the noses, and sometimes in the back yards, of the town police. Sixty years later, local magistrates still spoke fondly of the illegal liquor makers, and of the summer days when the brewers were given several hours' warning before federal agents made their swoops. July and August were months when hostilities and tensions could be forgotten, when guards were let down, souls renewed, and thirsts satisfied.

Before the twenties ended, resorts had codified standards of behavior and dress, and quite often they were more demanding than those of the city. Then again, there was more at stake: Manhattan only offered employment; in the Mountains there was the possibility of marriage. The Yiddish *Tageblatt* recorded the situation: The girls "live on Forsythe, Eldridge, Henry and

Madison Streets and work in the offices of the large corporations on Broadway and Wall Streets. . . . At home they hear how their parents struggle to pay the rent; at the office they are trusted with secrets of millions of dollars. Swimming between two worlds they struggle heroically to maintain their balance. Their vacation is short—only two weeks. In the country they act like daughters of the rich. Young men attach themselves like bees to honey. But soon enough their poverty is found out. The girls who thought themselves in the company of bankers discover that a few fine neckties and a silk shirt may just have been the product of a Canal Street clothing store. Then back to the office to pound the keys."

Indeed, says Hart, the men lived through the season "with complete anonymity except for the initials on their luggage; and when they decked themselves out in their . . . finery for their first appearance in the social hall or the dining room, it was impossible to tell whether a shipping clerk or the boss' son had arrived." Summer was a sunlit costume party, and it was up to the participants to discern how much was sham and how much could be believed. Since vacation "had as its goal sex on the part of the boys and marriage on the part of the girls," Hart goes on, "there was a better chance for the achievement of these goals if both partners gave no hint of their true status while in camp, but played the game of letting the other assume that each was heir to a junior executive's job or a wealthy father. It was a game of endless variations—a stately minuet of lying and pretense, and the social staff watched it flower and blossom every two weeks with no little delight and a good deal of malice."

If the parents came along, they had to play their parts in the drama, usually engineered by the mother. It did no good for a father to gripe, as one did in *The Forward*, "At home I can walk around in a bathrobe, without a collar, I can go where I want, sit, stand, etc. I am free." In the Mountains, "I have to wear a high collar all the time, and a different suit every day. I have to spit stylish and cough stylish, and if God forbid you catch cold you have to blow your nose stylish." At the new Jewish hotels, he complains, "you only get style, nothing else. In the old days they served you a big piece of gefilte fish, a big portion of chicken, served not so stylishly. Today you get flowers on the table and napkins, but fish and chicken—tiny portions. In the old days, hotel keepers knew that people came to get fat and regain their health, so they prepared good, Jewish food. Now they know that people come to show off their stylish dresses and good manners, so they prepare napkins and flowers, stylish conversation and smiles." With a melancholy, disdainful reference to this environment controlled by females, he concludes, "I hate the country, it's like a prison, and a lot of men feel like I do."

No doubt protesting in the public print alleviated his irritation, but the writer and his colleagues shrugged and took their daughters to the country all the same. They knew what their wives knew, that girls had to acquire husbands, that boys needed help to get on in the difficult world beyond the woods, and that the Catskills was considered the prime place to begin.

No one knew more about the importance of the Mountains than the entertainers who stepped up to join the tummlers onstage. For them it was an ideal arena, far enough from Broadway to allow the freedom to fail, but so close to the Main Stem that agents and producers could come to examine new acts. Those acts were taking a different shape and tone from the customary vaudeville fare.

From its scruffy beginnings in tents and barrooms, the twenties variety show had evolved into respectable family entertainment. Jugglers and singers, formal dancers, barbershop quartets, animal acts, magicians, light comedians now looked out over the footlights at the audience that Oscar Hammerstein II called the Big Black Giant. It was whimsical and cruel, and it had to be appeased at every show. On some occasions, mildly suggestive material could be used: FATHER: "If you plan to take out my daughter, be aware that our lights are put out at ten-thirty." SUITOR: "You can expect me at eleven o'clock." And there was the customary mockery of foreigners and blacks, usually with broad dialects. However, there were to be no assaults on the ticket holders, no attempt to jab them into awareness of themselves or their society. Backstage at all Keith theaters a sign was posted:

Don't say "slob" or "son-of-a-gun" or "hully gee" on this stage unless you want to be cancelled peremptorily. Do not address anyone in the audience in any manner. . . . If you have not the ability to entertain Mr. Keith's audience without risk of offending them, do the best you can. Lack of talent will be less censured than would be an insult to a patron. . . . If you are guilty of uttering anything sacrilegious or even suggestive, you will be immediately closed and will never again be allowed to appear in a theater where Mr. Keith is in authority.

None of these rules prevailed in the mountains. There, audiences could be addressed frontally and insulted constantly. Rabbis and diets, money and sex became the staple subjects of comedy; double entendre was the order of the day, and when energy vied with taste there was never a question of which would win. Every master of ceremonies reproduced the same phone conversation as if he had just overheard it in the lobby:

MAN: Hello!
WOMAN: Hello, Sam?
MAN: Who is this?
WOMAN: This is Sadie.
MAN: Which Sadie am I having the pleasure?
WOMAN: This is the Sadie with which you *had* the pleasure.
MAN: Oh, that Sadie. I remember you and that weekend we spent together. What a weekend. I'll never forget you. And I forgot to tell you, you're a good sport.
WOMAN: That's why I'm calling you, Sam. I'm having a baby, I'm going to kill myself.
MAN: Say, you *are* a good sport. (*Hangs up*)

This brand of comedy seldom sat well with friendly Gentiles who spent occasional weekends in the resorts. They could never get used to seeing the tummlers making fun of their own people. It seemed to run against the American spirit and smacked of the troubled past. Somerset Maugham describes that universal discomfort in "The Alien Corn" as he listens, squirming, to a fund of dialect stories told by an expert. Fred Robenstein has mastered the Yiddish intonations and ghetto mannerisms and the other listeners are weak with laughter. It was as good as a play, says the narrator, because Robenstein himself was a Jew. And yet the listener cannot join in the amusement: "I was not quite sure of a sense of humor that made such cruel fun of his own race."

Why self-abnegation is so much a part of a people's humor has been the subject of speculation for centuries, and of course became one of Freud's favorite topics. In a letter to his colleague Wilhelm Fleiss in June of 1897 he wrote: "Let me confess that I have recently made a collection of deeply significant Jewish jokes," psychical productions that he found analagous to dreams. All the items Freud collected made their way to the tummler's stock of tales. Sometimes stupidity was the topic: "A horsedealer was recommending a saddle horse to a customer. 'If you take this horse and get on it at four in the morning you'll be in Pressburg by half-past six.'—'What should I do in Pressburg at half-past six in the morning?' " Sometimes the joke portrayed the classic sloven: "A Jew noticed the remains of some food in another one's beard. 'I can tell what you had to eat yesterday.'—'Well, tell me.'—'Lentils, then'—'Wrong: the day before yesterday.' " And always there were stories of the Jew hidden under layers of pretension: "The doctor, who had been asked to look after the Baroness at her confinement, pronounced that the moment had not come, and suggested to the Baron that in the meantime they should have a game of cards in the next room. After a while a cry of pain from the Baroness struck the ears of the two men: '*Ah, mon dieu, que je suffre!*' Her husband sprang up, but the doctor signed to him to sit down: 'It's nothing. Let's go on with the game!' A little later there were again sounds from the pregnant woman: '*Mein Gott, mein Gott was fur Schmerzen!*'—'Aren't you going in, Professor?' asked the Baron.—'No, no. It's not time yet.'—At last there came from next door an unmistakable cry of '*Oy vay!*' The doctor threw down his cards and exclaimed, 'Now it's time.' "

In his paper *Jewish Wit*, Freud's disciple Theodor Reik offered stories to fit every conceivable category.

The Nouveau Riche: "A lady friend . . . complained that she had to go to *The Marriage of Figaro* tomorrow. Mrs. Pollack said, 'Can you not send them a telegram?' " The Uncultured:

"Teitlebaum asks for a room in a hotel. The man at the desk says, 'With bath?' Teitlebaum indignantly returns, 'What do you mean? Am I a trout?' " "A gentleman asks his neighbor at the table in a summer resort, 'Did you take a bath this morning?' Cohn is astonished: 'Why? Is there one missing?' "

The Guilt-Producing Mother: "She gives her son two neckties as a present. The son, who wants to show his appreciation, wears one at their next meeting. Noticing it, the mother says, 'What's the matter? Don't you like the other one?' "

New World Worship: "A number of Jews debate whose synagogue is the most progressive. One of them says that in his temple an ashtray is kept near the Torah so that those who pray can continue to smoke. The second man says: 'We are much more progressive. At Yom Kippur we serve . . . ham sandwiches.' The third Jew claims, 'We are so progressive that we are closed on the High Holy Days.' "

Assimilation: "Little Ilse asks her mother, 'Mommy, do the Gentiles have Christmas trees, too?' "

Bodily functions: "A Jew . . . complains, 'Doctor, I cannot pee.' The physician offers him a urinal. There is no difficulty and the doctor expresses his astonishment that the patient complained. . . . The Jew explains, 'Of course, I can if they let me.' "

Marriage: "Isidor Meyer had apoplexy of the heart while playing cards in a coffee house, and died. . . . The delicate task of informing the widow is entrusted to one of the players. Arriving at the apartment he greets her, 'How do you do, Mrs. Meyer? I wanted only to tell you that your husband played poker today in the coffee house and lost a good deal.' 'He should have a stroke,' Mrs. Meyer shouts, full of anger. 'He already had it,' the messenger says."

Prayer: "A Jewish mother comes to the rabbi and laments that her child suffers from diarrhea. . . . The rabbi tells her, 'You must say Tephillim [i.e., read the Psalms].' Three days later the Jewess appears again, complaining that the child now suffers from the opposite symptoms. The rabbi recommends: 'Say again Tephillim.' 'But, Rabbi,' cries the horrified woman, 'Tephillim are constipating.' "

Gallows Humor: A man is "led to execution on Monday and remarks, 'This week has a fine beginning already.' "

These Jewish jokes, Reik says, serve various purposes. At his most desperate, "the Jew sharpens, so to speak, the dagger which he takes out of his enemy's hand, stabs himself, then returns it gallantly to the Antisemite with the silent reproach, 'Now see whether you can do it half as well.' " In less threatening situations, the humor acts "to bring relaxation in the ardour of battle with the seen and with the invisible enemy; to attract him as well as to repel him; and last . . . to conceal oneself behind them. Jewish wit hides as much as it discloses. Like the seraph in the Temple of the Lord it covers its face with two of its wings."

In *The Seven Lively Arts*, one of the earliest studies of popular American culture in the twenties, Gilbert Seldes attempted to place this comic energy. He called the force "daemonic," and theorized that "in addition to being more or less a Christian country, America is a Protestant community and a business organization—and none of these units is peculiarly prolific in the creation of daemonic individuals." He narrowed his focus to two individuals whose over-the-top performances had made them stars: Fanny Brice, who mocked her own origins with Yiddish dialect ("The Chiff is after me . . . he says I appil to him"), and Al Jolson, whose burnt-cork-mammy act never disguised the urgency of the cantor's son longing for approval. Both singers were "racially out of the dominant caste." Seldes thought that "possibly this accounts for their fine carelessness about . . . politeness and gentility."

In other words, they were loud, vulgar, and Jewish. They were also symptomatic of a time. Before the war, men who were manifestly of foreign background like Jolson or Eddie Cantor or Ed Wynn, or women like Brice and Sophie Tucker, would have been regarded as curiosities or grotesques. Now their gestures and intonations had a familiar resonance: they were the children of immigrants, educated on asphalt, divided between the religious background and the secular life, full of fears and drives that found their release onstage.

The daemons spawned hundreds of Catskill imitators. In

the tones and timing of vaudeville headliners, tummlers delivered the favorite vaudeville Jewish jokes of the twenties. They spoke of the yenta who was asked if she had passed through the menopause. She replied, "I ain't even been to the Raleigh yet." And of the owner whose little boy asks him for the definition of ethics. "It's when a woman hands me a bill and I give her change and we think it's a single. Later I discover she handed me a ten. Now the ethical question comes up: should I tell mine partner?" Of the guest who complains to his waiter, "The food at this hotel is poisonous. And such small portions!" Of Mrs. Sexauer calling her husband by his last name, only to be informed by a staffer that "in this place we don't even get a coffee break." Of the difference between a Frenchwoman, an Englishwoman and a Jewish woman in bed with their various husbands. The Frenchwoman swoons, "Ah, Pierre, your kiss! *C'est parfait.*" The Englishwoman sighs, "By Jove, Clive, that was a wizard kiss." The Jewish woman says, "You know, Jake, the ceiling needs a good painting." Of the man who wandered into a jewelry store with a broken watch in hand. "Here I do circumcisions," he was told. "If you're a *mohel*," the customer demanded, "how come you have jewelry in your window?" "You can suggest maybe something better I should put in the window?"

An allied daemonism was present among the owners. Russian immigrant Morris Weiner of White Roe, for example, spent the mornings instructing his social staff to "Pep Op De Peepul" at any cost. In the code of the Mountains this meant that the lights must not go out too early, the music must always play, the gags must never grow stale. At the end of their stay, customers must feel as if they could not have eaten and laughed one more time without prostration. All was subordinate to the Schedule. The tempo had picked up to presto, and no one who paid good money for a vacation would henceforth be allowed to draw an unorganized breath.

Like their competitors, the operators of Loch Sheldrake Rest announced that their resort was "meeting the requirements of the Time. It shall be conducted as a modern CAMP in every respect. A noted social director shall provide entertainment in the morning, afternoon and evening," and a nearby hotel was pleased to advertise that on its premises there was "something doing every minute." Among the most important of those things were meals; nature could not hope to compete with them. As one brochure had it, "Parties can walk past the Glen . . . to the Catskill Mountain House after breakfast and return by dinner time."

It did not take a sociologist to find the cracks in the stucco or to detect a melancholia underneath these regimented pleasures. A journalist up for the weekend observed that "efficiency enslaves the summer boarders; joy lives by the clock at Camp Legion," as if to let down for moment would readmit the darkness of Europe or the demands of the Bosses. These were very real fears; the guests knew all about the vagaries of luck and opportunity. They had a rich tradition of cautionary proverbs: "Wealthy man down, poor man up, it's not the same." "Ever since dying came in fashion, life hasn't been safe." "Jewish wealth is like snow in April." "From fortune to misfortune is but a step; from misfortune to fortune is a long way." Why should this wisdom fail to apply in America?

The guests were hardly sophisticated people; they lived on sidewalk rumor and newspaper sensations. But their more educated children were just as uneasy. The young people spoke about Klan meetings and the rantings of Henry Ford, and about a newer and more disturbing phenomenon. In the country's past, writers and intellectuals had rallied to the side of the Jews. Not this time. The Great War had left vendettas and scars. Someone had to be blamed for the destruction, and for the profits. The wrong people seemed to have money these days, and without much warning, beaky caricatures of the predatory Jew were back in fashion. Look at the new books and there was Meyer Wolfsheim, the conniving gangster of *The Great Gatsby*: "He's the man who fixed the World Series back in 1919." . . . "Why isn't he in jail?" "They can't get him, old sport. He's a smart man." There was Robert Cohn, the vain and unpleasant Princetonian of *The Sun Also Rises*, who was overmatched in a boxing ring: "It gave him a certain satisfaction of some strange sort, and it certainly improved his nose." There was e. e. cummings's little lyric:

beware of folks with missions
to turn us into rissions
and blokes with ammunicions
who tend to make incitions

and pity the fool who cright
god help me it aint no ews
eye like the steak all ried
but eye certainly hate the juse

At the outset these literary productions were of little concern. But books are sometimes felt as well as read, and they are often only a step or two ahead of national sentiment. The resentments described by many postwar writers served to make the Catskill vacationers a little more insular, and their laughter a bit more forced. In America these were only small signs of unpleasantness; Europe, as always, could provide stronger signals of distress. The entertainments like John Buchan's *The Thirty-nine Steps* provided sinister hints of what lay just ahead: "The Jew is everywhere, but you have to go far down the backstairs to find him. Take any big Teutonic business concern. If you have dealings with it the first man you meet is Prince *von und zu* Something, an elegant young man who talks Eton-and-Harrow English. But he cuts no ice. If your business is big, you get behind him and find a prognathous Westphalian with a retreating brow and the manners of a hog. . . . But if you're on the biggest kind of job and are bound to get to the real boss, ten to one you are brought up against a little white-faced Jew in a bathchair with an eye like a rattlesnake. Yes, sir, he is the man who is ruling the world just now, and he has his knife in the Empire of the Tsar, because his aunt was outraged and his father flogged in some one-horse location on the Volga."

And there was Graham Greene's vicious plutocrat Sir Marcus in *This Gun for Hire*, who "gave the impression that very many cities had rubbed him smooth," who "bowed with the very slightly servile grace of a man who might have been pawnbroker to the Pompadour" and who "gave a small tired sign as if there were too many things to be seen to, to be arranged, revenges to be taken, stretching into an endless vista of time, and so much time already covered—since the ghetto, the Marseilles brothel."

All very amusing, and very logical. For it was not the man but the caricature that had been rubbed smooth by very many cities and very many writers. There was surely no reason to invent a new villain when the old one did just as well. And what if he was offensive? the word went. Didn't the Jews tell even worse stories on themselves? You ought to hear them when they're with their own kind and think that no one is listening.

CHAPTER 7

MALAISE IN

THE MOUNTAINS

Park View House, Liberty, N. Y.

Until the mid-twenties, major criminals had no place in the Catskills. They flourished in the overfilled city across the river. As Frank Moss's *American Metropolis* had expressed in lurid detail, the Lower East Side was a primary breeding ground of Jewish delinquency. And yet all of Moss's investigations had failed to expose a single instance of homicide. The commandment not to kill was inviolable. In some thousand years of history, the Eastern Europeans could remember only one recorded case of premeditated murder of a Jew by a Jew. The killer's name was Reinetz, and the incident was so remarkable that in the shtetls of Russia the man's name became a verb: "to Reinetz" someone, as the Czar's rioters so often did, was to take his life.

Tradition lost its hold in the new climate; wherever immigrants reached out their hands they touched enticements. The ghetto produced its share of thieves, swindlers, prostitutes, pimps, racketeers. The surprise was, Irving Howe reports, that "in the life of the immigrant community as a whole, crime was a marginal phenomenon, a pathology discoloring the process of collective assertion and adjustment; most of the immigrants had neither training in, nor understanding of, nor appetite for, imported or native criminal methods. Crime was a source of shame, a sign that much was distraught and some diseased on the East Side; but it was never at the center of Jewish immigrant life." The notion of a professional killer among the Jews was unthinkable until the days of Louis Buchalter.

His large and fond family referred to him as Lepkeleh, later abbreviated to Lepke, Yiddish for dear little one, and nothing in his background suggested the sociopath. His father was a blameless hardware dealer; one of his brothers became a rabbi, another a pharmacist, the third a dentist. The only Buchalter daughter graduated from a local college and taught high-school English. The family attempted to stay together after the father's death when Lepke was thirteen, the age at which Jewish law declares the end of childhood, but there was no insurance and no future in New York. Mrs. Buchalter took her younger sons and sought charity from relatives in the West. Their sister agreed to stay in an apartment on the Lower East Side and see to the upbringing of Lepke. She was to testify later that once the family left town her brother proved unmanageable.

At seventeen he was arrested for stealing and served time in a reformatory. Perhaps it was there that he learned the skills that were to make him one of the most hunted men in America. Certainly the detention home only increased his bitterness and removed the last remnants of remorse. He was apprehended within two years of his parole for burglarizing lofts, and this time he was confined in Sing Sing prison. When he returned to the streets in the early twenties, his manner was as shy and remote as in the days of his youth. His eyes remained soft and, to the casual acquaintance, sympathetic. It was impossible to tell that Lepke had no moral sense at all.

In a recollection of crimes past, former District Attorney Burton Turkus reminds his readers that "contrary to the general belief that Prohibition spawned the underworld gang on the American scene, the criminal mob actually sprang from the wars between labor and management . . . subsequent to World War I." He offers the case of Louis Buchalter as proof. Lepke was an insignificant hoodlum until the first great industrial disputes. Sometime in the mid-twenties he befriended the Russian-born Gurrah Shapiro, an intimidating hulk whose nickname came from difficulties he had experienced with the English language. When the boy was asked a question he could not understand, Shapiro used to shout, "Gurrah'da here," his version of "Get out of here," usually accompanied by a blow or a kick.

Together the men found new methods for getting illicit money. Charles "Lucky" Luciano, one of the most prominent gangsters of the period, contemptuously bore in mind that "with the rest of us, it was booze, gambling, whores, like that. But Lepke took the bread out of the worker's mouth." Especially the Jewish worker. At first a contractor named Little Augie Orgen used Lepke and Gurrah to break strikes for factory owners. When demonstrators carried placards in front of a workplace, the two men and their hired thugs descended on the strikers with iron pipes wrapped in *The Daily Forward*. "The paper muffled the noise," one of the mercenaries said. "Besides, it gave the shmuck something to read in the hospital."

The pair, now referred to as the Gorilla Boys, moved to the other side of the disputes. During an intraunion crisis, a labor organizer hired Lepke to "break some heads." He stayed on to place his own men in office. "What can stop us from taking over an entire industry?" he asked Gurrah. The trick is "a captive union and a captive trade association. That way you got both the boss and the worker in your pocket."

With a combination of wiles and terror, including murder and acid-throwing, Lepke moved his men into factories "to help keep the books." No one dared to stop him. Orgen, his first employer, might have tried, but he was standing on Norfolk Street with his bodyguard, a handsome Irishman who called himself Legs Diamond, when the Gorilla Boys called out. When Little Augie turned their way, they shot him down. He was one of some hundred deaths ordered by Lepke for what was later called Murder, Inc., the enforcing end of the mobsters' organization. Even Albert Anastasia, a high-placed criminal, told friends: "I don't ask Louis any questions. I just go along. It would be healthier that way."

At the height of his power, Lepke controlled the clothing workers, leather workers, bakery and pastry drivers ("one slice out of every loaf for us"), motion-picture projectionists, flour and clothing truckers, taxis, the handbag and shoe industries. His income was prodigious, but beyond the customary big car and chauffeur he seemed to care little for the public swagger of the twenties gangster. Instead, he led a conventional home life with a plump wife and their little stepdaughter, occasionally traveled to Europe, and, like many men of his age and income, made journeys from his Manhattan apartment to the Mountains. The Buchalters were soon joined by Gurrah and his mother and some other associates at their favorite hotel, the Plaza, in Fallsburgh.

In part this was because the men derived some comfort from specifically Jewish surroundings. Shapiro's devoted mother, Joey Adams recalls, was the " 'Queen Bee' of the hotel. Everybody catered to her. Her son . . . lined her path with gold. She was a lovely woman but only aware that her son must be a big man because everybody was so nice to her and she got everything she wanted." On summer evenings Mrs. Shapiro listened impatiently when the mothers of Adams and Leonard Lyons, then beginning his career as a columnist for the *New York Post*, boasted about their sons' achievements. One night, says the comedian, "Mrs. Shapiro couldn't stand it any longer. She yelled to her friends so everybody in the casino could hear, " 'That's all I hear, Leonard Lyons, Leonard Lyons. He's only got his name in small letters in one paper. My son got his name in big letters and his picture on the front pages of all the papers almost every day, but do I say anything?' "

The gangsters had another reason for vacationing in the Mountains. Rum-running from Canada was a full-time occupation for some Mountain entrepreneurs. A big-league bootlegger gives his biography in William Kennedy's historically accurate novel *Legs*: " 'Jack Diamond's got a future in the Catskills. You can carve a whole goddam empire up there if you do it right. . . . And it's not like I got all the time in the world. The guineas'll be after me now.' "

" 'You think they won't ride up to the Catskills?' "

" 'Sure, but I'll be ready. That's my ball park.' "

The stadium was large, and except for the occasional swoops by federal agents, policemen chose to hear and see nothing; the small towns were officially sanctioned hideaways. Federal investigators once let it be known that they were looking for Lepke's lieutenant, Max Rubin. They were informed that he had gone to the Mountains on a "holiday." No further questions were asked. On his own, Rubin decided that it was safe to make a few round trips to Manhattan. When he was spotted on the city streets, Lepke set him up for execution.

The official atmosphere of laissez-faire encouraged a powerful group of Jewish and Italian criminals. They were referred to as the Syndicate, and their gambling casinos and slot machines soon sprouted all over the Catskills. The operation had begun with local concessionaires appearing in the spring to rent out boats, set up card tables, and sell cigarettes and candy. They and their equipment disappeared at the first sign of frost. After a few years, says Adams, "the concessionaires got greedy. They started running crap games and giant poker sessions. They sold liquor and booked horses. When the hoods tumbled to all this action, they naturally moved in. It wasn't too hard to convince the concession operators that they needed 'protection'—a few broken arms and one or two bodies in the lake were enough to start a whole new partnership."

The criminals installed their own bookies in selected hotels. These men could arrange for bets to be laid down on racetracks as far away as Churchill Downs in Kentucky. Some candy concessions operated under mob protection, and the Cherry Lawn, a bordello near Hurleyville, was owned and operated by the Syndicate.

The Yiddish theater star Seymour Rexcite, then a struggling young entertainer, remembered that "the story was, the big Syndicate figure Meyer Lansky controlled the places where you could play dice or cards. I stayed away from gambling but, like many other young performers, I was taken up for a time by the Jewish gangsters. Once Lepke sent a $50 bill to my table to have me sing 'My Yiddishe Momme.' You can imagine how far fifty dollars went in those days. Well, I sang it, but I turned down the money. Still, Lepke liked me and he would have me around as sort of a mascot. He encouraged me to gamble and kept after me and kept after me and finally I played at a casino and won about $800. I realized later it was probably rigged. But I kept the money and when I got back to the city I gave it to my father. He had no use for gamblers or crooks of any kind, but he took the cash without comment."

Rexcite also remembered Gurrah Shapiro: "There was an incident once at Singer's restaurant in Fallsburgh. Some locals came in and began insulting the girls at Lepke and Gurrah's table. Lepke got some of his men to clear out the girls, and then they had somebody get rid of the kid, meaning me. Then they tore the restaurant apart and sent the insulters to the hospital. Next day the police came around but nobody knew anything. There are bodies still at the bottom of Loch Sheldrake from those days."

Sheldrake and some of the other small deep lakes of Sullivan County served as a place of warning and execution. Adams "used to play pinochle with a sweet, soft-spoken man who brought me special cigars every weekend. He was particularly kind and tender to his mother. One day they found his body at the bottom of Swan Lake with a slot machine tied around his neck. It turned out he had been the leader of the toughest bunch of killers in the East."

An element of pride is evident in such recollections. Phil Silvers, then the tummler in the Evans Hotel, was drinking a cup of coffee in Trachtenberg's, a Monticello luncheonette, with a gangster named Jerry Polan. "I recall vividly an irrelevant detail," he said. "Jerry's thick, crepe soled shoes. . . . As we came out, two New York state troopers walked in. Tall, hulking men, they knew Jerry but couldn't touch him because the gambling was protected by their superiors. 'Oh, Christ,' one of the troopers mumbled, 'the Jews are out again.'

"I froze. No rational hoodlum wants to slug a policeman. Jerry gave the trooper a chance to save face. 'You weren't talking to me, were you?'

"The trooper grunted, 'What's it to you—?'

"That was as far as he got. Jerry launched himself at the troopers, kicking, slugging, strangling. This was the job he knew best. The thick crepe soles gave him the speed and leaps of a panther. One trooper pulled his gun. Jerry snatched it away and pistol-whipped the man. A carload of Jerry's boys pulled up to join the battle. A moment of stunned silence, as both sides realized what had happened: Nobody looks good when a state cop has been beat up. By one man. Jerry tossed the bullets out of the gun, slipped a hundred-dollar bill into the barrel and tossed it at the inert trooper.

"He immediately went into seclusion for a few days—on a cot in our scenery room—while thousands of dollars were spread around to soothe the troopers' bruised egos."

No discomfort was felt by the witness. Silvers concludes: "I respected the Jewish musclemen and racketeers. We must have had a soft-focus mutual attraction. They saw in me the gambler who takes his risks and pays his debts; I saw them as the only militant Jews. After thousands of years of racial indignities, the only ones who struck back were the outlaws."

One entertainer felt more ambivalent about entertaining outlaws: "In the beginning most of us got a kick out of performing for our own gangsters. They gave off a clear signal that the Jews were no longer to be pushed around. We not only had doctors and lawyers, we had powerful criminals just like the Italians and the Irish. It gave us some peculiar kind of stature. But then, sometimes a few days after we had all laughed together, a man we might have entertained was being fished out of the water, probably killed by another Jew. And that was sobering. It didn't take long for the glow to wear away."

Some of the victims were obscure; others, like Walter Sage, were known to the readers of tabloids. The body of Sage, a Syndicate member, was found floating in Swan Lake roped to a slot machine and a thirty-pound stone. And the sash-weighted corpse of Maurice "Frenchy" Carillot, a narcotics peddler, floated to the surface of Loch Sheldrake during one Decoration Day weekend. He had been shot five times and stabbed another seven.

There were periods in the twenties and early thirties when the Catskills was referred to as "Chicago with pines." In the summer of 1926, seven men armed with revolvers emerged from a stolen Buick and a Ford roadster. They entered the Seiken House two miles from Liberty, posing as authorities searching for slot machines. None was in evidence. Irritated, the men held up all 186 guests and, said *The Liberty Register*, climbed back in their cars "firing 15 or 20 shots as they left to keep guests in a quiet mood." Two summers later, holdup men came into the Loch Sheldrake casino on a silent Sunday morning, proclaiming their arrival with a volley of pistol shots. The bartender was Morris Steiglitz, who, the local paper delightedly said, moved "according to the traditions of the old school bartenders of less effete days." Steiglitz pulled his own pistol and shot the gunman nearest to him. The bandits peppered the bar and back wall with bullet holes, and fled empty-handed in their Packard, the twenties getaway car of choice.

And so it went in Sullivan County: a daylight jewelry robbery in the lobby of the Ambassador Hotel at Old Falls; an exposé of gambling devices at White Lake; a gun duel at Fallsburgh; widely publicized seizures of stills; and, in the case of the sleepy little railroad depot of Winterton, the discovery of a boxcar loaded with "cereal beverage" that turned out to be seventy-eight half-barrels of beer. The vagaries of Prohibition could always inspire an indulgent smile in the Mountains, but the citizens were growing impatient with the style and violence of the professional criminals. A 1931 headline in the *Hurleyville Sentinel* tried to smile trouble away: REGION STILL POPULAR WITH GANGSTERS, BUT SUMMER PASSED WITHOUT FATALITY. Citizens were not reassured when Waxey Gordon, one of the Syndicate celebrities, was apprehended in a cottage behind the Mansion House at White Lake, nor were they certain of Sheriff Ben R. Gerow's angry promise: "The lid is going down on slot machines in Sullivan County and it is going to stay down."

The lid never did close on the machines; they could still be found in scattered Catskill locales thirty years later. The criminal population eventually dispersed, not because of vows, but because state and federal authorities finally built substantive cases against Lepke and many of his associates, and because the gangsters could not stop killing. Two talent agents, Al Beckman and Johnny Pransky, had started to book actors and singers into the resorts. Beckman, whose clients were sometimes behind in their 10 percent fee, hired a former fighter named Billy Tosk as his collector of delinquent accounts. When the Syndicate heard about Tosk, Beckman was informed that he had acquired new partners. A mobster told him, "You don't need no collectors, that's our job."

According to Adams: "This took all the tough guy out of Al in one treatment . . . he ran for help." Beckman tried to get some aid from the gamblers . . . He reminded others that he once represented the girl friend of an executive in Murder, Incorporated. No one was willing to intervene. Still Beckman would not go to the federal authorities and Pransky refused to open his books to the Syndicate. There was a brief, hazardous period, says Adams, when it seemed likely that "they would either give or get the business. Al and Johnny . . . were saved by the lake. One day the police found several bodies floating around the Neversink, and the hoods were forced to change their locale to a less noticeable vacation spot."

By the time the lower-level gangsters returned, some of them as legitimate businessmen, the worst was over. Gurrah was in jail, and Lepke was on his way to the execution chamber. The young poet Robert Lowell, serving a sentence for conscientious objection, remembered him:

> *A fellow jailbird . . . taught me "the hospital tuck,"*
> *and pointed out the T-shirted back*
> *of* Murder Incorporated's *Czar Lepke,*
> *there piling towels on a rack,*
> *or dawdling off to his little segregated cell full*
> *of things forbidden the common man:*
> *a portable radio, a dresser, two toy American*
> *flags tied together with a ribbon of Easter palm.*

Malaise in the Mountains

Flabby, bald, lobotomized,
he drifted in a sheepish calm,
where no agonizing reappraisal
jarred his concentration on the electric chair—
hanging like an oasis in his air
of lost connections. . . .

Even during the period of their greatest influence, through Prohibition and the beginnings of the Depression, the Syndicate found pockets of resistance. When the trouble seemed to outweigh the profit, the criminals backed off. At the White Roe Hotel, for example, a shadowy figure who leased pinball machines was told by owner Morris Weiner that he and his paraphernalia were unwelcome. The man never called again. "Pop Weiner was aware," says one of the early tummlers, "of the manner in which the gangsters gained a hold. They would come in to service the machines, request and get a piece of the concession, place prostitutes in residence and then put themselves in position to loan the owners money. That would be bad for the owner and worse for the guests. Money was tight, and Pop didn't want working people to lose their hard-earned salaries at gambling."

As federal prosecutions began in earnest, more owners came to agree with Weiner. They closed ranks against the Syndicate, and against the hard times that threatened to destroy all they had built. In the early thirties the most ambitious of them founded a newspaper, *The Mountain Hotelman*, partly in Yiddish, mostly in English, to express a new philosophy. "Shall We Organize and Exist or Compete and Destroy Ourselves?" asked one editorial. "The last ten years of unscrupulous and untrammelled competition have brought us nothing but misery. Can we—dare we—enter into the next year and years with the same individualistic, anarchistic spirit, of everybody for himself and the devil take us all?"

The paper argued for the railroad to assign a separate place on platforms for each hotel, doing away with the angry chaos that greeted passengers. It lobbied for easier credit and aid for the less fortunate. When it was not opposing the criminal element, it was offering readers promotional and merchandising tips: "Give Reunions More Attention, Watch Them Pay Dividend," advised one feature. "Most generally, the old guests bring new ones—which adds to your acquaintance, your 'prospects' and your mailing list, if you're wise." There were editorial cartoons: Inefficient hotel man, fishing with a line marked Promises: "How come you have so much better luck than I?" Efficient hotel man fishing with Performance: "It isn't luck, brother, it's efficiency." There were columns by the reliable Yiddish humorist B. Kovner, still at his familiar Catskill stand after nearly thirty years: "I asked a guest how many children he has. 'Four,' he said, 'two are married and two still live.' "

But there was a new moral tone. On one occasion Kovner abandoned his sarcastic tone to run a melancholy letter verbatim. The *cri du coeur* came from a hotel owner. The guests, says the writer, eat and drink, inhale the fresh country air, "take walks in secluded places, hidden paths, secret nooks, and often times steal themselves into dense, green bushes to make love, enjoy life . . . but we, the hotel keepers, cannot eat, we cannot sleep, nor can we make love. We can't have foolishness in our minds. Often we don't know the date of the day. Only creditors come with bills to collect. That's all they do is put out their hands, 'Give me, you owe me.' " The writer goes on to commemorate a fellow owner who died suddenly of appendicitis. "When his wife received the news of his death (it was 11 a.m.) she gave orders to the musicians not to play at dinner time, not until the funeral was over.

"But the guests began to grumble.

" 'We came here for pleasure,' they said, 'and we must have music at our meals.'

" 'Be reasonable,' cried the widow, 'my husband is dead and not buried yet. How can we allow to have music at this time? Aren't you human?'

"Eighty per cent of the guests checked out and ran away . . . the business had to go on. The widow and the orphans with tears in their eyes were compelled to plead with the remnant of people to remain. They were given the music at the dinner; the orchestra played jazz while the dead body of the owner was not buried yet.

"The crowd ate, asked for second helpings, for more chicken, more cake, more pudding, and the waiters were sweating while serving them. Meantime the widow was sitting in the kitchen with a broken heart and streaming tears, and the music played on.

"Oh, God, where is the pen, the skill, the talent to describe the pathos?"

A malaise now seemed to hover over the Mountains. Maurice Samuel's poem "Al Harei Catskill" describes his ancestors, Talmudic students, merchants, honey-gatherers:

> *While I, who live in Babylon the New,*
> *Preach the Return to startled Jews, and spend*
> *This summer in the Catskill Mountains here . . .*
> *And here in Catskill what do Jews believe?*
> *In* Kosher, *certainly; in* Shabbas, *less,*
> *(But somewhat, for they smoke in secret then.)*
> *In* Rosh Hashana *and in* Yom Kippur,
> *In charity and in America.*
> *But most of all in Pinochle and Poker,*
> *In dancing and in jazz, in risqué stories,*
> *And everything that's smart and up-to-date.*

It should be noted that, censorious as he was, Samuel stayed where he was. Like the vulgarians he railed against, the writer needed an affordable oasis. The Mountains had a thousand. In the Depression years of the early thirties, resort fees included three meals a day plus snacks. The entertainment was well rehearsed and professional, and the kitchen and athletic staffs consisted principally of college men at work for the entire summer to earn their tuition.

For an epoch of breadlines and soup kitchens, the *kuchaleyns*—spelled in a variety of ways depending on the writer's country of origin—represented one of the country's greatest bargains. "Child from its beginnings of the shrunken pocketbook," says Harry Gersh in his study of the "Poor Man's Shangri-La," "the decade of the Depression was its opportunity. Suppose stocks plunged downward and the dresses hung customerless on the racks, a man must still fix himself—indeed all the more reason."

The price was fixed no matter how many people occupied a room: "It is the same money if mama and the kids come up alone, and it is the same money if the whole family comes along. So one can afford to be a sport. For the Fourth of July week one has brother Jake and his family as guests and two weeks after that Joe and his kids. It sounds very nice, 'Come up for a couple weeks to my summer place.' "

As the snows began to melt, ads appeared in the daily papers: BUNGalows, hskpg apts, all impvmnts, all spts, 75m N.Y., reasonable." Improvements, housekeeping, sports, miles, all were abbreviated. Only the key word "reasonable" was spelled out. Anyone who had been to the *kuchaleyn* the year before knew that the ad was an encoded message. The sports were mainly pinochle, mah-jongg, and hikes. The improvements—new stoves and refrigerators to replace the old iceboxes and overflowing sinks—were unlikely to be in place; and crows were the only travelers who could make the trip from the George Washington Bridge to Monticello in less than ninety miles. But the price was within reach of almost everyone.

The *kuchaleyn* owners could set their watches by the procession of renters. Bargainers came in early spring. Times were getting worse, they argued, the season had not yet begun. Who knew how many bungalows would be empty by July? In May a second batch appeared. They happened to be out for a drive and thought they might drop in for a look at the "less expensive" dwellings. The regulars arrived in June; the latecomers in July. They assumed that anything unrented would be let go at a discount. All four groups paid exactly the same rate.

Not everything was inexpensive: "Vegetables, home grown, and staples, city imported, are available from the landlord's own store," says Gersh. "It's not really a store. The landlord is the first to admit it. It's a service to the renters run—almost—without profit. The vegetables are good, vine-ripened. They come from the farm down the road. By some peculiarity of capitalist economics they cost just a little more than the same vegetables—picked, packed, and shipped to New York—bought at a high-rent greengrocer's.

"The landlord explains it this way, 'But this is fresh picked. All the vitamins. It's not worth a penny more?' "

Country staples were augmented by husbands arriving on Friday night for the weekend. Their luggage was packed in the accepted Mountain manner: leisure clothes in paper bags, meals in the suitcases. This was to avoid insulting the owner. "He doesn't hold with food from the city," reports Gersh. "It's not that he minds losing the business, but bringing food from the city is a personal reflection on his prices and his quality. City food brings mice, too. The landlord's displeasure is important when it comes to small repairs—the rent is already paid. So the lox and corned beef ride in the suitcase."

Most of the men washed and changed into slacks and sport shirts, though almost every *kuchaleyn* featured at least one rigid figure who wore a white shirt and tie all weekend. The decibel level in the dining room was notorious: "Fifty per cent adult women noise. Forty-nine per cent piping children noise. And one per cent 'yes,' 'hum,' and 'uhhuh' from the men."

After a luxurious supper—fresh-killed chicken, local produce, and imported delicacies—the men drifted outside and lowered themselves onto the porch rockers. In the dark they surreptitiously loosened their belts, inhaled the scented air, and praised the country life. In half an hour they wandered back inside to the dining room. Presently, cigars were ignited, tables rearranged, and poker, pinochle, gin rummy, and mah-jongg games begun.

Saturday nights were another matter. "It's a peculiar fact," Gersh says, "but with all the space in the Mountains, ninety-three per cent of all *kuchaleyns* are within walking distance of a hotel or summer camp that has professional entertainment and a dance band. One explanation is that the rent of the *kuchaleyns* is determined in part by the quality of this nearby—and free—entertainment. One enterprising entrepreneur even used it in his advertising. But that's misrepresentation. He couldn't guarantee entrance.''

In earlier times the owners benignly looked on as their neighbors helped themselves. Then paying guests began to complain about freeloaders who took the best seats and crowded the dance floor. Guards were posted, fences built, rules enforced. The owners were unaware that what one mind can conceive, another can solve. Some intruders had boats cached away and knew of secret landing places on the lakeshore. From there they made their way up the beach to the recreation halls. Others trained their children to find penetrable spaces in the steel fences. A hotel owner remembered the invasions: "You could always tell when they were coming. Far off down the road there was a strange kind of illumination. It came from flashlights as people worked their way to the outskirts of the hotel. When the little beams went off, you knew they had somehow worked their way in.''

In 1929 Moss Hart moved up to the great Flagler Hotel. After years as an impoverished tummler, he reflected, "I was now the most highly paid, the most eagerly sought-after director of the Borscht Circuit." By the early thirties, Hart had a retinue of twenty-six, including a solemn young man of quiet but unswerving ambition named Dore Schary. Hart's chief competitor was Don Hartman, social director of Grossinger's, "a curious quirk of circumstance considering the fact that Dore Schary was to become head of Metro-Goldwyn-Mayer and Hartman the head of Paramount Pictures. Not one of us would have believed this to be in the realm of even remote possibility.''

The Flagler theater seated fifteen hundred, and its electrical switchboard, fly loft, and scenery dock were the equal of Broadway houses. "It was the pride of the Catskills," says Hart. "Its audience dressed to the hilt for the Friday and Saturday night shows. At the height of the season, such was my weighty reputation as a social director by then, overflow crowds came from other hotels from miles around to see the shows, even though they were charged an admission fee, and on Saturday nights a couple of hundred were always turned away.''

Only the owner remained unimpressed. Old Man Morganstern, as he was called out of earshot, habitually wandered the
grounds of the Flagler, loudly remarking on each improvement.
In his theater he liked to walk down the aisle, smoothing the
seats, touching the wood, and appraising his own decor, often
during a performance. At the close of one summer, Hart presented a drama set in a cathedral, with a choir chanting prayers
upstage. As the play neared its denouement, Morganstern shuffled down the aisle, up the stairs, and across the footlights. While
the actors strove to maintain the mood, the old man fingered
the luxurious velvet drape. He showed it to the audience and,
as the action continued behind him, explained, "This is an expensive piece of material—it cost me five hundred dollars."

The suffering Hart made notes, swore vengeance, and
stayed on to perfect his craft. It was, he concedes, "the ability,
week after week, to present full-length plays like *The Show-Off*
and *The Trial of Mary Dugan*, and short ones like *The Valiant*
. . . that kept the social hall jammed and kept Don Hartman, a
few miles away at Grossinger's, well up on his toes."

News of these glossy professional shows traveled rapidly,
and even the smallest resorts were put on notice. Their guests
became discontent with round-the-clock food and jokes. They
wanted Broadway in the Mountains. White Roe, concentrating
on a younger clientele, presented audiences with socially significant pieces like Clifford Odets's *Waiting for Lefty* and Irwin
Shaw's *Bury the Dead*. At Totem Lodge, social director Henry
Tobias raided the current musicals—*Good News, Ziegfeld Follies,
Connecticut Yankee, Whoopee, Girl Crazy*—and condensed them
without the authors' permission, "eliminating," as he saw it,
"the weak spots of Cole Porter, George Gershwin and Rodgers
and Hart."

Still, no stage production ever eliminated the Catskills' con-
suming need for tummlers. The theatrical presentations only
occupied one or two nights a week. The rest of the time, guests
were to be prodded, cajoled, and teased into laughter and activity, forever informed that they were having the vacation of
their lives.

In her paper, "Shylock's Mispoche," Ellen Schiff points out

that in "the borscht circuit . . . the entertainer's stock in trade included making all of Jewish life the subject of parody." A decade earlier, Al Jolson and Eddie Cantor had subtly mimicked their cantor fathers; now they were doing it openly. The voluminous Sophie Tucker "started interpolating Jewish words in some of my songs, just to give the audience a kick"; Fanny Brice would come on as a Yiddish Mme Du Barry: "I'm a bed voman, but I'm demm good company"; Irving Berlin wrote "Yiddle on Your Fiddle" and "Cohen Owes Me $97"; George Jessel telephoned the first of an endless parade of Jewish mothers: "Hello, Mama? This is your son Georgie—yeah, from the checks every week . . . Mama, what's gonna be with Anne's fella already? . . . I know he's such a nice boy, but he hasn't worked in three years . . . Oh, now he's going in with his father. What does his father do? . . . He's on strike . . . I see . . . He worked in a five-and-ten-cent store but he got fired? . . . Oh, he forgot the prices!

"What's that? You have spots in front of your eyes? Put on your glasses . . . Oh, now you can see the spots better? . . . What's that? Cousin Maxie swallowed the five-dollar gold piece you gave Sammy for Christmas? What are you gonna do? . . . Oh, he's gonna live with us for a while."

Tummlers caught the spirit of these routines, and as their confidence grew, they began to make contributions of their own. One talked about the livestock in the Mountains, where a Holstein was crossed with a Guernsey to get a Goldstein. Another spoke of the time he was delivering ice to a Gentile resort, only to discover his father, an Orthodox rabbi, in the arms of a beautiful blond shiksa. "You, Papa! You!" The old man broke from his embrace: "Yes, my son, but I don't eat here."

The stand-up comedian interacted with guests who shared his attitudes, his outlook, his vocabulary. In a way he *was* his audience, emphasizing faults that were theirs as well as his, at once overambitious, oversensitive, and, he insisted, oversexed. Hostile and self-deprecating, insulting and ingratiating, he was afflicted with what Saul Bellow was later to call "Pagliacci gangrene."

The tummlers' reservoir of Jewish phrases overflowed from the Mountains to the lexicons of Americana:

Malaise in the Mountains

Get lost.
You should live so long.
My son, the physicist.
I need it like a hole in the head.
All right already.
It shouldn't happen to a dog.
Okay by me.
He knows from nothing.
Do me something.
From this he makes a living?
You should excuse the expression.
Go fight City Hall.
On him it looks good.
Wear it in good health.

The large stock of phrases was further enriched when news-paper columnists added three more, Borscht Belt, Sour Cream Sierras, and Derma Road. All were references to the Catskill resorts. Owners were ambivalent about these labels. They hoped for a more ecumenical crowd once the Depression passed, and the sobriquets seemed to invite a strictly kosher clientele. On the other hand, it was the Jewish guests who kept the Mountains in business. "In the thirties they would do anything to be here," says an owner. "They shared kitchens, had communal bath-rooms and showers. We rarely had an empty bed. In 1931, for example, we grossed $46,000. Of course, our profit was $1,200. But it didn't matter. We were all poor together, and we all believed that we would have our arrival the day after tomorrow."

"Arrival" meant recognition outside of the Mountains. To that end the owners observed dietary laws but tried to attract goyim with names like The Raleigh, Goldberg's Spanish Villa, Ginsberg's Retreat, the Avon Lodge, The Laurel. Entertainers regarded Catskill jobs as auditions for the Big Time. Audiences cried when singers finished their act with "My Yiddishe Momme," but wanted the jokes told in English so that they could repeat them at the office. By the middle of the thirties everyone in the Catskills was pondering the question openly or uncon-

sciously: Should I stay true to the ancient Jewish laws and traditions? Or should I put both feet in the American mainstream?
It was not a trivial predicament. There was no correct answer.
Although hardly anyone was wise enough to see it at the time,
either option would put a finish to the Catskill way of life.

CHAPTER 8

SEX, LOVE, AND

EXPANDABLE TIME

Nowhere was the Jewish dilemma more apparent than in the disordered field of courtship. In earlier times, Mountain resorts represented the Lower East Side with its guard down, places where for a few weeks youth could disregard the national demand for assimilation and restraint. Now a fresh generation was coming up to the Catskills. Their voyage had begun in the New York ghettos, but it had continued outward to the far reaches of the city: the stately apartment houses of the Bronx, the attached homes and vibrant street life of Brooklyn and Queens—even in rare instances the sacred and once-restricted suburbs. English was the first tongue of these young American Jews. The majority of them were uncomfortable with the singsong of the Yiddish they heard at home. Tales of the old country had no significance. The past meant oppression and despair; it had nothing to do with them. They were free to choose what they laughed at, whom they saw, what they wore, or where they vacationed. And then came the Depression. Before it was finished, young Jews were observing social customs as rigid as any their grandparents had experienced in the shtetl. In two years, economic crisis had undone the work of two generations.

The thirties were particularly cruel to single females. With a third of the nation out of work, young women were not welcomed into any profession except homemaking. For them, marriage remained the one acceptable exit from the class into which they had been born. Single males enjoyed marginally better prospects: they could enter the professions, but only after an expensive education. This meant working their way through college and graduate school, unless they could find that great prize, the bride with the dowry. The European *shadchens*, the marriage brokers Sholem Aleichem had called "dealers in livestock," were obsolete, remembered only in stories circulated by the tummlers:

After a big buildup, the *shadchen* trots out a prospective fiancée. The young man hisses into his ear: "You said she was young. She's forty if she's a day! You said she was beautiful, and she looks like a duck! You said she was shapely, and she's fat enough for two! You said—"

"You don't have to whisper," says the *shadchen* proudly. "She's also hard of hearing."

Or: "You said the girl's father is dead. I just found out he's in jail for embezzlement."

"So? That you call that living?"

In private, parents were quick to admit how much they missed those old Jewish arrangers. For all their crafty salesmanship, the professionals were on the side of the single, dangling their long lists of "boys of exactly the right age and background, and no guesswork," and girls whose fathers had "a fortune from stores, investments and real estate holdings." Today, in the trough of the Depression, marriageable Jews were on their own. They looked around them and, by common consent, decided that the Catskills offered the richest hunting ground.

"Up there, accounts of fabulous weddings were repeated

like prayers," according to the wife of a retailer who stayed in the Catskills after her marriage. "Everyone had learned of the N.Y.U. scholarship winner who met the daughter of a costume jewelry factory owner. Everyone got wind of the stenographer who borrowed her whole outfit from her older sister and married a heart specialist. That was the trouble. Everyone knew *of*. But no one knew personally. I certainly didn't know. Still, I met my husband here. In those days, that was a success story in itself."

A partner in a prominent Manhattan law firm has his own wry memories. "I went up to the Catskills, quite frankly, to get rich. There was a slow way, by becoming a professional and working my way up. But I was in a hurry. I thought the best thing to do was to marry well. In the hotels that catered to families, it was pretty easy to tell who had money and who didn't. After all, you saw the girl with her parents. She might put on airs, but *they* rarely did. What you saw was what you got: a fat mama and a tired papa blowing their year's savings on two weeks in the country.

"In the singles resorts it was a lot harder to separate the fake from the genuine article. You have to remember that in the thirties all the great department stores were Jewish-owned: Macy's, Gimbels, Bloomingdale's, Stern's. And the rumor was that every young woman was a relative of someone who owned one of those emporiums. To find out the truth you tried to listen to her vocabulary, see the way she carried herself, how she acted with her friends. When you were satisfied you made your move. After waiting on her table for five days, I pounced—the girl in question knew so much about merchandising she *had* to be an heiress. By the time I discovered that she was only a secretary to a buyer at Bloomingdale's it was too late: I was smitten. The marriage lasted five years, and I paid alimony and child support for fifteen more. Then, at last, she remarried—someone she met in the Catskills. So I guess it had a happy ending after all."

A secretary from the Bronx spoke in great detail about her favorite Mountain romances. "One of the girls, Shirley, and her boyfriend, Jackie, the trumpet player, had a very interesting understanding between them. Shirley was nuts about Jackie, but she was looking desperately for a better-class catch. Like my mother, she considered musicians lowly characters. What she wanted was a lawyer in the making, but meanwhile, she didn't want to let go of her trumpet player until she had a better deal. As the saying goes, a musician in the hand is worth two attorneys if you can't find one.

"Shirley was very frank with Jackie. She told him she would accept his friendship ring with the understanding that if she met the guy she was looking for she would return it. He was so in love with her that he accepted her terms.

"The payoff is that the following summer she went to Copake for Memorial Day weekend. There she met a waiter who was studying law at Columbia. She married him on Columbus Day and returned the ring to Jackie like she promised. Shirley's lawyer became vice president of a big department store in New York, and Jackie later used the same ring to marry the daughter of the owner of the hotel. He's now one of the biggest tycoons on the Borscht Belt. As for me . . . I married the poor but happy musician who still works for scale."

As the playwright Marc Connelly saw it, owners of the Mountain playgrounds had but one purpose in life. It was their duty to demonstrate that "for two weeks one is alive after 50 weeks of sleeping."

Here, the owner informs his clients, "are life, adventure, joy, rest. . . . Here clocks are forgotten." For the guests, "there are no Monday mornings, or weary Saturday nights. . . . The accent on romance is assiduously stressed . . . [including] free vacations the following year to brides and bridegrooms who met in camp the summer before."

We have noted Moss Hart's description of the uniforms of the day, blazers and white flannel trousers for the men; elaborate outfits, changed three or four times a day, for the women. Unimaginable sacrifices were made by poor families in order to furnish those wardrobes. In the thirties, says a veteran of the bungalow colonies, "if you were not married by nineteen, which I was, you were considered an old maid." Candidates for marriage were lured by the usual means of plumage and mating calls. Then came a gavotte with more than two dancers. The third, and sometimes the most important participant, was the proprietor. It was he who was responsible for the Catskills' two most vital illusions. The first, male superabundance, was created by hiring college men as waiters and members of the social staff. The second illusion, female wealth, was accomplished by promoting rumors and gossip to the effect that nearly every unmarried woman stood to inherit her family's unpublicized but burgeoning fortune. The owner had many collaborators. As one of Hart's colleagues told it, "Since both sexes were vying for the best catch, it was natural that both would try to enhance their status to make the chase easier. All around the grounds you heard whispers of: 'See that fella with the clipped haircut? His father is worth millions,' or 'That blonde with the skinny legs is the daughter of a very wealthy Wall Street broker.' Of course, it was the boy with the clipped haircut and the blonde with the skinny legs who started the rumors, which were fanned by friends who expected you to do the same with them."

The social director never started the gossip; he merely amplified it. One young man took Joey Adams into his confidence: "Look, don't tell anybody, but my friend Charlie Davis is here incognito. He just inherited a million bucks from his old man and he wants to relax and enjoy it. So keep it quiet, please.' If I had kept it quiet the bum would never have applauded me. . . .

"Of course, the big heir was doing the same thing for his friend: 'I'm telling you 'cause you're in show business, but let's keep it to ourselves. My buddy is here looking over the local scene to get some girls for a picture he is producing about the Borscht Circuit. Don't let on or he'll get mobbed.' Who am I to break a confidence? So naturally I spread the word everywhere."

Throughout the Mountains, owners who catered to singles called their places "camps" and designed the landscapes so that they were spatially, temporally, and physically miles apart from the familiar world of the inhabitants. No family life could be found here, no squalling children or grandparents rocking their way through the summer. Vast and pretentious lobbies were out; in their place were community dining rooms, dormitory accommodations, outdoor meeting places under the sky or beneath the canvas roof of a tent. In *Camping Out*, a contemporary book for camp owners, the Playground and Recreational Association of

America offered some canny advice: "In order to provide the maximum of restful recreation, adult camps should be located as far away from the environment to which the campers are regularly accustomed as is practicable. In general the more completely the camp site is shut off from the normal environmental condition the better." Everything was made to seem different in the Catskills. Time itself was redefined. No longer the river into which no one could step twice, it had become a lake one could constantly revisit, like the body of water a few hundred yards down the hill from the recreation hall.

The Hebrew Education Society, which established summer camps for the children of Brownsville, expressed the idea in its bulletin: "When one stops to consider that 14 camp days (15 hours per day) are comparable to 52 school days (5 hours per day) the full impact of camp as an intensive experience becomes doubly evident." Arthur Kober's 1937 Broadway comedy of summer camps, *Having Wonderful Time*, put it another way. On the grounds of Kamp Karefree, a suitor named Chick romances a girl, Teddy, for six days. Then he articulates a thought that must have occurred to thousands of lovers in the Catskills:

CHICK: Supposing a fella was seeing you in the city. Regularly, I mean. Let's say two or three times a week.

TEDDY: Go on.

CHICK: Of those two, three times a week he spends, let's say, four hours a night. But . . . he doesn't spend those four hours solidly with you. I mean, you take in a lecture here, a movie there—you know. So of the four hours, he spends two solid hours with you. Now two hours times two nights a week, that's four solid hours you're in each other's company. Follow me?

TEDDY: Proceed.

CHICK: Let's multiply four hours a week by four weeks a month and we have sixteen hours a month he sees you. Suppose, merely for the sake of argument, it's a close relationship. Say six months. Right?

TEDDY: Continue.

CHICK: Sixteen times six months—six, three to carry—ninety-six hours you've known each other to warrant a steady relationship.

Sex, Love, and Expandable Time

TEDDY: So what's the point?

CHICK: Simply this. Up to and including today I've been seeing you
for breakfast, lunch and supper. I've been with you till two, three
o'clock in the morning. Correct?

TEDDY: Granted.

CHICK: That's fifteen hours a day we've been seeing each other really
solidly. Multiply that by six and that's—that's ninety hours!

TEDDY: Proving?

CHICK: Proving a very significant fact. Namely, that we've known each
other the approximate equivalent of six months in the city! Six
months! Think of it, Teddy!

Teddy does think of it, and after the requisite complications,
she marries him. The argument of expandable time was irresistible, especially when it was articulated by that most influential
figure the college man. Usually he was seen in the outfit of a
waiter, a busboy, or a social staffer. His position was symbiotic.
He needed the job, and the job needed him.

David Katz, owner of the Totem Lodge, made a policy of
hiring future doctors, dentists, and lawyers for his dining-room
staff. Each week he called a meeting to remind the male employees that they were not on salary for their abilities to balance
plates: "I hire you to socialize with the guests. You're all clean-
looking boys. You're all eligible for marriage. You all have big
futures. Remember, heiresses I got here as guests." The young
men were expected to dress up at night and mingle with the
paying customers. Aware that this would lead to complications,
Katz advised his listeners: "We want you to romance the girls,
but be discreet." The President, he reminded them, "sleeps with
his wife but you don't read about it in the papers."

Adams remembers that "Katz's big worry was . . . he had
eighteen canoes and twenty-five waiters. 'What am I going to
do about the seven other waiters?' This meant that you had better
not be caught in a boat unless you had a female guest with you."
To make certain that those guests had an escort, Katz forbade
his staff to leave the premises at night without permission. For
a time he actually locked the gates at dusk. After four weeks at
Totem Lodge, one employee rebelled. A few hours before dawn,

he went to the waterfront, stole a boat, and rowed across the lake to freedom. From then on, wags privately referred to the Lodge as Katz's Koncentration Kamp.

Few of them tried to break out. The Depression was a more formidable wall than any gates or decrees. Max Wolff, a prominent Long Island surgeon, thought of the day he applied to a camp in Livingstone Manor where, the year before, a friend had worked as a waiter and earned $500. That was enough to pay tuition and expenses for an entire academic year. It would cost Wolff $50 to get the job, the owner said, because "I will have to buy you several uniforms and this money guarantees my outlay." When Wolff hesitated, the owner pressed on: "It's a good investment. Two of my waiters married millionaires' daughters. It'll happen to you, too, I promise." Much later the student learned that "most of the waiters and busboys never got their deposits back. He always found some excuse to fire them before the end of the season. It was a financial means to help open the hotel for the summer."

The dining-room staff was considered third-class help. "Our accommodations were . . . old Army tents, no floors or plumbing, pegs to hang your clothes. . . . Our hours were interminable and the food was yesterday's menu. . . . I didn't meet a millionaire's daughter [as] promised. In fact, with the fifty-dollar-a-week secretaries at my tables, I didn't make enough to keep me in stethoscopes—but I sure developed a bedside manner."

That manner was assiduously cultivated in every adult camp, often under the most difficult conditions. The female guests usually shared rooms; the male staff, installed in dormitories, had almost forgotten the meaning of the word "privacy." At White Roe, as in many other places catering to the unmarried, some couples explored the parked, unlocked cars in a vacant area across from the baseball field, or rowed to a secluded section of woods across the lake. Others made use of the "silver room," a place where dining utensils were shelved, along with huge soft bags of dirty linen, temporarily stored en route to the laundry. The room had numerous liabilities: there were no locks on the swinging doors leading in, or on the exit at the rear of the building; many staffers used the shadowy chamber as a shortcut on their way to the casino, lake, or back lawns. Even so, it became a favorite trysting place with its own etiquette. "A lot of exploits took place among the spoons, forks and dirty linens," says the former social director, Dr. Saul Gladstone. "Anyone hurrying across the silver room while a 'session' was taking place simply kept on walking through the room and out the back door, never turning his head, but remarking enthusiastically, 'Enjoy!' "

The aura of sex and money gave the Catskills a new, and largely inaccurate, reputation as an upstate Gomorrah. It was true that Shawanga Lodge, an adults-only resort, was dubbed "Schweinga Lodge" (pregnant in Yiddish), and that the arrival of the "husband" or "bull" trains on Friday night could cause embarrassment to some of the more estrous wives. And it was true that the tummlers made much of this very raw material in their routines. Adams reported a conversation in the men's room:

" 'How you making out with Rhoda?'

" 'That box? No score—a waste of two Cokes. How about Laura?'

" 'Looks good. Now remember, I got the room for the first two hours.'

" 'Well, how will I know if I can come in or not?'

" 'If the rubber band is around the doorknob, you know I'm busy, so get lost.' "

Meantime, the ladies were doing their own planning:

" 'Don't leave me alone with that creep,' Rhoda was saying. 'His hands sweat . . . So what if his father is a big contractor? He's too damn anxious. He brought me one lousy Cuba Libre and he's looking to squeeze it outta me all night.' She took one sip of the Cuba Libre and continued without missing a beat. 'How do you like Marvin?'

" 'He's okay. A long distance call to my mother I wouldn't make. But . . . it's better than nothing.'

" 'So what are you gonna do?'

" 'I don't know. I'll see. Meanwhile you got any perfume in the room?'

" 'Yeah, it's in the third drawer in the bureau, under the pajamas. Why?'

" 'Well, in case he comes back to the room . . . Do you mind?'

" 'No, but what'll *I* do?'

" 'Well, can't you stay with Ira for an hour or so?'

" 'What'll I do with that jerk? How will I know when I can come back?'

" 'The shades will be halfway up.' "

Married couples also provided tummlers with hours of material. One described a proprietor walking by as an eight-year-old speaks to his father: "On weekdays Ma loves up the dancing instructor." The embarrassed father looks at the proprietor and stammers, "Don't listen to him, he's a little kid." The owner assures his guest, "Who's listening?"

Another comedian spoke about the husband who takes an early train and surprises his gorgon of a wife in the arms of a musician. "Max," he cries, "I *must* . . . but you?"

The tale of a prominent ophthalmologist was a favorite at every resort: After he learns that his much younger wife is enjoying a liaison with a swimming instructor, the physician demands a confrontation. The lover confesses, then goes on to explain that the wife is merely human, that she feels isolated and deprived of the affection she so sorely needs. He advises his listener to bring the Mrs. along to medical conferences, to take regular evening walks with her, to be more demonstrative. The doctor nods sagely, rises, and grasps the athlete's hand: "Thank you. And what do I owe you for this visit?"

For all of the rumored activity, a sense of propriety and decorousness pervaded the Mountains. Herman Wouk, who had been the children's waiter at Tamarack Lodge in the thirties, looked back in his novel *Marjorie Morningstar*. At the imaginary camp South Wind, a social director, Noel Airman, informs Marjorie that among the campers, "there isn't as much sex here as you think. Among the staff, I grant you, being cooped up together all summer, it does get to be a bit of a barnyard. But the guests are entirely different . . . The fellows do come here with the usual bachelor's dream of seducing a pretty girl . . . but they don't have much luck. The nice girls, the Shirleys, come with their tight bathing suits and bright flimsy dresses, intent on trapping a husband, and not inclined to settle for less. It's the pigs who mainly benefit from the tension that ensues. Their hopes are low and humble. They only want some attention, and they'll pay with their messy bodies for it. A few of the men really do break down and get interested in some nice girl. A few more, the less fussy ones, end up coupling with the pigs. . . . The wonder is not that there's so much sex at South Wind, but that there's so little of it. Most of the people get nothing more in the way of sex than a few fumbled kisses and hugs, and the handful who do go further with it skulk and crawl in the dark as though they were committing a crime." Then he adds the ultimate indictment: "That's Moses for you. At a remove of forty centuries he still has these poor young Jews under control."

It is significant that in the late thirties, a time of supposed personal liberty, so much of the sexual character of the Catskills was so furtive. The air was charged with double entendres, the games and exercises aimed to titillate, but there was always a great ambivalence about letting go. The climax of *Having Wonderful Time* focuses on the efforts of Teddy to return to her bunk and avoid spending the night in a cabin with a lover; it takes Marjorie Morningstar longer than the summer to relinquish her virginity. "Certainly many boys and some girls did it—and did it easily," reports the *Journal of American Jewish History*, "but there were others who clung (with slipping grasp) to the path of righteousness." The *Journal* goes on to speculate that "the downfall of many high-minded women" might have been due to the effects of strong drink. There was, it says, an "impressive array of alcohol served on camp premises." In fiction, Marjorie Morningstar "always has a beer in hand and the vacationers at Kamp Karefree drink scotch." And in the actual world, many places including an "intellectual arts-and-crafts camp featured a well-stocked bar."

Throughout the Mountains custom quarreled with the spirit of liberation. A wish to observe dietary rules was overrun by the appetite for once-forbidden foods. The seriousness of the human predicament, the sadness of history, clashed with the idea of enjoyment for its own sake. A preponderance of adult camps dared to offer a combination of kosher and non-kosher food.

Although Yiddish was still spoken at a variety of Jewish cultural camps in the thirties, English was the language at Kamp Kare-free, South Wind, and their non-fictional equivalents. Some family camps continued to maintain small synagogues on their premises, but at places like Camp Utopia and the Blue Moon Country Club, the once-sacred Friday evening was musical comedy night, and the Sabbath was special for a new reason: it was the occasion for a full-length play, the most elaborate presentation of the week.

A joke from Hollywood worked its way into the tummlers' monologues: After years in New York a man returns to the old country. His mother, peering at him in his Brooks Brothers suit, is aghast.

"Nu?" Mama asks. "Well? What happened to your beard?"

"Nobody wears a beard in America."

"But you observe the Sabbath, of course."

"Mama, in America almost everybody works on the Sabbath."

She sighs. "Of course you keep kosher."

"I . . . eat out a lot."

The old lady whispers confidentially: "Tell Mama, my boy. Are you still circumcised?"

Very few resorts could resist the trend toward secularism. The Pioneer in South Fallsburgh attempted to remain strictly Orthodox: it forbade its guests to register or to drive cars on the grounds during the Sabbath. On that day all labor, from the switching on of lights to the washing of dishes, was performed by Gentile help. For their efforts the hotel was cited by the State Commission against Discrimination for refusing to employ Jewish bellhops.

The most successful of the kosher resorts remained Grossinger's, the only establishment to become a brand name during the worst years of the thirties. Its expansion was due to an infallible sense of timing, and a personal hospitality that bordered on self-destruction. When an employee was observed pocketing a handful of bills from an open cash register, the founding mother, Malke, told the informer, "Don't get excited. So he's stealing. Maybe he needs the money. *A bissel fur ihm and a bissel fur uns*—a little for him and a little for us." A chambermaid indignantly reported that departing guests were packing towels, pillowcases, and sheets in their luggage. "Don't be upset" was the old lady's advice. "If it wasn't for the guests, you and I wouldn't be here. As long as they don't take the buildings."

In addition to purloining, the clientele at Grossinger's delighted themselves with food, nature, and each other. One of the most amusing guests was a stage mother who had encouraged her son Milton to shorten the family name and get into show business. At Grossinger's, unbidden, Sandra Berlinger organized an amateur show, worked out the choreography, rehearsed dancers in the dining room between meals, and badgered guests to participate. The first presentation lacked a certain polish: the grand finale featured the Hungarian folk singing of a kitchen worker, Frank Hajak, and a massed chorus. Dizzied by applause, Hajak went on to produce dozens of unrehearsed verses from memory until the curtain was charitably rung down.

Amateur nights were only one of Mrs. Berlinger's inspirations. "Why don't we have a whole guest day?" she suggested to Jennie. "Let the guests take over the whole operation of the hotel, from the morning till night."

Jennie demurred: "Why should people paying for vacations want to work? I wonder if it would even be fair to suggest it. I don't want to take advantage."

Sandra assured her: "Don't worry. the way they'll do the work, it won't be any advantage to you."

"Well, if you're sure it won't be too hard . . ."

The next week, guests and staff reversed roles and a Marx Brothers pandemonium was the order of the day. The chambermaids *pro tem* short-sheeted the beds of all the staff members. "Simon Says," the children's game of commands, was played with new rules. When I say "Simon Says," went the instructions, "don't do a thing. Just take life easy."

At the hotel desk, the unfortunates who had just arrived were greeted with the Groucho approach. A woman set down her luggage and announced, "I have a reservation."

"Can you prove it?" the clerk demanded.

"What do you mean?" She identified herself. "Look it up."

"Impossible. We don't keep records. The clerk can't read and write."

At lunch the chaos continued. Nobody was served what he ordered and complaints were met with "You eat too much anyhow." At several points the guests grew indignant and announced their intention to leave. At another resort they might have. At Grossinger's every one of them was persuaded to stay. There is a proverb in Galicia, the country of Malke and Selig's origin: It is not enough to be lucky, one must have a talent for luck. Jennie had inherited the family trait. Instead of a disaster, Hajak's bungled presentation became a kind of family joke, and when a new show was presented the following summer, it was again closed by the interminable folk chant. Guest day became another tradition; people accustomed to Catskill overindulgence actually welcomed a twenty-four-hour period of insults and practical jokes. It seemed to justify the gourmandise of the next two weeks.

Luck touched every phase of their work. Selig and Malke had bought a neighboring farm in the twenties, betting that an increase in business would more than offset their steep mortgage. When he heard about their increasing profits, Eddie Cantor urged the family to buy into the stock market. "I have everything I could raise in it," he told them. "So does Al Jolson, George Jessel . . . a year from now we'll all be millionaires." Selig resisted. A luxurious resort in upstate New York had been brought to his attention, and he dreamed of imitating it. "All I want," he said, "is a golf course."

His daughter Jennie argued, "This time next year we could build one out of the profits. It wouldn't eat up all our cash the way it would now." Her father meekly countered, "I know it sounds good, I can't argue against it," and meekly shuffled off to bed.

Malke took her husband's part after Cantor left. "If it makes Eddie and Al Jolson and Georgie Jessel happy to buy stocks, then let them buy stocks. What will make Pop happy is to build a golf course. I want Pop to be happy." In the end the Grossinger family decided to honor Selig and to forget about the 1929 mar-

The Jewish struggle for fresh air and food began in the crowded holds of ships and continued on the teeming streets of New York. *Top:* Produce and meat are hawked from stands and pushcarts on the Lower East Side, c. 1906; *inset:* Steerage on the *James Foster Jr.*, c. 1869; *bottom:* Yiddish signs and cries greet thousands of immigrants on Orchard Street looking south, c. 1898.

Right: Major Mordecai Noah, carver, diplomat, journalist, soldier, politician, pamphleteer, attacker of Shakespeare, and promoter of self, vainly attempted to build a home for World Jewry on an island in the Niagara River, c. 1825. But Noah's fame rests on his record as the first of his religion to visit a Catskill resort.

LIBERTY FALLS, SULLIVAN CO.
117 Miles from New York. Local Fare, $3.00 ; Excursion, $5.09.

Left: The 1887 issue of *Summer Homes*, published by a New York State railway, attempts to lure passengers with evocations of nature, sport, and, most important, an abundance of attractive members of the opposite sex. *Below:* The platforms of small towns burgeon with visitors and their "all summer" trunks, c. 1900. *Opposite, top:* A typical "health" advertisement run by the Ontario and Western. *Center:* "The straw ride" at Liberty Falls during the unhurried nineties. *Below:* The exercise mania hits the Catskills as young campers go through sets of calisthenics dressed in the leisure outfits of the period.

Above: White Roe Lake House in the twenties, when Danny Kaye made his debut as a tummler. *Opposite, top:* The original Ratner House, established in 1902, was later called the Winter House (right) when it was refinished during the epoch of stuccomania in the thirties. *Center:* The Nevele Falls Farm House grew into the imposing structure known as the Nevele Hotel and Country Club, on the Shawangunk Mountain Trail in Ellenville, New York. *Below:* The Hotel Biltmore, a style typical of hotels built during the Depression and later dubbed Sullivan County Mission.

EXTRA **The Liberty Register** EXTRA

THE LEADING NEWSPAPER OF SULLIVAN COUNTY

Vol. XLIII. No. 39   Liberty, New York, Saturday, June 14, 1913   Price Five Cents

HALF OF LIBERTY'S BUSINESS SECTION WIPED OUT BY FIRE!

Most Destructive Conflagration Ever Known in History of Town. Opera House, Baptist Church, B. F. Green's, Jafnel's Pharmacy, Kniffin's Stationery Store, B. E. Misner's Grocery Store, Roosa & Lancashire's, James Mance's Pharmacy, Wm. Fahrenholz's Stationery Store, Roosa & Lancashire's Barn, Hasbrouck's Apartment House, Sherwood's Barn and other smaller buildings burned to ground; Very Little of Contents of buildings Saved. Other buildings greatly damaged.

Total Loss Will Reach From Three to Five Hundred Thousand Dollars. All Will Rebuild at Once

Left: Conflagrations were a hazard of Catskill life from the earliest days of the resorts. By 1913 stories like that of the great Liberty fire were all too common, and they were to be repeated for the next sixty years. *Below:* Refused fire insurance by major companies, Jewish merchants formed their own cooperatives.

The
NEVELE
Hotel and Country Club

Above, top: The Saxony, formerly the Hotel Glass, built in 1919 and made increasingly elaborate until its heyday of 1969. *Below:* The main building of the Concord in 1942, complete with the mandatory exercise class, and as it originally appeared (inset). *Opposite, top:* The Brickman House, c. 1935, showing a touch of the Mission influence. *Center:* More vigorous aerobics at the Lakeside Inn in Sullivan County, c. 1944. *Below:* The slow track. Groups of visitors play pinochle at Cutler's Cottages in South Fallsburgh in the 1940s.

Top, inset: The Welworth, formerly the Wadler, product of the Stucco and Mission eras, stood deserted in the sixties, then met a spectacular end (top) in 1969. *Bottom:* The Concord's new wing, added in 1948, adds an imposing, if impassive, façade. *Inset:* The rest of the Concord Hotel in 1978, bringing the city to the country.

ket. Black Tuesday came and went on Wall Street, and while others were ruined, Grossinger's had cash on hand. The dream of golf had saved the family fortune. The course was completed in the early thirties, and Jennie regarded it as a signal for further alterations. She reminded her father, "We're not only a hotel, but a country club . . . it's time to act more dignified. No more milk lines at the barn. People can get all the milk they want from the kitchen. No more practical jokes in the dining room. And for the prices they pay, the people who come to us aren't boarders anymore. They're guests, just as if they were at the Waldorf."

Selig promised to bear it in mind when he made his dedication speech. But when the old man mounted a speaking platform and looked down at the familiar faces he had seen each summer, he blurted out, "I was supposed to tell you that this . . . is for the pleasure of our guests . . . But when I look around me, I don't see fancy guests. I see all my old boarders. It was you . . . who made it possible to build it, and this golf course is for you, our boarders." All that was missing was a thousand violins, but the sentiment was genuine and the listeners knew it. It was Selig Grossinger's last public address; he died that December, breathing his last words to the hotel's maître d': "Abie, make sure that everybody eats."

If the family possessed a coat of arms, that line would have been its motto. The chief cook complained that "we give bigger portions than anyone can eat," but followed orders to serve lavish meals at a time of breadlines. After the Eighteenth Amendment was repealed, the resort conformed to public taste and put in a bar, although neither Selig nor Malke nor Jennie had ever tasted anything stronger than Passover wine.

The bar did not entice new guests, nor did the promise of golf, swimming, or food. By 1932 money was growing scarce and visitors shortened the length of their stays. Some confessed that the Crash had wiped them out. Jennie assured them that they could pay later, "when things got better." It was an act of faith. Nothing appeared to be improving in the Mountains. Like many hotels, Grossinger's adjusted its rates downward. It was now barely breaking even.

Around the Catskills, hotel bankruptcies and foreclosures became commonplace. Overexpansion had done them in: too many tennis courts and swimming pools had been built in anticipation of booming times, too many orchestras and social staffs had been engaged in advance. In February 1933, a petition signed by six hundred owners was presented to New York State governor Herbert Lehman. The petitioners sought to "remove penalties for non-payment of taxes and provide for tax payments in installments." Some one thousand resort operators reinforced that plea during a meeting at the Flagler Hotel. According to their findings, "ninety percent of the hotels in Sullivan and Ulster were in straits." The financial bind, they said, was worsened by development of a "weekend season," with nothing but children underfoot during the weekdays, sent to the Catskills to avoid the summer polio epidemics.

While they were waiting for federal and state relief, a few Catskill resorts found unofficial sources of revenue. One was arson. For more than a century, fires been a hazard in the parched hill towns. Spectacular blazes had consumed half of Liberty back in June 1913; a month later, the Grand View Hotel in Mountaindale, one of the largest in the county, had burned to the ground. In 1926, a fire in Schindler's Prairie House, near Loch Sheldrake, took twelve lives. Still, these were isolated incidents, carefully reported by journalists and inspected by insurance companies. After 1929, fires of suspicious or "unknown" origin became regular occurrences. "Even when a fire was legitimate," says a historian of the Grossinger era, "—and many of the structures in those days were tinder boxes—everyone assumed automatically that it was a way out for a failing establishment—especially so since these fires always seemed to ignite immediately after the season when buildings were empty and bills were pressing."

These conflagrations, most of them accidental and some of them fatal, were derided by locals as "Jewish lightning." As proof, they quoted the tummlers, who had coined a joke for the occasion: "Max," one owner commiserates with another. "I hear you had a bad fire." Max raises a finger to his lips: "Shhh. It's not till next week." That exchange was soon repeated by Gentiles in the Catskills, this time without amusement.

During the period when so many hotels were in the process of collapse, Jennie received a disturbing letter from a restaurant equipment dealer with whom the family had done business for years. "Dear Mrs. Grossinger," it began. "We have had numerous letters asking us what we know about the Grossinger family having gone into bankruptcy. We are replying with the following note: 'The Grossingers have always paid their bills on time. But this year they have paid their bills ahead of time.' May we continue to be of service?"

The note was meant to be reassuring. The owners were not soothed. Even a whisper of insolvency could be ruinous. They mailed out cards that read: "There is a rumor about that Grossinger's has gone bankrupt. Please pay no attention to it. There is absolutely no truth to it. We are open as always and look forward to welcoming you on your next visit."

At the end of summer the rumors were traced to their source. A neighboring owner, referred to only as "Mr. Gordon" in the resort history, was the one in financial distress. The rival hotelier had hoped to stampede the Grossinger crowd to his place. Once Jennie discovered the scheme, she dispatched a guest to act as middleman. He offered to buy the Gordon place, settled on terms, and then sold it to the Grossingers. It was the last feud anyone had with the family. When Jennie decided to hire professionals in the early thirties, the luck held. Sandra Berlinger's son was never to forget Mama's favorite resort, and the attendant publicity of Milton Berle's visits always brought in more business. From the staff of part-time musicians, Grossinger's hired Shepard Feldman, later Shep Fields, the dance-band leader whose celebrated Rippling Rhythms were inspired, he said, by the sound of Catskill brooks. Grossinger's first full-time social director was Moss Hart's great rival, Don Hartman, soon to be head of production at Paramount Pictures.

When the news was bad, the Grossingers managed, by some show-business judo, to make it work for their profit. Broadway producers finally put a stop to the pirating of shows, because one of Jennie's stenographers was too adept. George White, whose *Scandals* was enjoying a long run at the Winter Garden, seized the young woman as she was furiously and accurately transcribing the text of his show. He bullied her into a confession and then threatened every Catskill resort with a lawsuit. Overnight it became necessary for the social directors to provide original entertainment, with songs and plots written on the premises, and so another Mountain tradition began.

After Hartman left the resort to try his luck in Hollywood, Jennie personally supervised the hiring of talent. It was not a success. She preferred scrupulously clean material, and if the comedian seemed to be, on her terms, "a nice boy," she signed him on regardless of talent, and was puzzled when his act failed onstage.

During her administration a nightclub owner phoned from Monticello: "I have a terrific show, but it doesn't open until Saturday. I'd like my boys and girls to go through a dress rehearsal before a crowd. How about letting me put on my show in the playhouse Wednesday night? It won't cost you a cent. I'll bring my own musicians." That Wednesday Jennie was called away just as the band struck up the overture. Half an hour later she returned to see an angry guest leading his young son away.

"Get to bed," the man was saying. "I never should have brought you in the first place!"

Jennie understood what he meant as soon as she got a glimpse of the show. The chorus line was in very abbreviated costumes, and the girls were singing a song filled with double entendres. By Jennie's orders the curtain was immediately rung down.

On another occasion, a young comedian was hired on the recommendation of a theater manager in Newark. That the theater was a burlesque house was unmentioned. The comic used risqué material, and on Jennie's word Jackie Gleason never again played Grossinger's. These misadventures, coupled with the pressures of managing a resort in the trough of the Depression, put an end to Jennie's career in show business. She turned the job over to Milton Blackstone, a hyperthyroid public-relations man. Here was another instance of the Grossinger luck.

Blackstone had entered as a guest, graduated to house publicist, and then left the resort to learn the brokerage business. He later told friends that Wall Street was not nearly as profitable as Route 17, and he returned to handle the Grossinger account in his own advertising agency. He warned the family that "in these days hotels are luxuries. A lot of people are eliminating the word 'vacation' from their vocabularies." To lure customers into the tent, he decided, "the obvious answer is to advertise in the big New York newspapers, but we can't afford that. You *can* afford my kind of inexpensive letter-and-phone-call campaign."

It became the most imitated onslaught in the Mountains. To the unmarried, Blackstone wrote, "Even if you are coming by yourself we know you'll have a wonderful time. You will meet a lot of fine, friendly people, and you can be sure that you will get our personal attention."

If price seemed to hold a customer back, he wrote what he called his "three-hundred-acre letter." In it, Blackstone extolled the huge grounds, the swimming pool, the sports and entertainment, all of it gratis. To induce parents, he described cots for children placed in the room at a reduced rate. And in every communiqué he went on in enthusiastic detail about the voluminous menus, all carefully selected to observe dietary laws.

Blackstone hired social directors, collared prospective guests in New York City, and served as Jennie's personal trouble-shooter. One Saturday night, she telephoned him at his city apartment. A headliner was too drunk to go on. The public-relations man consulted his watch. It was 7 p.m. He told her to inform the guests the resort was going to give them a surprise this evening, a midnight show with a mystery headliner. Then he went out to ransack the nightclubs. At the Paramount Hotel Grill he found a fire-eater and sword-swallower. Dangling a large fee, he persuaded the man to pack his gear and get in a taxi.

"Where we heading for?" the driver asked.

"Grossinger's." Blackstone handed him a twenty-dollar bill by way of introduction.

"What's Grossinger's?"

"Who cares? I'm paying you twice what your clock shows if you get us there by midnight."

In a time of ill-lit highways and unimproved roads, he beat the deadline by fifteen minutes. Sometime during the ride Blackstone received his greatest inspiration: the merchandising of winter. Until the thirties, Grossinger's, like all its competitors, regarded the Season as, at most, four months long. After the autumnal High Holy Days of Rosh Hashanah and Yom Kippur, leaves were raked up, lawns reseeded, pipes drained, staffs laid off, and facilities prepared to lie in wait until spring. For the few guests who lingered on, cold weather activities consisted of a walk in the snow and perhaps some tentative figure eights on a frozen pond. This schedule dramatically expanded after Jennie ran into Irving Jaffee late in 1932. Here was the Winter Sports Director the family had been looking for without realizing it. Every credential was in place. Jaffee was young, Jewish, and an Olympic Gold Medalist.

Early in 1933 Blackstone announced to the press that Grossinger's newest employee would attempt to break the world's twenty-five-mile speed record on the hotel lake. Over five thousand spectators came to watch the champion shave a few seconds off the old mark and set a new one of 1 hour 26.9 minutes by dizzily racing around a third-of-a-mile track seventy-five times.

There always had been money in sport, but it was Blackstone who sensed that a hotelier willing to stoop could pick up a lot of small change in the off-season. The next Jewish athlete to appear at Grossinger's was a scrappy lightweight champion named Barney Ross (né Rasofsky). There were no worthy contenders in his weight class, and in 1933 Ross agreed to fight Jimmy McLarnin for the welterweight championship. Blackstone had little trouble persuading him to train at the fully equipped Grossinger's gym; the difficulty came with Malke. When she was told a prizefighter would be staying at her place, the old lady inquired, "What is he, a drinker, that he must do such a thing? He can't hold a steady job?" She refused to meet him or to watch him train, until one afternoon when the boxer was given a tour of the kitchen. She suddenly recognized Ross: "This is the box-fighter? He was Friday night in the synagogue." After that, all doors were open to Barney.

Joel Pomerantz, who charted Jennie's rise, says that, during the weeks of workouts, "the best-known sports writers of New York, Chicago, Philadelphia, and the wire services were all there. With a nudge from Milton Blackstone, instead of datelining their daily stories 'Liberty' (home of the nearest Western Union office), they datelined them 'Grossinger, N.Y.' When rain canceled Barney's workout, they would write feature stories on the hotel, about Jennie, about how it all began back in 1914, and about the invigorating air." It was no longer another Catskill resort; it was, as New York *Daily News* sports columnist Paul Gallico wrote, " 'The Big G' and . . . when Damon Runyon dubbed the hotel 'Lindy's with trees,' Broadway knew Grossinger's was in." It was to remain so until the rumors of insolvency surfaced in the fifties, when they were downed, and in the eighties, when it was impossible to deny them.

During the thirties two opposing forces tugged at American Jewry: the involvement with radicalism and an increased participation in the American experience. Howard Fast, who had spent much of his adolescence in a relative's Catskill bungalow colony, discarded the ethnic display he had seen all around him. Communism was his choice. "A Jew is nothing special," he said. "I see him as no better, no worse than other human beings— no wiser, no more foolish. If he is distinguished by anything, it is by the fact that through his religion and situation he offered a fine target for political reaction. Then I say—let him fight that reaction. . . . Let him join with all others who fight reaction, who fight for decency and democracy."

For novelist Michael Gold, the answer to millenniums of yearning came from a soapbox speaker, proclaiming that "out of the despair, melancholy and helpless rage of millions, a world movement had been born to abolish property. I listened to him:

" 'O Workers' Revolution, you brought hope to me, a lonely, suicidal boy. You are the true Messiah. You will destroy the East Side when you come, and build there a garden for the human spirit.

" 'O Revolution, that forced me to think, to struggle and to live,

" 'O great beginning!' "

* * *

City College, with its predominantly Jewish student body, was the scene of ceaseless political harangues. One of the undergraduates remembered bitterly, "Anyone who has not lived through it . . . cannot fully appreciate the intellectual terror . . . that the Communists exercised on the campus. Always small in number, they were the most dedicated and fearless of missionaries. In the basement alcoves at City College . . . the party adherents held regular sway with booklets on tables, placards announcing rallies, speeches going on to nobody in particular. In this atmosphere, it took unusual courage and unusual apathy to remain outside the church, especially since joining up was supposed to be a practical demonstration of idealism and humanism."

Undoubtedly the radical movement had an influence far out of proportion to its numbers. Yet staying in lockstep with the Party would only suffice for a few, most of them lower-middle-class shopkeepers facing bankruptcy, and intellectuals convinced that Marxist dialectic held an answer to the renegade business cycle. Most Jewish working men and women had no use for the promises of Stalin and the screeds of the Comintern. Instead, they found salvation in the New Deal. Unionism, social work, politics, journalism, and education provided enough excitement for a generation.

The Hasids with their moral fables, the wonder rabbis, the lessons of Talmud and Torah receded into the shadowy past. What did these references have to do with a people born in America, where the excitement was in making over the world? The prattle of parents and grandparents, the talk of pogroms and persecutions were the stuff of myth. Everywhere one turned these days, there were Jewish names, Jewish accomplishments. Despite his name, the mayor of New York City, Fiorello La Guardia, was half Jewish; Herbert Lehman, the grandson of Southern peddlers, was governor of the state; Louis Brandeis and Benjamin Cardozo were on the Supreme Court. President Franklin Delano Roosevelt's advisers included Samuel Rosenman and Henry Morgenthau, Jr.; the big department stores, Macy's and Gimbels, were owned and operated by Jews; there was even a Jewish baseball star, Hank Greenberg, leading the Detroit Tigers to pennants. Everyone knew Hollywood was run by Jewish producers, and American bookshelves and theaters were crowded with new talent, one generation removed from the ghetto. It was only on closer examination that this renaissance of Jewry was revealed as a reformation.

As Irving Howe notes, "The most striking feature of literature by Jews between the two world wars is the absence of its Jewishness. The children of immigrants sought to Americanize themselves as quickly as possible, and they were careful not to betray their ethnic origins or heritage. In the twenties and thirties they divorced themselves almost completely from formal religion, and it seemed as though Judaism could no longer sustain itself in America." As for playgoers "who wanted to see Jewish life on the stage, [they] had to go to Maurice Schwartz's Yiddish Art Theater. . . . The roster of Jewish dramatists is long and impressive . . . but the work of these playwrights is so Americanized that . . . it scarcely draws upon their Jewishness.

"During the twenties and thirties, novelists, short-story writers and essayists were less overtly Jewish than entertainers."

But only some entertainers. When a director petitioned Harry Cohn to hire a particular actor, he refused. The blunt vulgarian who ran Columbia Pictures decided that the man "looks too Jewish."

"But he's a good actor."

"Around this studio," Cohn replied, "the only Jews we put into pictures play Indians."

That was typical corner-office noise; Jewish actors played many other roles besides Sioux and Kiowa. Theaters were full of people like the enchanted ticket holder who later reminisced about the "wonderful afternoons . . . spent in the darkened houses watching John Garfield [Julius Garfinkle], Edward G. Robinson [Emanuel Goldenberg], Melvyn Douglas [Melvyn Hesselberg], Theda Bara [Theodosia Goodman], and Paul Muni [Muni Weisenfreund] make my fantasies come true." Still, it is worth noting that in every case the name was anglicized and that in no production did the actor impersonate anyone of his own background.

If the newly prominent American Jews were anxious to get out of the shadows, they were just as eager to avoid direct sunlight. The comic villain of *The Butter and Egg Man* was Lehman in the stage play; in the 1937 film adaptation, *Dance, Charlie, Dance*, he was named Morgan. *The Front Page* featured a befuddled character named Irving Pincus; by the time it was filmed at the end of the thirties as *His Girl Friday*, he was Joe Pettibone. On screen, Roxie Gottlieb, the boxing promoter in Clifford Odets's *Golden Boy*, was converted to Roxie Lewis. In *Kind Lady*, Rosenberg was Roubet; in *Success at Any Price*, Ginsburg and Glassman became Martin and Griswold. Irwin Shaw's *The Gentle People* was retitled *Out of the Fog* and the Jewish tailor Goodman altered into an Irish tailor named Goodwin. A proletarian novel of Jewish life, *City for Conquest*, was made into an investigation of Irish life, starring James Cagney and Arthur Kennedy.

All these changes were not the result of some Anglo-Saxon decree, or even of a secret understanding between powerful figures in the Establishment. The men who ordered all Semitic traces removed from the screen were themselves Jews. They were men like Cohn and Samuel Goldwyn and Louis B. Mayer, William Fox and the Warner Brothers, Adolph Zukor and Marcus Loew. Some of them were former pushcart peddlers or furriers or song pluggers or owners of nickelodeons. None of them was secure in his sudden prominence, or in the country that had given it to him. But they all had a vision of what might be, and they produced it in every sense of the word. The message was made clear in every one of their films, and articulated by one of the town's favorite executives, Dore Schary: "America is a 'happy ending' nation." Contrary to the anti-Semites who saw dark and un-American forces coming over in steerage, says Paul Johnson in his *History of the Jews*, it was the immigrants "who stylized, polished and popularized the concept of the American Way of Life." In essence that concept meant no exotics or obvious members of minority groups in leading parts, particularly if they looked like young versions of Goldwyn, Fox, Mayer, Loew, Cohn, or Warner. The best example of the unspoken code occurred when the greatest performer in Borscht Belt history was given his first screen test at Metro-Goldwyn-Mayer. Yes, the tummler had talent, Samuel Goldwyn conceded, but his nose was too large and it would have to be abbreviated. The actor refused. Goldwyn brooded about it for days. The man looked too—foreign. *Something* would have to be done. The hair, that was it. If the nose was to stay, the dark locks must be bleached. This would remove the curse of the ghetto and make him an American. Goldwyn, as his associates knew, was not always right, but he was never wrong. An appointment was made with the hair-dresser, and ever afterward, Danny Kaye was a blond.

CHAPTER 9

THE FIFTY-HOLE GOLF COURSE

White Lake, N.Y.

Every resort area has its fund of local myths, stories of ghostly dwellings and unexplained disappearances, legends about hidden gold coins and ancient Indian burial grounds. By the time the Jews arrived, the Catskills had already served as backdrop for scores of intriguing fantasies. Rip Van Winkle was internationally recognized as the first American to sleep through history. In life, Captain Henry Hudson had been set adrift by mutinous sailors. In Mountain lore he was a ghost playing bowls with a group of elves whenever a thunderstorm hovered, their ninepins echoing in the valleys. Satan himself was buried in the region. The Devil's Tombstone, a natural outcropping rounded at the top by eons of rain and wind, was visible then as it is today near Hunter Mountain.

Like the stories of Captain Hudson, Jewish tales were based

on fact and then distorted beyond recognition. They concerned three basic groups: couples, entertainers, and owners. Stories about those who had married well were told by those who had merely married. Other tales focused on entertainers who had vaulted from the Mountains to the sound stage. These were elaborated by tummlers who would never go farther than the local recreation hall.

The central figure in most of these legends was born David Kaminsky, on the Lower East Side. Thirty years after his last film and many months after his death in Hollywood at the age of seventy-five in 1986, Danny Kaye was still a Catskill cynosure. Those who saw him in the early days always spoke of the comedian with the same awe physicists use to describe the time they worked with Robert Oppenheimer on the Manhattan Project. It was because they knew that long before the television specials and the global tours on behalf of UNICEF, before Danny appeared Live at the Palladium and became the darling of London, before the days of *Wonder Man* and *The Inspector General* in Hollywood, even before he stole the stage musical *Lady in the Dark* from Gertrude Lawrence, he had been one more young and untried tummler in the resort country.

"This was one case where we really knew at the start we were watching a superstar," says Dick Diamond, who first supervised Kaye at White Roe. "He started as half of a duet, with a man named Lou Reed, a ukulele player. Danny became a musician. He didn't know how to dance a step, but he joined two dancers, Kathleen and Mack, and became part of a trio. It was immediately apparent that he had so much talent that no one would be able to use it all. Least of all the movie studios. The fact is, Hollywood missed the boat on Danny. Yes, he was a fine comedian. But he was much more. He was a serious actor. He could play anything. And I was in a position to know. I cast him in anything."

Metro-Goldwyn-Mayer could hardly be blamed for making Kaye their prime comedian. Although the White Roe players featured him in the standard repertory—*Journey's End, Private Lives, The Guardsman,* and *Juno and the Paycock*—he was always liable to take a profound bow at the finale, and without

warning launch into a throaty version of "Minnie the Moocher."
And if Kaye's initial salary of $25 a week included some general
tummling along with the straight acting, his "porch sessions"
were what brought the first celebrity. A lack of outside illumination made no difference to the young entertainer. Visitors'
cars were parked in a semicircle around an outside porch, and
in their glassy light Danny Kaye cavorted and sang until the
audience, the staff, and even the owner were convinced that they
were in the presence of a natural force. Pop Weiner was so
certain that he awarded Kaye a $100 bonus and brought him
back the following year for $125 a week. Kaye remained for
three more seasons. During that time he assumed new characters, polished his timing, and consolidated his reputation as a
clown. One routine was so celebrated that when he became
famous he repeated it *in toto* at fund-raisers for the New York
Philharmonic.

"He would arrive with his hair disheveled," a fellow tummler affectionately recalled. "He carried a phone book under one
arm and several batons under the other. Then Danny proceeded
to break the batons as he banged on the lectern to attract attention and gain quiet from a noisy, practicing orchestra. He started
to lead, but no one responded. When he dropped his arms to
his sides, exasperated, they began to play. Then the saxophone
player blew a sour note. Danny stopped the orchestra, walked
up to the offending musician, peered into the sheet of music,
flicked a spot from the page, looked up toward the sky, and
shook a threatening finger at an imaginary bird." At the appropriate time, and this Kaye always knew to the nanosecond, he
attempted a dignified return to the podium.

En route, the conductor tripped and managed to break his
fall by knocking over a music stand and scattering all the sheets
of music. "Apologetically, Danny gathered up the paper and
replaced it. Then he'd try to regulate the height of the stand,
making it necessary for the musician to gradually rise from a
sitting position until he had to stand on a chair to read the
music—the stage crew had to build a special music stand for
this piece of business. When the next musician played incorrectly, Danny stopped the orchestra, asked for the instrument,

played it himself—incorrectly—and then beat the musician over the head. When he tried to blot the perspiration with a pocket handkerchief, it turned out to be an endless sheet of music. Many other musical pieces went awry. The conductor would walk up to a player and turn the sheet of music over. So that was what was wrong! The fiddler had been reading upside down! For variation, he would take prop music and throw it wildly into the air. The program always ended with 'The Stars and Stripes Forever.' As the last strains were played Kaye turned to bow to the audience, whereupon the orchestra started to play the ending again. The conductor had to turn back hurriedly and lead his men. This action was repeated so many times that Danny would fall down, exhausted, still leading the orchestra, as he crawled off the stage."

Not all Catskill material would submit to recycling years later. The distance of Kaye's epic journey from White Roe to MGM may be charted by watching, say, *The Inspector General*, and then imagining him in a segment of "The Prizefight Sketch," a perennial Mountain favorite, reconstructed by Kaye's former aide Dr. Saul Gladstone:

REFEREE (*Addressing ring opponents*): I want you to fight clean. No
   hitting in the clinches. No hitting below the belt. (*Comic lifts his
   loose trunks up to his chest*) Shake hands, go back to your corners,
   and when the bell rings, come out fighting. (*Big fighter squeezes
   the comic's hand with both of his gloves. Comic falls down immediately on the floor, gets up whistling and whining like an injured
   dog. He returns to his corner complaining as the bell rings for round
   one. Big fighter takes three large paces toward the center of the ring.
   Comic starts toward the center and recoils*)

COMIC: Where are you going? Do you want the whole place? Stay over
   on your side. (*Large fighter stands in the center of the ring in a
   fighting pose as comic jumps, swings wildly, and dances around*)

MANAGER: What are you doing?

COMIC (*Out of breath*): I'm tiring him out . . . (*Falls to floor*).

REF. (*Counting over him*): Two, four, six, eight.

COMIC (*Jumping up*): What's the matter with one, three, five, seven,
   and nine?

REF.: I don't like odd numbers. Get in there and fight . . . (*Comic obeys, pointing toward audience: "Hey, Smitty!" Big fighter looks away, in Smitty's direction. Comic hits him a resounding smack, with an open glove, on his shoulder. Big fighter falls to the floor. Referee approaches the fallen man and gives him a straight count*)

REF.: One, two, three, four, five, six, seven, eight, nine, ten. The winner and new champion! (*Comic, bewildered and tired, staggers around ring. Fallen fighter rolls over and begins to get up from floor with only his hands and feet touching the floor, as his rear end extends in a reversed V position. Comic is asked to say a few words into the microphone dangling from the top of the stage*)

COMIC (*Wobbles toward the fallen fighter, leans over him, and talks confusedly into his rear end*): Hello, Mom. Hello, Pop. It was a tough fight, but I'm going to bring home the bacon. (*Big fighter rises off the canvas just far enough to fall over comic's shoulder. He lifts the big fighter up and unsteadily carries him off the stage*)

BLACKOUT

Although Kaye left the Mountains in the late thirties, never to return, they continued to shape his career. White Roe's first paying guest was a dentist named Benjamin Fine. A generation later, his daughter Sylvia was to become Kaye's most significant collaborator, as a writer of special material and later as his wife. On a spring evening in 1937, as Danny performed her works at the Martinique Club on Fifty-second Street, the suddenly prominent Moss Hart paid a visit to his old Catskill friend Richard Diamond at his Manhattan apartment.

According to Diamond, "the conversation got around to *Lady in the Dark*, a new musical Moss had written about his psychoanalysis. He and his collaborators, Kurt Weill and Ira Gershwin, were looking for someone who could sing a song called "Tchaikowski." It was a number in which the performer had to sing a list of Russian composers ["There's Malichevsky, Rubinstein, Arensky and Tchaikovsky, Sapellnikov, Dimitriev, Tcherepnin, Kryjanowksy, Godowsky, Arteibouchev, Moniuszko, Akimenko, Soloviev, Prokofiev, Tiomkin, Korestchenko," etc.]—something like forty-nine Russian composers in thirty-nine seconds. I suggested Kaye. Moss knew of him, but he also knew and hated the Mountains. 'I don't want a Borscht Belt comedian,' he said. I convinced him to go four blocks north and catch a few minutes of Danny's act. That's all it took. He watched the movements, heard some wonderful original patter songs, and a few days later he hired him. There was no more mention of Borscht Belt."

After Kaye's legendary Broadway debut, references to the Mountains were to be found, uncredited, in his fluid and manic movements, his metronomic delivery, and in his sudden mastery of foreign tongues. It was only upon closer examination that the fluency turned out to be a torrent of the nonsense syllables he used with such effect in the porch sessions, spoken with such authenticity that they passed for German, French, Chinese, or whatever other tongue was called for in Catskill sketches.

Linguistic play was used to great effect by the Mountains' second most prominent graduate, Sid Caesar, who was to dominate postwar television for almost a decade. In weekly performances he parodied scores of foreign films, speaking his own brand of Catskill gibberish shaped to the needs of the moment. His headlong mimicry was the tummler's heritage, a mix of chutzpah and the urge to please. Like Kaye, Caesar had brought it to the resorts from his neighborhood: his parents owned a restaurant, the St. Clair Buffet Lunch, just north of the Bronx. There, he said, "I would just be fascinated by the customers. Nearly all of them were young, single immigrants who would segregate into groups speaking Italian, Russian, Hungarian, Polish, French, Spanish, Lithuanian, and even Bulgarian. I would go from table to table listening to the sounds. I learned how to mimic them, sounding as if I were actually speaking their language."

Caesar recorded his first attempts at parody: "I went over to a table of Italians. When I began, they all smiled happily at me as if to say, 'Hey, this kid is one of our own.' Then they cocked their heads, listened carefully, and looked at one another, jabbering away. They must have realized what I was up to and they roared with laughter. . . . One of them asked, in English, 'Hey, kid, can you speaka Polack like that, too?' When I said yes, he sent me to do my act at a nearby table of Poles. Before it was over, the whole place was breaking up and it was the beginning of a comic device that helped me earn millions later on."

The device was given considerable sharpening at Vacation-land near Swan Lake, where Caesar was booked as an adolescent clarinet player. "I offered to help out with the sketches," he says. "The only thing that continued to bother me was the quality of comedy. . . . I said to [the social director] these people laugh at the old skits because they know them by heart and are just waiting for the punch line to come up. Why do just that? Let's start with two guys going into a bakery to shop, for example, and take it from there, making up funny situations that can happen in a real bakery. Who's going to kill you here? Let's try.

"He thought about it for a long time. Then he said 'OK, let's try.' We did. Some things worked and some things didn't. But people started coming over from other hotels to see our improvisations, and he finally conceded that we were on the right path. He particularly liked some stories I made up from my days in my father's luncheonette, using the foreign-language double-talk."

Long before their ascents, Kaye and Caesar had become the most imitated comedians of their time and place. By the late thirties, in homage and envy, almost every major hotel offered an entertainer who could exaggerate the voices and gestures of movie stars, local celebrities, or, better still, one or two of the guests. Imitators had been neglected since vaudeville days, when nearly every tummler was expected to put on blackface and do Al Jolson, or assume a bowler and crayon mustache for a parody of Charlie Chaplin. Suddenly they were back in vogue.

The ability to duplicate another's style has never been confined to a single group; in a sense every actor in a role is copying someone else's locutions and mannerisms. If the gift of imitation seems to have occurred disproportionately among Jews, perhaps it is because they were so frequently forced across national borders, absorbing attitudes and postures in order to do business with foreigners who had suddenly become neighbors. A century before the clowns of the Catskills, the scholar Ahad Ha-Am had noted in an essay on eighteenth-century assimilation that his co-religionists had "not merely a tendency to imitation, but a genius for it. Whatever they imitate, they imitate well."

Such Jewish "genius" was never to be regarded with complete equanimity. Those who were amused by mimicry were outshouted by some who dismissed it as a rudimentary tool of survival, and by others, like the composer Richard Wagner, who had a more malign view. In his influential paper *Jewry in Music*, published pseudonymously under the name K. Frigedank (Free Thought), Wagner opened fire on his rival Giacomo Meyerbeer, reigning operatic composer of the day. Meyerbeer was a Jew, and therefore, according to Frigedank, "owned no mother tongue, no speech inextricably entwined among the sinews of his innermost being: he spoke with precisely the same interest in any modern language you chose, and set it to music with no more concern for the idiosyncrasies than the mere question of how far it was ready to be a pliant servitor to Absolute Music." And indeed, as historian Chaim Bermant suggests, Meyerbeer might well have pleaded guilty to the ease with which he traversed boundaries and languages. The son of a German-Jewish banker derived so much of his inspiration from Italian opera that as a young man he changed his name from Jacob to Giacomo. Later his most enthusiastic support came from France, and in homage he composed most of his songs to French librettos.

Felix Mendelssohn, baptized a Christian, was the son of Jews and therefore a candidate for Wagnerian contempt. After all, he had also shown a predilection for styles other than those of his native country. His *Scotch Symphony* and "Hebrides" and *Midsummer Night's Dream* overtures were testament to what Bermant acknowledges as "a roving eclecticism, a ready ear for new sounds." He elaborates: "Jewish adaptability is perhaps seen in its supreme form in the operettas of Jacques Offenbach, for no one more embodies the spirit of *la vie Parisienne*, or rather enhanced it, than this son of a Rhineland *Hazzan* who became to France what Arthur Sullivan was to England."

The debate about Jewish imitation lay moribund for some six decades after Wagner's death. Then in the thirties it was revived. The old question was put: If the Chosen People were so adaptable, if they could slip into a culture like a hermit crab entering another's shell, were they truly creators? Or were the best of them merely popular entertainers, unable to rise to the demands of Art? Influenced by older cultures, Americans spent some little time thinking about the problem. Europeans, as always, had more to say. Germans thought about little else. All too soon, action would take the place of obsession.

The third kind of Jewish legend was built around the great resort rivalries. At the end of the thirties Jennie Grossinger found herself displaced as the greatest impresario in the Mountains. Arthur Winarick had first visited the Catskills a few years before, as a privileged guest. The Russian immigrant had prospered by selling bottles of his concoction, Jeris Tonic, guaranteed, users were encouraged to believe, to grow thick, luxuriant hair. The inventor was wise enough not to display his picture on the label. He was bald.

To *Fortune* magazine's way of thinking, Winarick resembled "an unkempt Samuel Goldwyn . . . with as much side as a professor of economics." He had begun as a barber on Madison Avenue, developed a tonic, and invested the profits in a series of salon supplies, including La Crosse manicuring cutlery, Herpicide, Dr. Ellis' Hair Products, and Duragloss Nail Polish. No matter how long the breadlines, people wanted to groom themselves—perhaps they needed more assurance than ever from the mirror—and while other businesses went under, Winarick's endured and prospered. In 1932 he spent a brief vacation at the Kiamesha Ideal House. The place was not doing well, and the guest loaned his hosts $15,000. That and a fresh identity as the new Concord did them little good; three years later he assumed control of the mortgage.

Gradually the rich man's hobby became something of an obsession. Winarick was apprised of Grossinger's increasing reputation; he decided to make his place a year-round hotel and the most luxurious resort in Mountain history. "The Concord's progress," *Fortune* noted, "became a blend of shrewd economy and equally shrewd extravagance—the economy where nobody notices it, the extravagance where everybody notices it."

The Fifty-Hole Golf Course

Winarick borrowed little capital, and paid for most construction out of depreciation and profit. The man who had built his fortune on the growth of other people's hair was not in a rush. He arranged to take three years to pay for furniture, fixtures, and decorations. When local profiteers came to call, the smiles froze on their faces. Arthur Winarick, they learned, was to be his own general contractor. He would award the contracts; he would oversee the labor.

Year by year the hotel expanded. In the Grossinger style, contiguous properties were acquired, until the original holding of 3½ acres expanded to a 2,800-acre estate. Formerly there had been but one cesspool; Winarick brought in a complicated sewage system commensurate with his grand vision. He added fifty large bedrooms with a unique provision. "Everybody has a bathroom in the city" began the owner's epochal decision. "On a vacation, they deserve something better. Something they can go back and talk about." He gave them something to talk about: *two* bathrooms. Then he gave them the Cordillion Room; a 15,000-square-foot dining area decorated in what was labeled the Catskill Queen Mary style; a large upstairs lobby with starlight roof and gold-and-beige carpeting; a curved 150-foot Night Owl bar with dozens of mobiles fluttering behind it; a Tropical Sun Valley swimming pool. Not every improvement was triumphant; a lobby with white marble walls and a dark red ceiling had to be redone immediately because it intimidated the guests. Once the interiors were completed, Winarick turned his attention to the grounds. Neighbors heard of a conversation between Winarick and his Scottish landscaper:

"How big a golf course has Grossinger's got?"

"Eighteen holes."

"Then build me a fifty-hole golf course."

He eventually came up short of his goal: two luxurious eighteen-hole courses and a smaller one of nine. But in other ways Winarick realized his oddest ambitions. He had always distrusted the way the weather was made. If he were in charge, he told associates, matters would be different. One October day he was approached by a salesman who had stumbled upon the divine secret of snow making. It was not exactly a miracle, he

explained, simply the result of a happy accident: one day a sprin-
kler went off in cold weather and started producing flakes. Intrigued, Winarick encouraged further experiments with various
temperatures, heating the water to the precise degree to keep it
from freezing before it issued from the nozzle. In the end the
Concord succeeded in laying a foot of snow over a five-acre hill
in twelve hours. Later the hotel added red, yellow, and blue dye
to the water and offered ski slopes in primary colors. The feat
was the talk of the Catskills. It was no surprise that once me-
teorology was taken out of the customary hands the competition
began to blaspheme in their advertising copy: "You wouldn't
have liked the Garden of Eden anyway—it didn't have a golf
course," read one advertisement. "Kutsher's, on the other
hand . . ."

Winarick was never content to let his achievements speak
for themselves. His was a familiar figure, roaming the grounds,
greeting visitors, and indicating features. He held out his hand
to one unfamiliar young man climbing the front stairs: "Shake.
This is your first time here?"

The man nodded.

"How do you like it? Some grounds, huh? Look at that
lobby, better than the Waldorf, no?"

"It seems pretty nice."

"Come here. I'll show you something. See over there, that
new gorgeous building? Last year it was an old building. All the
rooms not so good. Adjoining baths, not enough. My guests
wanted two bathrooms for everybody. Look here, over there is
a new indoor swimming pool which is in addition to the two
outdoor pools we have. Here, see that golf course? It's a new
one. Everything bigger and better for my guests." He searched
the listener's face, seeking a reaction. "So. You like the place?"

Another nod.

"You got a nice room?"

The young man spoke for the first time. "I don't know. I
haven't checked in yet. I'm the new busboy."

Pride of ownership extended beyond the acreage of the Concord. In a minor labor dispute three picketers walked outside
the front gate, an affront to the imperial Concord. It was not the

UNFAIR placards that bothered the owner, it was their demeanor and attire. The picketer in the middle was threadbare, his jacket pocket torn, his faded trousers supported with clothesline instead of a belt. Winarick appraised him closely and withdrew. Presently he appeared carrying a newly pressed navy-blue suit. He summoned the shabbiest of the trio. "Here," he told him. "Put this on. If you're going to picket in front of the Concord, you've got to look good."

Winarick knew that his resort lacked the homely *haimish* quality of its competitors. It enjoyed little of Grossinger's warmth and history. There would be no stories dated Concord, N.Y., no tales of the old days when Mama and Papa scrimped to build a dream. The G and many other places had long and complicated roots in the Catskills. His Concord was only a little older than the New Deal. Still, when you came right down to it, what was tradition? Only a gathering of objects and ceremonies. Winarick could accumulate as well as the next hotelier, and faster.

To this end he recruited the Mountains' most aggressive talent agents, Al Beckman and Johnny Pransky. The partners were temperamentally suited for the assignment. They had begun as Catskill musicians; one was a saxophone player, the other a violinist and leader of Pransky's Troubadours. In the summers they met every resort owner; in the winters they got acquainted with the talent in New York City. Soon they were booking themselves and their colleagues onto hotel stages, and by the early thirties they had abandoned instruments to become full-time ten-percenters. Their first clients were the obscure Latin Americans Canay and His Orchestra, and the Mexican film star Filipe de Flores. But once they had convinced Winarick to pay higher wages Beckman and Pransky were able to lure more illustrious names to the Mountains, and ended by watching Judy Garland and Marlene Dietrich perform at the Concord. By then the agents had grown wealthy from their fees, but they never failed to act like men in search of their first dollar, recruiting, promising, cajoling, threatening until their demands were met. Joey Adams records an instance of their double-teaming:

" 'I may be able to get you a certain band leader for the summer,' Al would tell an unsuspecting owner. 'That is, if I can steal him away from Grossinger's. He's a pal of mine and owes me a favor.'

" 'Don't be silly,' Johnny butted in. 'He has five new records coming out. Besides, they offered him a network radio show for the summer. He won't take the job for that kind of money.'

" 'I'll get him,' Al bragged. 'He's my friend. Didn't I introduce him to Crosby and Jolson, who went nuts about him?'

" 'Get him,' the boss screamed. 'Get me that what's-his-name. I'll give him anything he wants. He can eat in the dining room with the guests, even. Just make sure you don't give him to Grossinger's.'

"Now they had to go out and find a band. The boss was ready to sign anybody after the . . . bookers did their routine.

"Whenever I bumped into them on the street Johnny would say, 'Huh? Al? Who were we just talking about? Is that a coincidence? Come up to the office . . . we have a job for you for the summer. It's made to order for you.' Now he had to rush back to the office and look for a hotel that he could con into booking me."

As the resorts prepared for more bounteous seasons, the tragedy of European immigration was being rewritten, this time with a savagery unprecedented even in czarist Russia. Ironies again played themselves out in New York, where the Jews of Eastern European descent warily regarded the new refugees from Germany. Suspicions and feuds, forgotten since the days of World War I, burrowed their way to the surface. Many of the German Jews had been comfortable bourgeoisie only a few months before—who else could have afforded the prohibitive costs of bribes and transportation to the United States?—and their attitudes offended those who had crossed the Atlantic a generation before. These Poles and Russians had seen enough prejudice to last them a lifetime. They were not going to tolerate anti-Semitism from Jews, and when they spoke of the Upper West Side, where the new arrivals were settling in, they spitefully referred to it as the Fourth Reich.

Jacob Kaminsky, a Manhattan bagel baker, could recall the mutual disdain more than forty years later. The German immigrants "always had this air of superiority," he said. "They made nasty comments about those of us who still spoke Yiddish. And they never missed an opportunity to flaunt their education or the fact that they held important positions in their native country. It's amazing how many of them still spoke of Germany, not the Nazis of course, with affection. They simply couldn't reconcile themselves to the fact that we wouldn't accept them at German values."

By way of illustration, the old identity jokes were revived in the Catskills: A German dog refuses to talk to a Boston bull terrier: "Don't tink I alvays vas chust a dachshund. Back home in Düsseldorf I vas a Saint Bernard."

Tasteless no doubt, but tummlers were not paid to make their patrons weep. Most of them were conscious of what was happening overseas. Stories of *Kristallnacht*, of roundups, racial laws, curfews, and later of death camps were covered first in the Yiddish press. However, the social directors and comedians could hardly be expected to confront the vacationers with facts. Instead, they spoke in Catskill code, tincturing the overseas news with oblique and bitter commentaries.

To hear the jokes of the period was to be given an eccentric history lesson. They began with the story of the sad-faced little man with the Star of David patch on his arm. He alone is willing to climb into a lion suit and wrestle the most ferocious tiger in the Berlin circus. As the crowd gathers, he enters the cage, faces the animal, and cries out the Jewish prayer recited when death is imminent:

"*Shema Yisroel!* Hear, O Israel . . . !"

"*Adonai, Eloheinu, adonai, echod!* The Lord our God, the Lord is One," returns the cat.

"Wh-why you're not a tiger at all!" gasps the pseudo-lion.

The tiger turns his back on the crowd. "*Landsman*, what makes you think you're the only Jew in Germany who's working?"

A favorite anecdote at The Laurel spoke of Adolf Hitler's visit to a fortune-teller. "He wants to know on what day he will die," the tummler explained. " 'On a Jewish holiday,' says the gypsy. 'What holiday? Rosh Hashanah, Yom Kippur, Hanukkah?' 'My führer,' she says, '*any* day you die will be a Jewish holiday.' "

At the Olympic Hotel, a comic told his audience of two Jews philosophizing in a coffee house. "How miserable is our lot," says one. "Pogroms, discrimination, and now the Nazis. Sometimes I think we would be better off if we had never been born." "Of course!" the other agrees. "But who has that much luck? Not one in a hundred thousand!"

And of the Storm Trooper who demands, "What group caused all of the fatherland's troubles?" He collars a white-bearded rabbi. "The Jews," admits the old man to the Nazi's satisfaction. "Also the pretzel bakers." The German is puzzled: "Why the pretzel bakers?" The rabbi gives the eternal reply: "Why the Jews?"

A discerning guest could have peered behind the anecdotes to see the flames, but very few dared to look farther than the next meal. One of the owners of a now defunct hotel regrets "how little we all had to say about what was happening to European Jewry. It was almost as if by not mentioning the event we might dismiss it from reality." Despite the growing popularity of the term "Borscht Belt," Jewishness was not a thing to be flaunted. The Grande Yenta, Sophie Tucker, liked to conclude her act by belting "My Yiddishe Momme." She found that it was no longer a crowd pleaser and finished with "God Bless America." The tone was merely an echo of the larger arena of show business, where the banishment of Judaica was reaching a new absurdity. In a contemporary study of Hollywood conventions, screenwriters Eliot Paul and Luis Quintanilla suggested that even when the presence of Jews was legitimately required they were not allowed on screen. If the current situation were to be filmed, they said, "it would be bad for the public to get the idea that the Nazis are persecuting Jews. . . . In the eyes of the producers, it is even worse to show a Jew in clover than one in the soup up to his eyes. The solution is not to show him at all. He becomes a Czech or some kind of Central European the 40,000,000 [moviegoers] can view impersonally."

Perhaps the ultimate purgation occurred in the film adaptation of Arthur Kober's Catskill-based *Having Wonderful Time.*

The Fifty-Hole Golf Course

The lovers were portrayed by Douglas Fairbanks, Jr., and Ginger Rogers. Stern became Shaw, Kessler was Kirkland, Aaronson was Armbruster, Sam Rappaport was Emil Beatty. This was too much even for the staid *New York Times* critic Frank S. Nugent, who filed an appropriate critique. The cast of this once unabashed comedy of Jews at play was, he complained, "*alle goyim.*"

"We let it happen in the movies, and we let it happen in the Mountains," says a still-active owner. "There were all sorts of whispers and stories about the persecutions of Jews, of course. Hitler was no secret. But the extent of the crime, and how it might be alleviated—we spent little time discussing that. When the time would come to fight the Nazis in uniform, of course, we were ready to go. In the meantime, if we thought at all about what was later to be known as the Holocaust, it was not how we could get arms or aid to the sufferers in Europe. It was how we could send money to get Jews out of Europe to Palestine." Broadway producer Manny Azenberg agrees: "At camp we thought in terms of Eretz Israel. It animated our songs and speeches and rituals. Zionism: that was what might give the refugees a chance to live."

In the Catskills, as in the city, the notion of a Jewish homeland took on a new urgency. Years before, Theodor Herzl, the founder of political Zionism, had written: "One of the major battles I shall have to wage will be against the Jewish spirit of scoffing." It was being won in an arena the show-business agents commonly referred to as "the cage of mocking birds." Slotted blue-and-white canisters from the Jewish National Fund appeared on checkout counters, to overflow with coins. No one made jokes about them. Safe or not, the old dream of a national home was being reinvigorated.

With the dream came responsibilities. Outrageous sums were required to convey Jewish adults out of Germany to the hostile British protectorate of Palestine. Their children were in every sense a smaller matter, and it was for them that an agency called Youth Aliyah was created. One of its principal benefactors was Eddie Cantor, an entertainer who had never forgotten the deprivations of ghettos on either side of the ocean. Cantor proceeded to do grandly what more obscure men did quietly. During one Grossinger reunion, held at the Hotel New Yorker, he was so persuasive that virtually every alumnus made a contribution. The next morning Jennie phoned Cantor to inform him that the receipts came to more than $3,000.

"I'll send you a check, Eddie," she promised.

That was not good enough. "Every minute counts," he told her. "Bring the cash over to my hotel."

The money, most of it donated in one- and five-dollar bills, arrived in two shoeboxes and a hotel laundry bag. The cash was enough to pluck eight Jews out of the Holocaust, eight out of six million.

These rallies for Youth Aliyah were about as far as the vacationers were willing to go. Milton Plesur, in *Jewish Life in Twentieth Century America*, notes sadly: "Lack of further action or protest simply reflected the times: America was still relatively isolationist and American Jews were primarily concerned with their status as Americans. President [Franklin D. Roosevelt], following the cue of the State Department, contended that Palestine was a British matter and, in essence, his policy was to view the Palestine situation as a problem which could be solved only after victory." The presidential assumptions went unchallenged. For as the forties began, Roosevelt had assumed a mythic stature among the Jewish population of New York. His closest confidants were said to be Jews, and he had appointed a Jewish Justice of the Supreme Court. He alone, said the legend, abolished the Depression and strengthened the labor unions, to which so many of the vacationers belonged. A Tammany politician, Jonah Goldstein, wryly observed: "The Jews have *drei velten—di velt, yene velt, un Roosevelt*" (three worlds—this one, the other world, and Roosevelt).

That trust was to prove fatal for their brethren. FDR never spoke out in favor of a bill, co-sponsored by New York State Senator Robert Wagner, that might have saved the lives of 20,000 refugee children between 1939 and 1940—a vital re-election year—and it died in committee. The White House had no comment about Nazi atrocities before the war, although they had been secretly documented. The reasons are now pathetically clear. As Irving Howe points out, "The Jewish organizations lacked political leverage with the Roosevelt administration precisely because the American Jewish vote was so completely at the disposal of the President. Had they been able to threaten that, unless the government took more courageous steps to save the refugees, crucial swing votes in crucial states might be withdrawn, it is at least possible that they could have had some effect."

Instead, all was silence. But not ignorance. On January 30, 1939, Hitler had announced to the world that "if international-finance Jewry inside and outside Europe should succeed once more in plunging the nations into yet another world war, the consequences will not be the Bolshevization of the earth and thereby the victory of Jewry, but the annihilation of the Jewish race in Europe." Actually, the annihilation had begun by that time; the Führer, in another of his inventive diatribes, was merely putting a *fait accompli* in the shape of a warning. Although the horrific details of the Final Solution were not fully revealed until the invasion of Auschwitz, American Jews knew one fact in their bones: a lethal hate had once again become the policy of a nation, and, once out of its cage, anti-Semitism never stays at home.

In the United States it took the shape of resentful cracks about Jewish war profiteers and their mink-coated wives. Then the professional haters produced a new doctrine, and it immediately found an audience: the Jews, with their notorious international cunning, had somehow maneuvered the United States into a war it did not have to fight. In the way of the *badkhn*, comedians tried to deflate the opposition by telling stories on themselves: George Jessel said that the draft board had classified him 12-F: "That means I go when the Japs are in the lobby." The Catskill audiences dutifully laughed and applauded on cue. Others were not so enthusiastic.

The effect of home-front anti-Semitism is impossible to calculate. Certainly it made the victims excruciatingly defensive. The father of Sergeant Seeger in Irwin Shaw's story "Act of Faith" expresses a sentiment that few were willing to say aloud: "I am loath to praise any liberal writer or any liberal act and find myself somehow annoyed and frightened to see an article of criticism of existing abuses signed by a Jewish name. And I hate to see Jewish names on important committees, and hate to read of Jews fighting for the poor, the oppressed, the cheated and hungry. Somehow, even in a country where my family has lived a hundred years, the enemy has won this subtle victory over me—he has made me disenfranchise myself from honest causes by calling them foreign, Communist, using Jewish names connected with them as ammunition against them.

"And, most hateful of all, I find myself looking for Jewish names in the casualty lists and secretly being glad when I discover them there, to prove that there at least, among the dead and wounded, we belong."

So the hotels in the Mountains posted their lists of former guests now decorated with blue and gold stars. They opened their doors to convalescent GIs, and held vibrant War Bond rallies. The indefatigable Eddie Cantor sold a quarter of a million dollars' worth of bonds one August evening at Grossinger's, and Secretary of the Treasury Henry Morgenthau, Jr., presented a special citation to Jennie. A week later, the hotel was appointed a direct issuing agency for bonds, a designation usually accorded only to banks and post offices. When pledges reached the million-dollar mark, the Treasury outdid itself: to celebrate the event it ordered the legend "Grossinger" painted on a bomber's fuselage.

There was much laughter about that, and about life in general on the home front. It would be incorrect to characterize the comedy as gallows humor. The resort staffs were ordered to make the guests forget the war and its consequences, and audiences were willing accomplices. A former busboy remembered that "the laughter was a little too loud and the tummlers were a little too relentless for comfort. It wasn't that everybody was laughing to keep from crying. They were laughing to keep from dying." And the mother of an adolescent girl was made so uncomfortable that it was years before she returned. "Men were in short supply," she said, "just as they must have been in the old days of the sweatshops. There was a subtle hysteria to the place: too many single women, too much inane chatter, and too much loud entertainment. It was as if thinking had suddenly gone out of style."

Something else went with it: a sense of being at ease in America. For the duration, the Catskills was a place of haunted accomplishment. Many of its most successful people bore a spiritual resemblance to the slave Mark Twain cited in his reminiscences: "He sang the whole day long, at the top of his voice; it was intolerable, it was unendurable." Young Sam Clemens went to his mother to complain. She told him, "Think . . . when he is singing it is a sign that he is not grieving; the noise of it drives me almost distracted, but I am always listening, and always thankful; it would break my heart if Sandy should stop singing."

CHAPTER 10

LAUGHTER A LITTLE TOO LOUD

North Main Street, Liberty, N. Y.

After almost a year overseas, the war came home to America. On December 1, 1942, gas rationing went into effect. The system was based on the simplified alphabet of A, B, C, and T. The owner of an A sticker received coupons enough for four gallons a week—60 miles of driving, according to official estimates. B stickers were granted a supplementary allowance, and holders of a C card, professionals such as doctors and undertakers, could purchase additional gallons. T signified the men of privilege, truckers who could buy and burn all the octane they wanted.

Almost overnight the nation's thyroid gland calmed down. In New York City, the notorious traffic jams were gone. The cruising taxi was a memory; department stores discouraged deliveries, urging their customers to heed the new home-front slogan, "Don't delay, buy it today, carry it away." Sugar, butter, and coffee were rationed or in short supply. The government commandeered 60 percent of the prime and choice cuts of beef and 80 percent of the utility grades. Much of the meat supply that was left found its way onto the black market.

At first city dwellers were content to stay where they were, listening to the radio, marking Meatless Tuesdays with macaroni and cheese and vegetable stew, repeating the standard rationing joke: "I'm stocking up before the hoarders get here." Paperbacks, introduced just before the war by Pocket Books, moved rapidly from the shelves; mysteries began to sell at the rate of 150,000 copies a week. On radio, comedy dominated the evenings. Jack Benny, Fred Allen, Edgar Bergen and Charlie McCarthy, Fibber McGee and Molly beguiled listeners and helped them to forget the discouraging bulletins from Bataan and Corregidor. In an early service comedy, MGM introduced their new comedian, Danny Kaye, in *Up in Arms*. Records featured jaunty tunes by the Mills Brothers and the Andrews Sisters, and a new singer, Frank Sinatra, began to make a career of wounded arrogance. Nightclubs and ballroom dancing enjoyed a new vogue.

By summer most of these pleasures came to seem frantic and unsatisfying. For those on restricted incomes, overspending at some boîte was unthinkable. Besides, at the "21" Club a sign expressed rudely what most owners merely implied: BE COURT-EOUS TO OUR HELP; CUSTOMERS WE CAN ALWAYS GET. Added to this was the gray sameness of daily life, the insufferable heat unrelieved by air conditioning, the bland radio reruns or summer replacements, the blander cuisine, the dread of one more weekend on "tar beach," sobriquet for the melting black roofs of apartment houses. The real beaches of Coney Island and Rockaway, never empty, were so crowded that a low-flying seaplane could not see the sand for all the bodies and towels spread over it.

But there was hope. For the advocates of fresh air and exercise, the lack of wheels was a godsend. The naturalist Donald Culross Peattie described the rediscovery of walking: "I came back to my desk with blood tingling, with every stale, mundane concern washed out of my head. I had heard the titmouse calling his merry song of peet-o, peet-o and song sparrows turning up the alder branches where the catkins were hanging out all pollen-dusty and fertile. I had heard the brook gurgling." Those who were deaf to the peet-o of songbirds were preoccupied with thoughts of larger animals: chickens who could lay unrationed eggs and cows who might contribute unlimited sour cream. All this was available to those bus and train riders, and to New Yorkers who pointed their cars northwest, provided that they possessed B or C coupons. Nearly half of them did, having proved to the Office of Price Administration—the official rationers—that their vehicles were essential to the war effort.

Once the guests arrived, according to one owner, "they would pull the Catskills up around their ears and shut out the rest of the world." The insularity was understandable. Outside of the Jewish community, reports of Nazi atrocities were widely held to be exaggerated. More than a few believed that they were total fictions composed by immigrants attempting to get by the inspectors on Ellis Island. A 1942 Gallup Poll asked a sampling of citizens to rate those whom they considered "good as we are in all important respects," "not as good as we are," or "definitely inferior." Only five nationalities (Canadians, English, Dutch, Scandinavians, and Irish) were considered by a majority to be "good as we are." Germans, with whom the United States was waging unconditional war, ranked seventh, just after the French. South Americans came in ninth. "Jewish refugees" were tenth.

In his ruminative *Men and Politics*, published at the outbreak of World War II, Louis Fisher noticed: "Most American Jews remain in the Ghetto even when they move to the fashionable suburbs and join country clubs." That observation was truer still when they vacationed in the small towns of New York State. Here the Jews were not only the visitors, they were the hosts and merchants, the makers of law and custom and marriage, the comedians and cooks.

A Frank Loesser–Arthur Schwartz song of the period neatly encapsulates the odds for romance in the Catskills c. 1943:

Laughter a Little Too Loud

They're either too young or too old;
They're either too gray or too grassy-green.
What's good is in the army,
What's left will never harm me . . .

The customers came anyway: the young women perpetually eager, the old and disabled men as randy as the G.I.s overseas. After all, there was really nowhere else to go. For Mountain proprietors and tax collectors, and for many guests, the war years were good. For the people who worked there, circumstances were not always so happy. The liberal newspaper *PM*, always curious about how life was lived below the surface of things, sent its correspondent Gene De Paris to Livingston Manor in search of work as a dishwasher. He was immediately hired by the White Roe Hotel at a salary of $2 a day. The De Paris account provides a bracing antidote to tinted belowstairs memoirs:

"My room," he reported, "was an attic of a guest cottage that fringed the lake. The attic contained nine cots."

Before he was put to work, the journalist was fed a lunch of spaghetti, liver, and vegetables. When the meal was finished, he asked the chef for orders.

" 'Keep away from this stove,' he growled officiously. 'And when you talk to me take your hands out of your pockets.'

"I didn't talk to him. I turned to the 'head' dishwasher . . . who, aside from smirking when he looked at me, was strangely nice.

" 'When the dishes come in you clean the food off the plates with him over here,' he instructed. 'Then pile them up in the right sizes.' "

With four others the apprentice began his routine: "For two solid hours, without even taking time out for even one word of conversation, the five of us worked like a machine, washing dishes for 300 guests. After a while I got a stiff neck.

"When we finally finished I was assigned to sweep the floor. I worked for about nine hours a day and after the last meal I thought I was never more tired in my life.

"I went to the head dishwasher.

" 'This is a pretty good place to work, isn't it?'

" 'Yes, I've been here for four years.'

" 'The food is good, the bed isn't bad and they treat the help like human beings?'

" 'Yes, of course.'

" 'That's what I wanted to know. I'm quitting.' "

Entertainers had a livelier time of it. Merrill Miller, a young singer, vividly remembered his efforts to pursue the big time while prospective in-laws plucked at his coattails. "I played almost all the large hotels in the Catskills. The entertainment facilities varied, but one show remained constant: the parents' acts trying to marry me to their daughter. The fact that I was a budding operatic singer added a cachet of culture that raised me, in their minds, above the budding pharmacist or accountant. My calculated determination to remain single at that time was only a minor complication in their scenarios."

Miller includes a memorable exchange:

SCENE: *The hotel lounge, after the show. I have been invited to tea and cake with Mr. and Mrs. A. He is an effervescent man who plays guitar and, incidentally, owns a chain of supermarkets.*

MR. A: I like your voice, my boy. A great gift.

MILLER: Thank you very much.

MR. A: Still, talent has to be nursed along, correct? You know my daughter, Anna? What a personality!

MRS. A: And a beautiful cook and a college girl. She studies piano with a teacher that comes to the house.

MR. A: Well, I just got word from my partner, he's retiring soon and I'll need help in the business . . .

MRS. A (*Brightly*): You'll always have groceries on the table.

MILLER: I make enough for my teachers . . .

MR. A: Fifteen thousand a year brings the best teacher.

MILLER: I don't want the complications of a wife—I need to be free to travel—

MR. A: Who's talking about marrying? So she'll wait. My Anna likes to travel. Already she's been to Miami.

MRS. A: Come over to the house. She plays so pretty—you'll sing, I'll make a sponge cake . . .

MR. A: Look. I can raise the job to $20,000.

MILLER: I'm going out to California . . .

MR. A: Keep in touch. Here's my card. (*He winks broadly*) What a smart negotiator you are, young fella!

Miller dismissed the flattery. "Negotiator . . . I was a notorious patsy for agents. They rented my voice out for cash, deducted 10 percent, and since I seldom knew what actual fee they received, often kept an additional $20. Sometimes I was booked into the Catskills on off-season weekends, with Phil Foster or Phil Silvers, and the agent would try to pay us off separately, so we wouldn't know the total fee. One of the Phils usually discovered what that fee was, and the agent would reluctantly pay us at the same time—under a bright light so we could count the bills."

Miller's most inventive agent was a man he refers to as the Machiavelli of the Mountains. Charlie Rapp was infamous for booking his clients into several resorts on the same evening— and frequently at the same hour. Henry Tobias, an old *Variety* hand, reported that "many . . . acts used to do six shows for $90 plus an extra $10 for the use of the car. Sometimes they were lucky and had to travel only a few miles between engagements. But sometimes Rapp . . . would send them more than 100 miles." The automobiles were old and inefficient, and high-speed traveling consumed far too much gasoline. "A common practice," says Tobias, "was to push the speedometer back so they could get gas from rationed tickets (determined by mileage). They drove the gas station man crazy coming back so often with the same car and a different story." During the war Rapp represented so many acts that he took over two hotels, the Willow Lane in Monticello and the Midwood in Hurleyville, to house his clients. On the rare occasions when the rooms were empty, he rented them to "civilians," people with no show-business connections. One slow Saturday two young secretaries innocently checked into the Willow Lane and asked about the amusements. They were presented, Rapp claimed, with "a show that will go down in the annals of show business. Those two girls, the whole audience, were entertained by 80 acts who had no other shows that night. And the headliners were Red Buttons and Merrill [Miller]."

It must have been one of Miller's rare nights off. A classic summer began with performances at the Young's Gap Hotel every Tuesday, Saturday, and Sunday evening. When these went smoothly, Rapp scheduled the singer for additional appearances on the same evenings. It was simple, the agent explained. All the talent had to do was clamber out of a men's room window: "You'll open the show here. Applause—thank you—walk out for some fresh air—your driver is waiting in the Plymouth—over the mountain to the other hotel, where you come on in the middle of the show—three numbers—applause—thank you—out for the fresh air—into the Plymouth—and back for the finale at Young's Gap."

"What if I can't get out for fresh air?"

"They have to give you time to wash your hands—it's in the contract. Then—out the window—into the Plymouth—"

"What if the window doesn't open?"

Rapp exploded: "I'll break it open!"

"I came home breathless," reported Miller, "and twice as rich. Next summer: same place, same scheme. Except that I was caught at the President Hotel by Mr. Leschnick, co-owner with Mr. Podolnick. Podolnick was the overseer of the kitchen who, it was rumored, slept in the walk-in refrigerator and allotted twelve potato chips to a plate. Leschnick was the impresario, a short, bald, volatile man."

He became choleric when he found Miller headed out the window of his music hall. The owner cried out triumphantly, "Ha! I'm going to trow you and your mudder off the show!"

For Miller this was a double embarrassment. His "mudder" had rented a place in a *kuchaleyn* close by the hotel. At such places the clocks seemed to have rusted to a stop in 1932. The guests still made their forays through the woods to the President Hotel as if nothing had intervened since the Depression, when gate-crashing was overlooked. "Guiding their way with flashlights over dirt paths and around trees," said her son, "these patrons of the arts moved silently onto the hotel grounds like a column of fireflies. The hotels retaliated with a security system, marking their registered guests' wrists with an invisible ink that could only be revealed by a special light. Often members of the audience with bulging pockets were searched by hotel guards for the incriminating flashlight, and interlopers would be ejected."

Months before, Lillian Miller had worked her way past the border guards, identified herself as a singer, confronted Leschnick, and persuaded him to give her a tryout. The audience responded to her Polish songs with surprising enthusiasm, and she had become a star in her own right. Bearing this history in mind, Miller dropped contritely from the window to the grass below. " 'Mr. Leschnick,' " he promised, " 'I'll sing two extra numbers on every show.'

" 'And no running to udder hotels.'

"I assured him his people came first."

Leschnick's warning showed how far the Catskills were from Broadway: "Remember—actors I can buy by the gross— people it's not so easy."

Miller remembered. It would be several years before he changed his name to Robert Merrill and signed on as the Metropolitan Opera's new baritone. His was the second voice to go from the Catskills to grand opera. A portly tenor named Pincus Perelmuth had made the journey a generation before. "Back in 1918," he writes in his autobiography, "I became addicted to the Catskills." After the summer of his debut as violinist Pinky Pearl and his Society Dance Orchestra, at the Breezy Hill Hotel in Fleischmanns, he "whiled away the winters and the school years as recesses [waiting] to get back to the mountains and greenery and full-time music making." Like most of the other musicians, Perelmuth found his salary diminished by hotel fees for housing and feeding his family. Then, he adds, "there were tips to our waiter and busboys, cigarettes, newspapers, and we still had to pay rent on our apartment in the Bronx. By the end of the summer we owed ourselves money, but at least I was giving my wife and son some good Catskill Mountain air.

"One weekend, a man in the jewelry business heard me sing. He had once been married to a showgirl and told me he could arrange an audition for me with Earl Carroll . . . then the

King of Show Business . . . his *Vanities* were comparable to the *Ziegfeld Follies.*" It was not a success. Carroll's chief booker offered an unlivable wage. When Perelmuth tried to negotiate, he held up a hand. " 'Kid, if you were as tall as I am, if you looked more like me, if you had a good profile, and if you didn't have to wear those big thick eyeglasses, and if you were handsomer, instead of having that big chest and even bigger stomach, and if you weren't short and stocky, then you could name your price, because the boss is crazy about your pipes.' "

As Perelmuth remembers it, "The tears were about to burst the dam. I . . . knew that he and I weren't going to do business. So without choking too much, I made a pretty prophetic speech of my own:

" 'You know something? . . . Maybe there'll come a time when a little guy like me, with glasses and a stomach—small, stocky, overweight, with not such a great profile—could buy a cup of coffee for a big handsome guy like you when you may need it.'

"With that, I turned and ran west on Fifty-fourth Street, with him yelling after me. I ran down Tenth Avenue, cutting over to Forty-second and Twelfth and the Weehawken Ferry to get the Ontario & Western Railroad, crying all the way back to the mountains, where I was making twice as much as Earl Carroll was willing to offer me."

The tenor might have returned to the resorts for the rest of his career, soloing profitably before undemanding guests. But Perelmuth was unwilling to settle for security. Upon returning from Swan Lake to New York City at the end of a miserable summer he sang in nightclubs and continued to audition before anyone who would hear him. En route he attracted the attention of Samuel L. Rothafel, an impresario better known by the nickname emblazoned on one of his theaters. "Roxy" agreed to hire the singer after a small adjustment. It was not the stomach or the profile. "Who wants to hear Pinky Perelmuth, the tenor?" he demanded. "Starting next Sunday, your name is John Pierce." A few years later he changed the billing for the last time. "Jan Peerce meant a new life in art," Perelmuth later acknowledged. "Pinky Pearl was left behind in another lifetime."

Few singers have made longer journeys than the one from the Mountains to the Metropolitan. Once they arrived on the opera stage, neither Peerce nor Merrill had any reason to go back to the Catskills. But if they discarded their names, they retained an indulgent view of their early years. Merrill dwelt on the lessons he learned as an apprentice, and long after he had sung *Don Carlos* and *La Traviata* he was still dispensing practical wisdom he had learned in the resorts. He told hopeful singers, for example, how to press a tie without an iron. "Sprinkle some water on it with your fingertips, then run the back side of the tie carefully over a bare electric bulb in the dressing room. The wrinkles steam right out."

He spoke of the time when "in the Catskills, I needed a white waiter's jacket for a comedy bit; the one available must have been used to wash the dining room floor. Simple, said the stage manager. He took it to the scenery shop and painted the entire jacket whiter than white. It was as crisp as if it had just been pressed."

Jan Peerce had a similar affection for his past. During the war he played Grossinger's with the same gusto he brought to *Pagliacci*. Despite his billing as the new Caruso, the tenor never lost his appetite for shmaltz or applause. His showstopper was the emetic and ungrammatical "Bluebird of Happiness" ("Be like I, hold your head up high"). Audience reaction to the song became so predictable that Peerce learned to carry sheets of the music wherever he went. Sometimes after a performance of *Aida* he would slip a copy to the orchestra conductor and provide an encore. Years later he liked to boast, "My RCA record of 'Bluebird' . . . has sold well over a million copies . . . and is second-ranked among all-time best-selling recordings by opera or concert singers. It is still gaining ground on number one, which is Enrico Caruso's recording of 'Over There,' released during World War I. I do earn royalties from store sales, so please remember this when next you visit your friendly record shop. Forgive my directness."

When he was not plugging songs and records, Peerce liked to bestow *mitzvahs*—kindnesses—in the Mountains. When the maître d' at Grossinger's informed Peerce that his grandchild had "a real voice on her," Peerce records, "I said very casually that I'd like to hear her sometime, and a few months later a girl named Roberta Peterman came down from the Bronx with her mother to see me . . . To my amazement, she was only about thirteen. To my further astonishment, her grandfather had been absolutely right. . . . A couple of years later I arranged for Roberta to audition for Sol Hurok." She, too, had to make a change, and it was as Roberta Peters that she appeared at the Met, and at Grossinger's, for the next twenty-five years.

The Chester brothers, Sam and Herman, had watched the Depression eat away at their real-estate business until they could stand no more and retreated to their country place in Woodbourne, New York. There they set up one of the most idiosyncratic vacation spots in the Catskills: an anti-resort. Chesters' Zumbarg—Sun Hill—was just down the road from Grossinger's and the Concord, but it had no tummler, no ostentatious over-stuffed lobby. The customers who found their way to Chesters' had seen the ads in *The New Masses* and *The Nation*. This was a pleasure dome with a conscience.

Some forty years after his death, Herman Chester's widow still cherished one part of her old place above all the others, the Poets' Corner. "Name the poet, we had a cabin dedicated to him," said Ann Chester. "Wordsworth, Byron, Keats. We had an intellectual crowd. Nevertheless, not every activity was high-brow. Even thinkers like a little romance now and then." For that reason, Chesters' closed the reservations for women and couples early in order to guarantee the presence of single men.

Once the season was under way, Chesters' became the Catskills' Jewish arts-and-crafts center. Workshops were set up for the making of copper jewelry; amateur landscape painters were supplied with easels, sculptors were given clay and wood. Instructors dispensed advice at no extra charge. Most important, wherever the guests wandered, they were presented with classical music, live and on record. String quartets rehearsed on the lawn, and strains of Beethoven and Brahms competed with the mating cries of the red-winged blackbird. "Our most unusual event," Ann Chester told her family in a long reminiscence, "was our annual June Music and Arts Festival. It began when Ray Lev, a pianist with an international reputation, visited Chesters' and decided that we needed other well-known musicians to concertize at our place. I reminded her that not only didn't I have contacts with these people but I couldn't afford them.

" 'Well,' said Ray, 'I can get them to come up. They'll enjoy the surroundings, we like to play together, and they will welcome a vacation in a friendly atmosphere.'

"And they did. We had people like Leonard Posner, the first violinist with the Casals Festival Orchestra; Charles Lubovic, second violin in the Paganini Quartet; Alan Shulman, cellist with the NBC Symphony under Toscanini; and David Nadian, concertmaster of the New York Philharmonic."

Every day guests could attend a chamber music concert; once a week the resident pianist gave a recital. In addition there were discussion groups, yoga and meditation lessons. When comedians appeared, they discarded the Borscht Belt staccato for a loftier approach. Zero Mostel imitated a coffeepot coming to a boil; Jack Gilford gave his impression of a fiddler crab and a chimpanzee; Sam Levenson, a former schoolteacher, gently evoked the old days: "On the Lower East Side we saw our dentist twice a year—once when he moved into the block and again six months later when he moved out. To keep our teeth white we chewed roof tar. This not only kept them shiny, but preserved them, especially those that remained in the tar." Perhaps the most distinguishing feature of the entertainment—and often, of the guests—was the presence of blacks. Other resorts booked what the agents called "colored acts," usually tap dancers or singing groups who were instructed to end their routines with "My Yiddishe Momme" to prove that, despite their ethnicity, they were certifiably kosher. Chesters' employed the folk singer Josh White and the dancer Avon Long, and welcomed Paul Robeson as a guest. No one could dispute the owner's claim: "We were a very, very different sort of place." Being different did not make the duties any lighter. "You had to learn to live with the help, all maintained on the premises. Some nights you would hear a drunken dishwasher coming by and wonder will he be in for work the next morning. Or the chef or the baker or the head salad man has to be appeased because a waiter coming from the dining room to pick up some orders called out to just one: 'Your beef (or your pastry or your salad) was great' and the others were not singled out for a compliment."

Then there was the clientele: Some would stop at the front to demand, "Whoever heard of a resort that says ART CAN BE FUN?" The owner, at ninety, could still remember her favorite complainers, like "the nudnik who sits near the office practically all the time and especially Sundays when people are coming and going. He is counting the money you are making—after all, how much does it cost to feed a guest? All else is profit, he thinks." And the "woman who read about us, came up, and attended a recital. In the morning she left, loudly indicating the headline in our ad. 'It was entertainment,' she said. 'But it wasn't gala.' "

As the war progressed, every Catskill hostelry saw itself as a bastion of freedom. Speeches, bond rallies, and USO dances became as common as Friday-night basketball games. Former busboys and waiters came by to display their uniforms and medals, and to be treated with new respect in the house newspaper ("IRV SHAPIRO IS A HERO: There's Truth and Poetry in that Headline, as Another Grossinger Man Wins Battlefield Honors. . . . That fellow looking at the windmills in Holland is none other than Pvt. Richard Dickson our former doorman. . . . Cpl. Philip Foster is not kidding when he says that one of these days he'll be playing a club date at Loew's Berlin").

A backhand salute to servicemen came in the form of a long-neglected ritual: the mock wedding. On Saturday nights a man, guaranteed to be out of the running as a candidate for marriage, dressed in a bridal gown. An unrelated woman got herself up in the formal clothes of the groom. Comic vows were read by a mock rabbi, played by whatever clown was available; songs were chanted; the traditional glass was trampled underfoot, symbolizing the destruction of the Temple. There were, however, no philosophical afterthoughts, only raucous laughter. A sense of the sacrilegious hovered about all this, and the mockery of tradition was imperiously criticized at Orthodox hotels. The less rigid resorts were defensive. What was wrong, the owners argued, with a line of bridesmaids played by middle-aged males, and a chorus of ushers impersonated by young women? Until the boys came marching home, this was as close as most of them would get to the bridal canopy.

Of course, it was not only grooms who were in short supply. During the war, almost all jobs were filled by the overaged or by youths. Even in the major leagues, adolescents were in evidence: Joe Nuxhall, aged sixteen, started a game for the Cincinnati Reds. And in the Catskills, a similarly inexperienced youth, Joseph Levitch, became a professional at the same age. He had watched his father Danny, a Mountain comedian, capering at Brown's Hotel. The boy found his own ways to parody the manic gestures, the unintentional pratfalls and lunacies of the kitchen help. He never forgot the "grueling time, rising every morning at dawn, hurrying down to the kitchen to find twenty busboys and waiters already there. You could hear them jabbering:

" 'Boy, am I sleepy.'
" 'Watch the doors.'
" 'Outta my way, simp.'
" 'Up your nose—'
" 'Hot stuff coming through—'
" 'Hey, who wants table thirty-three?'
" 'Oh, for the life of idle play—'
" 'Sure, sure . . .'
" 'Boy, am I tired.'
"All this, and one break between lunch and dinner."

On a Sabbath evening the hotel rabbi was delivering the traditional blessings. His rich voice sanctified the evening. Hundreds listened, hushed and reverential, says Levitch, "when out of some kind of unconscious fog I came waltzing through the kitchen door, bumped against a waiter on the other side and dropped a tray full of dishes.

"I wailed, 'Oh, God, I didn't mean it!'

"It was a wipeout. Even the rabbi laughed.

"At which point it seemed like an ideal thing to start clowning my way through every meal. The clown. The one guy who could make people laugh in spite of themselves, giving pleasure by creating an illusion of wild absurdity. It was all I wanted to do in the first place. So you can imagine the stunts I pulled during those busboy days at the Ambassador. Suffice to say, the more absurd, the more they liked it."

Levitch learned quickly. One of the most valuable lessons was absorbed the night he watched his father and a partner, Lou Black, work the audience, hoping for recognition from big-time agents like William Morris. "It was all there," recalls the son. "Dad's brilliant song-and-dance routines; Lou's hilarious comedy violin solo; the two of them combining in a knockabout sketch, rolling from joke to joke that worked the crowd into hysterics, then going off with cheers and bravos ringing everywhere.

"The only problem, nobody from the Morris office showed."

That bitter conclusion drove the young comedian out of the Mountains, but not before he worked up an act pantomiming the words and sound effects of selected records. As Joey Levitch and his Hollywood Friends, he offered "Cyril Smith and 'The Sow Song' (snorting, whistling sounds of the farm and barnyard; *Figaro* and *The Barber of Seville* by opera singer Igor Gorin; Danny Kaye's 'Deena' . . . *Is there anyone feena in the state of Caroleena, if there is and you know her, just show her* . . . Also, there were songs by Jerry Colonna, Louis Prima, Louis Armstrong, Kate Smith, Deanna Durbin."

The collector of adolescent gestures and tics worked on "a speed change, a hesitation or the effect of the crack in the record. . . . I did all those devices, always finding ways to do different things . . . wearing a strawberry fright wig and a tattered coat . . . I worked myself into a frenzy doing crazy things with my hands, eyes, lips, tongue; in fact, every part of my body that could move, moved all at once."

By day he was an impatient busboy, Levitch says, but the nights were dedicated to performing, "running to this or that hotel—the Waldemere, the Nemerson, the Laurel Park,

Flagler's, Young's Gap and how many others I don't remember."
If the promises and the profits were minuscule, the oedipal
drama was full-sized. Several years later Levitch dropped the
lip sync, acquired an agent and a partner, changed his name,
and wholly obscured his father's reputation. When the comic
triumphantly returned to the Mountains, his caricature grinned
from roadside billboards along Route 17. By then he had starred
in such headlong film farces as *My Friend Irma* and *At War with
the Army*. Many tourists had never heard of Brown's Hotel, but
every driver could identify the owner of the underslung jaw and
the gawky stare. Jerry Lewis had displaced Danny Kaye as the
Catskills' most influential graduate.

The end of the war introduced vacationers to some unfamiliar words: Auschwitz, Buchenwald, Belsen, Maidenek, Babi
Yar. In his undervalued novel, *Dusk in the Catskills*, Reuben
Wallenrod wrote of American Jewry in wartime: "Every morning
you read the papers, the heart thumping with fear of surprises.
You kept telling yourself that the Nazis would be beaten. It was
impossible otherwise. Your mind did not want to accept any other
end. But . . . here, in Brookville, in a little village in the Catskill
Mountains, Jewish men and women, brothers and sisters of those
tortured Jews in Poland and Holland and Slovakia, came and
demanded pleasure with eagerness, with anxiety. The little eyes
blinked with desire, the nostrils quivered: a little more pleasure,
a little more. The grounds were bright and colorful with flower
beds; on the tennis court young men and women jumped, one
opposite another; and no one paid attention to the monstrosities
that cut into the brain."

A few months after V-J Day, attention had to be paid. No
one could look away anymore. Photographs in *Life* magazine,
and in virtually all the major newspapers, showed the bodies
bulldozed into common graves, and exhibited the rooms of human hair and gold teeth and rings. Evidence of human flesh
made into soap and lampshades mutely presented itself, and
abruptly anti-Semitism acquired a bad name. The destruction
of European Jewry cannot properly be discussed in a social history; as Irving Howe points out, immediately after the war, "any

pretense of explaining the Holocaust, any theory as to its causes, was bound to crumble into inconsequence, a mere trifling with categories in the face of the unspeakable. There was nothing to do but remember, and that was best done in silence, alone."

Discussions, when they occurred, centered on the idea of a homeland. In the postwar climate Eretz Israel, the promised territory of the Jews, was no pious testamental ideal to be trotted out at Passover and forgotten the rest of the year. Palestine was in the headlines, fought over by the Haganah, the Jewish army, and the Irgun, a quasi-military group labeled as terrorist by the occupying British forces. A fragment of the emotions stirred up in the late forties can be discerned not from contemporary news bulletins but from an ad, LETTER TO THE TERRORISTS OF PALESTINE, inserted in New York newspapers by the screenwriter Ben Hecht:

My Brave Friends . . .

The British figured the sound of gabble before a world court would drown out the sound of Hebrew guns in Palestine.

It hasn't and it won't.

True enough, Jewish respectability is making a bit of noise at the moment. Our "Jewish Leaders" are pleading for a Jewish sanctuary in fine measured strophes.

They are not nearly as hotheaded about it as were the bird lovers of America who a few years ago pleaded for a sanctuary for the vanishing penguins.

But they are much alike. They want a sanctuary where the Jews of Europe can all stand on a rock and eat philanthropy fish until the Messiah arrives. We are ringing doorbells and peddling your cause and passing the hat.

Forgive us if our take is a little meagre—for the time. . . . Hang on, brave friends, our money is on the way.

Hecht watched "with awe" as sympathizers "rose out of stores and workshops . . . Jewish clerks and salesladies, garage workers, plasterers, elevator boys, Yeshiva students, policemen, garment workers, prize fighters, housewives; Jewish soldiers and sailors still in American uniforms, Jews from night clubs, tenements, farm lands, synagogues and even penthouses came boldly . . . [with] their dollar bills and five dollar bills."

A goodly portion of bills were contributed by guests in the Catskill resorts who, after years of insularity, saw themselves playing a global role. "We did what we could to help the Irgun [the Jewish underground in Palestine]," one of them remembered. "We talked it up, we spoke at rallies, but mostly we raised money. There were those respectable citizens who disliked violence, and they walked away from the appeals. But many were happy to help. Among them were a few leftovers from the thirties, men who had a criminal past, maybe from the Murder, Inc. days, and they liked the notion of outlaw soldiers. They heard about Cohen in California. They tried to copy his style, and they kicked in plenty."

The Cohen he referred to was Mickey Cohen. In the tabloids his name was always preceded by the title Gambling Czar. Early in 1947 Cohen held a meeting of some thousand bookies, ex-prizefighters, gamblers, jockeys, and touts. They were urged to contribute funds to Jewish fighters in Palestine. When he counted up their pledges, Cohen, never much of a public speaker, petulantly ordered his bodyguard to "tell 'em they're a lot o' cheap crumbs and they gotta give double." The bodyguard roared inarticulately for a time. Afterward Cohen stood up, silently glaring. Man by man the audience stood with him and increased the ante 100 percent. The evening, Cohen noted, raised $200,000 for "Jews ready to knock hell out of all the bums in the world who don't like them."

All the same, to most vacationers, the history of suffering, the fight for an ideal, were obscured by the summer light. The postwar climate of the Mountains is acutely recalled in two neglected novels, Harvey Jacobs's *Summer on a Mountain of Spices* and Martin Boris's *Woodridge, 1946*. Jacobs's novel measures the portions of horror and exultation as his hero gets ready for a season in the Mountains:

"Millions died in the war's fire. They had no voices. They lost their faces. Harry Craft could think sadly of the dead, but he celebrated the time he was born to, the crisis of battle, the tension of counter-attack, the newspaper maps with thick ink arrows tracing the blitz, the eruption of history. Harry Craft liked living on dates they would teach forever in schools not yet built. They jibed with his own throbbing history. . . .

"The fetal faces of Dachau . . . looked out through barbed wire. Harry looked back. Was it his fault that his testicles were full? Was it his fault that he had plans? Was it his fault that the morning was beautiful?"

In *Woodridge, 1946*, a Sullivan County newspaper arrives by rural free delivery. The protagonist opens it: "The front page contained its assortment of misery and disaster. The Malmedy massacre again. Forty-three German S.S. officers were sentenced to death for their part in the murder of seventy-one G.I. prisoners during the Battle of the Bulge. And at the upper echelons Robert Jackson was fashioning nooses for the top Germans in Nürnberg for their part in the murder of over ten million poor devils. Phil gazed at Goering's face; the Luftwaffe chief looked like a small-town bartender. He turned the page. Trouble with Russia. We were saying mustn't touch the Reds' dismantling of Hungary's industrial plants and the shipping of them back home to Mother Russia. Phil didn't care. To hell with the Hungarians for what they did to the Jews before the Nazis got there."

Phil's attention is arrested by an item on page 2: "An outfit called the Irgun had blown up the King David Hotel in Jerusalem. Now that was a showstopper: Jews barking back at the British lion. He quickly skimmed. Butter up to eighty-five cents a pound and eggs down to thirty-three cents a dozen, which proved . . . that the butter people in Washington were stronger than the egg people. Sleep came slowly or quickly to him depending on how much of his mind [Phil's girlfriend] cared to invade."

Near the conclusion, another Catskill youth has a sorry adventure with radicalism. He descends from the Mountains and crosses the Hudson River in order to attend a rally in Peekskill, New York. "Douglas wound the wires from the speakers through the branches of the tall elms and took note of the hate on the faces of the crowd. It surprised him. Weren't they all on the same side? Peace? Freedom? Jobs? Many were middle-aged, overweight, and wore American Legion caps. Simple people but smug, Douglas decided. . . . He discounted the hate and decided not to feel in danger. After all, they *were* Americans.

"The state troopers on the edge of the crowd were taller than the rest. They wore cowboy hats and wire-framed sunglasses that were mirrored so that no one might see their eyes. . . . The crowd pressed closer to the platform. . . . An egg whistled past Douglas's ear and cracked open on [a] senator's white suit. Soon eggs were all over the platform. Then a deep red tomato. . . . The troopers approached. . . .

" 'Son of a bitch Red,' the first policeman said, 'you're not so goddam brave now, are you?'

"Douglas was too terrified to answer. Although most of the crowd was still milling around, gawking and shouting curses at him, he had expected to be murdered on the spot by the police. They threw him into the back of a patrol car with such force his nose smacked the door handle on the other side. . . .

"In town a judge berated him for spitting on the American Way of Life and he was prodded off to a cell in the basement of the building."

Douglas returns to the Catskills in time for a lecture addressed to those who dabble in Causes. "You're always someone's towel," says the boy's father, Harry.

" 'Well . . . I don't think I can live your way.'

" 'Prepare yourself, then,' Harry said as he dumped four spoons of sugar into his second cup of coffee, ' for a pretty rough life.' "

Although the characters of *Woodridge, 1946* are fictional, the Peekskill riot did take place. It was far more ominous, and it occasioned a Catskill commute of an entirely different kind.

By the summer of 1949, the Cold War had reached far into show business. It had already provoked blacklists of entertainers suspected of leftist sympathies, and it encouraged yahoo anti-Communism among audiences for theater, film, and broadcasting. It was not a propitious moment to express radical sympathies. But the most prominent black singer and actor of his time was uninterested in proper timing. Paul Robeson had long been a celebrant of Josef Stalin's U.S.S.R. and a target of congressional investigators. Out of a combination of self-righteousness and perversity, he decided to give two outdoor concerts in Peekskill. He and his sponsors were greeted by more than a thousand protestors who, like the shouters of two generations ago, believed that radicalism and Jewry were one and the same. "Reds!" they called. "Jew bastards!" "Go back to Russia!" "Nigger lovers." "Go back to Jew City!"

After the second concert, demonstrators stoned the departing audience. Hundreds of cars were hit; eight were overturned. Chartered buses from Manhattan were attacked by rocks, some the size of footballs. Several vehicles were abandoned by their drivers. One passenger lost an eye; several arms were broken. New York City hospitals reported that nearly fifty injured concertgoers drove all the way into Manhattan before they dared to seek medical care.

The singer took a different route. Bulletins of the Peekskill riot were broadcast; Ann Chester heard them on the radio. She immediately dispatched a driver to meet Paul Robeson and bring him back to the resort, where he would be safe. "For more years than anyone could care to remember," she said, "the Catskills were a haven for Jews. Why couldn't they also be a place where a black man could feel safe?" In other years she would answer her own question by playing hostess to a number of black couples, and employing black entertainers. Only once did she allow her bias to show, and then it was not racial but political. The Negro folk singer Josh White, she said, "practically lived at our place for many years and had our guests spellbound so often until he became an informer for the House Un-American Activities Committee." In the Mountains there were all sorts of traditions to be maintained.

CHAPTER 11

ELBOWING HISTORY OFFSTAGE

After the war, survivors of the Holocaust became an increasingly common sight in the Catskills. They could be observed on the town streets and in the late-night cafeterias, whispering to each other and sometimes to themselves, the pain sealed up behind the eyes. "I try to understand my new country," one of them said. "In the newspapers, I see people still hate the Jews. In the movies, we are beloved. Maimonides himself would not be wise enough to interpret this."

Two of the films he referred to were playing the Mountains in the late forties. Both features dared to consider the long-forbidden subject of American anti-Semitism. In *Crossfire*, a sadistic bigot, Sgt. Montgomery (Robert Ryan), murders a Jewish war hero (Sam Levene). Later, he confides his private loathings to a tough, streetwise Sgt. Keely (Robert Mitchum): "I've seen a lot of guys like Samuels, guys who played it safe during the war, scrounged around keeping themselves in civvies, had swell apartments and swell dames. Some are named Samuels and some got funnier names." Keely replies, "There's a lot of names on the casualty list, too." After he helps police detective Finley (Robert Montgomery) trap the killer, Keely faces the sergeant and delivers an editorial: "My best friend, a Jew, is lying back in a foxhole at Guadalcanal. I'm gonna spit in your eye for him because we don't want people like you in the U.S.A. There's no place for racial discrimination now."

Finley—the most Christian of the film's good men—adds: "This business about hating Jews comes in a lot of different sizes. There's the 'you can't join the country club' kind. The 'you can't live around here' kind. The 'you can't work here' kind. Because we stand for all these, we get Monty's kind. He grows out of all the rest. . . . Hating is always insane, always senseless."

Crossfire was shot in twenty days for $500,000, and it showed, as expected, a very small profit. *Gentleman's Agreement* was different. The big-budget film was personally supervised by Darryl F. Zanuck, head of production at 20th Century-Fox. It was written by Moss Hart, based on Laura Z. Hobson's best-selling novel, and directed by Elia Kazan. Zanuck, head of the only "goy studio" in Hollywood, found some surprising opposition when he announced plans to proceed. "There was a terrific uproar from the rich Jews of the Hollywood community," a colleague wrote. "And there was a meeting at Warner Brothers, called I think by Harry Warner. At that meeting . . . all the wealthy Jews said, 'For Chrissake, why make that picture? We're getting along all right. Why raise the subject?' " Zanuck went ahead with his plans, sensing that the country was ready for a major film about social bias. "In a polite way, [he] told them to mind their own business."

The hero of *Gentleman's Agreement* is an investigative reporter, Phil Green (Gregory Peck), assigned to write a series of articles on anti-Semitism. To get close to the subject, Phil decides to make himself a victim, and Green becomes Greenberg. His bewildered son is brought on screen to ask Dad, "What are Jews?" Phil responds with the message of postwar brotherhood—deep down, everyone is exactly the same. "There are lots of different churches. Some people who go to them are Catholics. People who go to other churches are called Protestants. Then there are others who go to still different ones, and they're called Jews, only they call their churches synagogues and temples. . . . You can be an American and a Protestant or a Catholic or a Jew. Religion is different from nationality."

Wherever he goes, Green/Greenberg is made the victim of fear and loathing; he even confronts Jewish self-hate. His secretary, Miss Wales (née Walofsky), objects when he urges the hiring of more Jews: "They'll get the wrong kind, the kikey ones who'll give us all a bad name." Green confesses that he is not Jewish and comments bitterly on her slack-jawed disbelief that "anyone would give up the glory of being a Christian even for eight weeks."

Gentleman's Agreement was preening and self-congratulatory, and at previews the Hollywood doubters had their say: anti-anti-Semitism was definitely not box office. Good reviews it would get. But money? Then the receipts started to come in. By the end of 1947 the film had become Fox's most profitable production; it placed eighth in *Variety*'s annual tabulation of grosses. Early the next year it won three Academy Awards. *Gentleman's Agreement* had not only done well in New York and Chicago and Los Angeles, it had played in Pasadena, Tuscaloosa, and Peoria. Prejudice was unfashionable and it was unprofitable. The epoch of good feeling, characteristic of America's postwar periods, had returned.

The national pity and understanding were not to last. Perhaps, viewed at a remove of two generations, it was never really there. Sometime after the filming of *Crossfire*, the director remembered that one of his assistants had complained, "There's no anti-Semitism in America. If there were, why is all the money in America controlled by Jewish bankers?" *Gentleman's Agreement* provoked similar reactions. Its scenarist, Moss Hart, said that a stagehand loved working on the picture because of its "wonderful moral." Curious, Hart asked him what the moral was. The man replied, "I'll never be rude to a Jew again because he might turn out to be a Gentile."

Even the most authentic feelings of brotherhood were difficult to sustain in the late forties, when a jittery economy and a fear of subversion combined to elbow history offstage. Americans began to fret about what was in front of them, not what had passed by: the Market, the Bomb, the Russians. In 1948 George Orwell warned them about the dystopia coming in 1984, and Albert Einstein told them of his fears for the Atomic Age. One day they heard about Communist sympathizers in government, the next they were warned about the virulence of irresponsible witch-hunts for "Reds in the State Department." Public-school air-raid drills were reinstituted, and so were blacklists of entertainers suspected of radical sympathies.

John Rankin, congressman from Mississippi, revived many dormant suspicions when he implied that the Jew and the subversive were one and the same. Holding up a petition against the House Inquiry into Hollywood Communism, he described signers who had spent many summers in the Catskills: "One of the names is June Havoc. We found out from the motion picture almanac that her real name is June Hovick. Another one was Danny Kaye, and we found out that his real name is David Daniel Kaminsky. . . . Another one is Eddie Cantor, whose real name is Edward Iskowitz. . . . They are attacking the Committee for doing its duty to protect this country and save the American people from the horrible fate the Communists have meted out to the unfortunate Christian people of Europe."

Investigation embodied the spirit of the age. Senator Estes Kefauver of Tennessee sought with great headlines and fervor to find the roots of organized crime. Congressman J. Parnell Thomas of New Jersey led the House Un-American Activities Committee's probe of Communist influence in film and broadcasting. Senator Joseph McCarthy of Wisconsin attempted to find traitors in the State Department and later, at the cost of his career, in the army. Far too often for comfort, Jewish names appeared as suspects, and in New York, with the highest concentration of Jews in the nation, discomfort was palpable. A handful fought back; most sought to escape from the headlines. "It was a very difficult time," a resort owner recollected. "A few years before, we were the victims and everyone felt sorrow and regret for us. Now we were hearing the familiar old line: World War II was a Jewish war, and Jews were its biggest profiteers. Or, if people wouldn't buy that, the Jews were the big Reds out there in Washington and Hollywood. In the late forties and early fifties it got so people would come to the Mountains just to get away from the papers. On vacation they read the house organ and let the *Times* and the *World-Telegram* and the *Post* go to hell. Nobody wanted to talk news up there. They wanted to see a new dining room, a better swimming pool, fancier facilities. Believe me, we gave it to them. But they never really relaxed. You heard very little substantial conversation. It was all 'How's your son in medical school? I hear your daughter's getting married. Salt is bad for the blood pressure. Our basketball team is better than Grossinger's.' It was hard to believe what a different world we had been looking at only a few years before."

After an acrimonious debate, the United Nations General Assembly of 1949 decided that Israel was "a peace-loving State which accepts the obligations contained in the Charter and is able and willing to carry out these obligations." The new nation was thereupon welcomed as a fully accredited member.

For American Jews two sentiments accompanied this acceptance: euphoria and discomfort. Certainly there was a sense of moral recompense after the terrible arithmetic of the Third Reich; certainly pride attended the restoration of the land, the reinstitution of Hebrew as a national language, the knowledge that a Jewish state could field a victorious army in the early conflicts against British and Egyptian troops.

Even so, the Holy Land had a way of arousing pangs of guilt among its most avid supporters. On a fund-raising tour of America, the new nation's Prime Minister, David Ben-Gurion, stated flatly that a Zionist is one who settles in Israel. The assertion did not entice many immigrants. When the uncomfortable matter of Israel arose, Jews in the United States voted with their wallets and their ballots, not with their feet. For the first two decades of Israel's existence only 8,000 Americans chose to emigrate, and many of them returned dissatisfied with life on a kibbutz or in the growing cities of Haifa and Tel Aviv. In customary fashion, the Catskill tummlers put it succinctly: "A Zionist," they said, "is a New Yorker who pays someone else to live in Israel." The pay was generous. In 1945 the United Jewish Appeal raised $35 million for the Holy Land; in 1948 donations reached $150 million.

A large fraction of that money was raised in the Mountains, where fevered postwar expansion had begun. The Concord was redoing its lobby and dining facilities. At Brickman's, Murray Posner, son of the founder, announced plans for a new outdoor swimming pool. It would take the place of a neglected apple orchard. "My father was always for progress," Posner recalled. "But you know what my mother did? My own mother got all the guests to sign a petition to stop us from cutting down the trees. We had a family feud going here. She was sentimental: the apple trees, that's where the hooks were for the hammocks in the old days."

Mama lost; the romances that once took place under the apple trees now occurred around an oversized pool. Murray Posner called it the Marine Deck: "I remember going to the . . . hardware stores in downtown New York to buy all sorts of junk from boats—anchors, anything related to ships. I had portholes and I made it look nautical. I chose the right colors for it and it was copied all over the Mountains."

Grossinger's, as expected, topped all the competitors. The G built its own airstrip. Opening ceremonies included speed flying, field buzzing, a helicopter exhibition, and a parachute jump. These were loudly appreciated and quickly forgotten. The business of the chickens was not. The family had learned that the Holy Land, now crowded with refugees, was suffering from a shortage of eggs and poultry. A Major Aubrey (later Abba) Eban of the Haganah had once visited Grossinger's to speak about Zionism; in the Catskills, a poultryman named Max Brender presided over the largest breeding farm in New York State. The equivalent of a large incandescent bulb appeared over the heads of the Grossinger family, and Eban and Brender were brought together. The poultryman agreed to donate a thousand fertile eggs set to hatch within two days. Each one was guaranteed to mature into a prize breeding hen. The eggs were carefully wrapped in cotton batting to keep them insulated and unbroken, then crated and driven to Grossinger Airport. From there they went to La Guardia Field in New York, where Eban saw to it that they caught the scheduled flight of an airliner bound for Tel Aviv.

Precisely forty-eight hours after the selection at Brender's farm, a thousand prize chicks, unpacked in the Middle East, broke from their shells and began vigorously peeping. Not a single one had been lost. The hatchlings were later distributed to Jewish cooperatives. There they founded dynasties that continue to this day.

At about the same time Israel was being accepted in the comity of nations, Milton Blackstone, the resourceful publicity director of Grossinger's, decided that the story of Jennie was not enough: the resort needed a myth for the fifties. Lana Turner, it was said, had been discovered on a stool at Chasen's Drugstore. A shrewd agent had spotted Gary Cooper horseback on a ranch. Whatever Hollywood could produce the Catskills could embellish. In the great celluloid tradition, a star would be discovered at the G.

By this time Blackstone had become one of the most influential figures in the Mountains. His audacity was famous; one admirer characterized him as "a man with ideas, a builder . . . always willing to take chances even if the odds weren't always in his favor. Once, during the war, he jumped on the running board of the open car that was carrying Franklin Roosevelt in a motorcade and persuaded the President to make a detour to the nearby shipyard owned by Blackstone and his brothers to boost the workers' morale."

The agency that bore Blackstone's name was located on Fifty-seventh Street. It was the epicenter of Catskill advertising and publicity, the Jerusalem of gossip and hype, and therefore no place for a seventeen-year-old baritone just out of the slums of Philadelphia. Eddie Fisher, sent there by a mutual friend, looked around, intimidated by "a place crowded with desks and people, phones were ringing, typewriters clacking, and in a small office of his own sat the man in charge. . . . He was the puppeteer, and everyone danced and sang at his command." Blackstone listened to the adolescent, unsure of what to advise. "Well," he said finally, "I guess I could send you up to Grossinger's for the summer. You could sing there. Do you think you'll be lonely?"

It was a peculiar question. Fisher thought: "With all the people around in a resort hotel, how could I be lonely?" Friends deposited him at the hotel entrance. "We said our goodbyes in the parking lot and as I watched the car drive away, tears started streaming down my face. I *was* lonely. Milton Blackstone was right. He was always right."

To Fisher, Grossinger's was "part enchantment, part disappointment." The buildings, the grounds, the tennis courts, the golf course, the private lakes were not quite enchanting enough. Years later he thought of "those first moments, standing alone in the parking lot, looking down at the cracks in the cement. Somehow I expected that a place like Grossinger's would be paved in gold."

In a sense it was, once Blackstone completed his manipulations. At first Fisher merely took up space: "I ate in the staff dining room and slept in a room underneath the playhouse with a rabbi, a tennis pro, and a waiter. The rabbi scared me to death, and the tennis pro might as well have come from another planet. Later they moved out and two six-foot-six basketball players moved in. I had nothing in common with any of them and nothing to do but just wander around and consume three enormous meals a day. I was being paid twenty dollars a week to eat and sleep."

To keep him company Fisher secretly brought in Joey Forman, a friend from the old neighborhood. Their roommates changed yet again. This time there was a masseur, a waiter, and a trumpet player. "Four guys on the staff, including Fisher," says Forman. "He used to smuggle me food from the dining room—chicken wrapped in a napkin, seven days a week. Finally I said, 'Eddie, I'm tired of chicken, for God's sake. Can't you get me a steak?' Fisher explained the rule of the Catskill kitchens: "Chicken is easy to steal. They count the steaks." Gradually the singer was worked into the professional bill. He offered a sweet but untrained voice, and the starved presence that was

then a requisite of band singers. Tania Grossinger, Jennie's
young cousin, remembered the first months: Eddie "sang the
warmup . . . every night before the show went on. He learned
to sight-read. He also tried learning to dance, his dance instruc-
tress often complaining that he didn't have any rhythm, an observation heartily endorsed by many of the musicians in the
house band. But Milton Blackstone felt very strongly that, to
date, the one thing that Grossinger's had not done was spawn
a major star. That Labor Day of 1949, [he] set the machinery
in motion. It was then that I learned for the first time that stars
were made, not born. Made by working out deals behind closed
doors, staging events that were often less than they appeared to
be, and by creating fictions for the press."

The drama began with a whispered arrangement. Eddie
Cantor, headlining the bill, agreed to "find" the youth who had
been hanging about all summer. At the beginning of the Labor
Day weekend, Tania, along with a group of children and many
staff members, was summoned to a meeting. Blackstone's assistant instructed them to attend the show that evening, and to
"be demonstrative." Tania was puzzled, she says, "because usually on a big Saturday night we weren't allowed in the playhouse.
All the seats were needed for guests. I was soon to learn that
this Saturday night was to be unlike any other Saturday night.
. . . Some of us were to sit in the first row and clap and jump
up and down and squeal when Eddie started to sing." She adds
dryly, "Shades of Frank Sinatra. There the comparison ends."
Others in the claque were to fan out on all sides of the room
and, on cue, "applaud, scream and encourage the guests to do
likewise. We did. They did. And I saw a page written in entertainment history."

It was a page inscribed without the singer's knowledge. After
Fisher finished his second solo, Blackstone started the pseudo-
spontaneous reception. As the last cheers died, Cantor bounded
onstage and made a prediction: "Believe me, ladies and gentlemen, this boy is really going to be something."

Fisher was crestfallen. He believed that Cantor "had let me
sing as a favor to Milton Blackstone, and that was the end of it.
But then he said, 'I've heard many a crooner in my day, ladies

and gentlemen, but this boy isn't a crooner, he's a singer. I want him to join my show on our cross-country tour. Is that okay, Eddie? And when we get to Los Angeles, I'm going to take you home to meet my five daughters."

Columnists and radio interviewers battened on the Discovery in the Mountains. On tour, Fisher heard echoes of that Saturday night. "Like the audiences at Grossinger's," he found, "the people weren't merely applauding me; they were rooting for me." If Eddie Cantor sometimes felt that Eddie Fisher had been forced upon him, he was unfailingly paternal to his charge. Only once did the youth upset him. In Chicago Eddie looked up his mother's brother. Uncle Jack took him to a Paul Robeson concert. "It was so crowded," Fisher remembered, "that we had to sit on the stage, and suddenly Robeson entered from the rear of the auditorium, singing without a microphone, a handsome, powerful, dynamic man with an incredible voice. It was one of the most electrifying moments I had ever experienced and I couldn't wait to tell Cantor about it. He was horrified, 'You went there . . . ?' he said incredulously. 'Don't tell anybody, or your career is finished.' "

Fisher had other, apolitical ways of damaging his reputation, but the hard days of ruinous marriages, drug abuse, and bankruptcy were decades away. As the fifties began, everyone in his slipstream seemed to profit. By 1951, he had sold a million copies of his first big hit, "Any Time," and his price for a personal appearance had increased by 1,000 percent. When Blackstone decided that Grossinger's was incomplete without an Eddie Fisher fan club, Tania Grossinger's name was offered as president. "There was nothing I wanted to do less," she says. "Eddie's feelings were hurt but I finally convinced him I had too many other things to do. . . . The truth of the matter was I couldn't stand Blackstone and didn't want to be involved with him in any way. The job I turned down went to the columnist Rona Barrett, a youngster who then lived in the Bronx, had a crush, as did so many others, on Eddie, took a chance, applied for the job, and, much to her delight, got it."

Tania professed to be Eddie's "staunch defender," but her reminiscences are unkind. She recalls Fisher's triumphal return to the resort. Tania carried ice cream to him as he lounged at poolside. Fisher "suddenly . . . pressed a dollar into my hand. He was trying to tip me. I pushed him into the water. I was insulted. I was his friend, not a servant he was supposed to tip. Funnily enough, when I repeated the story to a bellhop years later he told me, 'Tania, you should have taken it. It was probably the last tip he ever offered up here.' "

Apparently, no one was more impressed by the Fisher ascension than Fisher himself. More than thirty years later he still refused to believe that his celebrity was a matter of connivance. In 1962 Dorothy Kilgallen informed the *New York Journal-American* readers that "for over a decade, truthful Milton and his boyishly truthful client have been telling the press that Fisher was 'discovered' by Cantor at Grossinger's in 1949. Now, in a confessional mood, the comedian says the whole thing was contrived for publicity and 'Milton Blackstone practically shoved him down my throat. I wasn't impressed by him.' "

Fisher acknowledges the controversy in his memoirs: "Someone wrote that Milton Blackstone had rigged the audience's response that night. . . . I didn't want to believe it but Joey Forman . . . said, 'It's possible, Eddie. You know the way Milton did things. I saw him strolling around the grounds with Cantor, probably talking about you, and if he persuaded Cantor to let you sing in his show, do you think he would have left the rest to chance? Milton was a manipulator. He had an angle on everything.' "

But no, Fisher decides, "Milton didn't operate that way. It wasn't necessary. That night the playhouse was jammed with so many paying customers, they had to stand in the aisles and even outside the doors, along the sides. The only room left for the staff was up in the back of the balcony where the spotlights were. If anything was rigged, the people in the audience did it themselves. They wanted Cantor to discover me as much as I did."

It took several years for higher education to recover from the war, but by the time Harry Truman was installed in 1949, the universities had returned to solvency and optimism. Veterans repopulated the campuses, studying on the G.I. Bill, and college styles influenced the fashion industry. The brilliant smiles of cheerleaders appeared on billboards; Big Men on Campus were featured in ads for spring suits and white cardigan sweaters. Once the World Series was over, varsity athletics dominated the sports pages. Initially, the big games were held in the Midwest, where college basketball was a traditional source of pride and alumni contributions. Then the East slowly began to take the headlines, as thousands of students rooted for outstanding teams from Long Island University, St. John's, Manhattan College, and the City College of New York. Many of the conferences offered ticket holders a phenomenon they had only heard about but never witnessed: the Jewish athlete, bred on the tar and cement of public-school playgrounds.

Basketball fever took no vacations. In the summer world of the Mountains every important resort fielded its own basketball team. The majority of stars were "ringers," college players on their summer break. They all held seasonal jobs—waiter, busboy, athletics counselor—with the understanding that assignments were purely nominal, a way of earning money without losing amateur status. Their real assignment was the weekend battle on the courts.

The Catskills needed no leagues, no standings, no champion. They offered something more compelling: the wager. For the first time since the thirties gambling became an unadvertised attraction of Mountain life. Bets were not made on the teams but on the number of points scored. Like all criminal schemes, the fixing had modest beginnings. Before the first whistle, a hatful of numbers was passed around the stands. Spectators could pick one for a dollar. The games, a forward later explained, were rigged with childish ease. A betting pool was set up "to match the total number of points scored in the ball game. The players used to split the pot with the winner and pocket an extra ten or fifteen dollars every time we played."

This air of lighthearted finagling lasted until the professionals moved in. The corruption soon became obvious even to fifteen-year-old Tania Grossinger. In midsummer, 1951, she sat in the stands of her cousin's hotel idly watching a basketball game: "Fouls by our team were virtually ignored whereas those that didn't exist were being called against the other team."

Half-time intermission sounded. Tania ran from the stands to the playhouse property box. She grabbed a pair of comically oversized spectacles and, before the game resumed, went out onto the gymnasium floor. Before an audience of several hundred, she impudently presented the glasses to the official, Sol Levy, "to make you an honest ref, as well as a good ref." The onlookers, she remembered, "broke up. Sol's face froze. I knew instantaneously I had done something terribly wrong. It wasn't that he just wasn't amused. It was worse than that. I had hit a nerve.

"Three months later I was to find out just where. I picked up the newspaper one morning after breakfast and there were the headlines screaming at me. The biggest basketball scandal ever to hit the metropolitan area had broken. Members of four university teams were arrested for throwing games. Half of those arrested had played on the Grossinger team that previous summer. Sol Levy was involved in the payoffs."

What unraveled in the sports sections had started in the Mountains three years before. Late in the summer of 1949, one of the backcourt stars of the L.I.U. Blackbirds was cooling himself in the Grossinger pool. Eddie Gard had learned to play basketball in a settlement house in Williamsburg. The youth required tutoring in academics and instruction in passing and layups. No one had to teach him the rules of the streets. As one sportswriter had it, "Eddie was lovable, but he was also larcenous."

Gard had been involved in basketball fixes since his sophomore year, when a teammate, Jack Goldsmith, showed him how to make games seem closer than they actually were. In gambler's parlance, Gard was point-shaving in order to defeat the spread. In layman's language, who won the basketball game was not nearly as significant as the size of the margin of victory. That margin, the point spread, was what attracted the bettors' money. A team might win five games in a row and still earn big money for those who bet against it, merely by seeing to it that the win was by, say, less than the ten points that the bookmakers were offering.

For Catskill players who had learned to score whatever number the resort chef held in his hand, no more and no less, fixes were absurdly simple. "A shot hits the side of the backboard," theorized a basketball writer, "a player zigs when he should have zagged." When Goldsmith moved on to extracurricular gambling operations, Gard was left in charge of the fixes. For a season he dealt with gamblers on a game-by-game basis; now he was looking for a more secure arrangement. He found it paddling in the opposite end of Grossinger's pool.

At forty-five, the Sicilian immigrant Salvatore Sollazzo moved with a bulk and authority that suggested powerful connections to organized crime. He had the requisite thinning hairline and underslept face; he was heavy but muscular; and he had a beautiful second wife, Jeanne, whom he liked to troll before young athletes. Actually, Sollazzo was a mere freelance corruptor, an inept businessman as well as a reckless gambler. In the past he had served time in Sing Sing for armed robbery; paroled, he became a jewelry salesman, then organized his own company. It had prospered until Sollazzo threw away his profits on horse races and basketball games. At the time of the meeting with Gard he was searching for a way to manipulate the odds.

Athlete and fixer conferred many times in the Mountains without coming to an agreement. Then in January of 1950, after prolonged negotiations at the King Edward Hotel on Forty-fifth Street, they settled on terms. Two weeks later, at Madison Square Garden, North Carolina enjoyed a close victory over the heavily favored L.I.U. Blackbirds, 55–52. Not all the losing players were in on the fix. One of the innocents, Sherman White, was a promising 6 foot 5 inch guard. Charles Rosen, in his somber and accurate study, *Scandals of '51*, calls him "the first big man with the skills, the quickness, and the savvy of a guard. When 'Dr. J' was still wearing Doctor Dentons, Sherman White's classic game and mirror-smooth inventions helped turn the game black."

White had spent a summer in the Catskills; he sensed that his teammates were playing a tainted game. Still, when he confronted Gard in the locker room, the fixer denied everything. So did his colleagues Adolf Bigos and Dick Feurtado. "We're doing the best we can," one of them said. "Why don't you let us alone?" White immediately backed away, but Gard knew that the entire season was jeopardized unless the naif was cut in for a share. "He's getting too good," Sollazzo was informed. "If Sherman's not with us, he can turn a game around all by himself."

A few days later, White and Gard were invited to dinner at Sollazzo's apartment on Central Park West. As they entered the lobby, a uniformed doorman offered a salute: "Good evening, Mr. Logan." Gard whispered, "It's an alias." Sherman White had entered a world he had only seen in the movies. Jeanne Sollazzo was wearing a low-cut dress, and all through dinner, served in the apartment, she kept leaning over to speak to her guest. After dessert her husband consulted his watch and got down to business. "You don't have to lose," he assured Sherman. "All you have to do is shave the points. It's easy enough and I'll give you a thousand dollars a game. In cash." His listener sighed and nodded. Now that he had capitulated, White saw smiles wherever he looked. Sollazzo added the final reassurance. "Everybody's doing it," he said.

So it seemed in 1950. Early that summer Gard went to the Mountains to seek out a City College player named Ed Warner. He found him at Klein's Hillside. Gard informed Warner that two of his teammates on the C.C.N.Y. Beavers, Al "Fats" Roth and Eddie Roman, were experienced point-shavers. Warner was persuaded to fall in with them. Gard moved on to Sol Levy's hotel, this time in the company of Jeanne and Salvatore Sollazzo. Gard, always intrigued by the use of aliases, introduced his friends as the Tartos. In the beginning there was no mention of gambling. "I'd like to arrange for my wife to stay here for the summer" was the only favor Mr. Tarto wanted. "Do you think you could help me with the details?" Levy was delighted to oblige. Jeanne was booked through Labor Day. Her husband would come up on the weekends.

When he arrived, Sollazzo seldom stayed in one place. Customarily he and Gard traversed the Mountain roads, scouting basketball teams for corruptible talent. In what seemed a series of happy coincidences, they kept running into Levy as he refereed at "away" games. Occasionally Sollazzo bought the official a drink. As the two men relaxed, the subject of betting was gently introduced. Sollazzo knew that Levy's NBA salary was $3,000 a year. The gambler represented himself as a high roller with unlimited funds, and then changed the subject. Later there would be time to discuss the inner game.

On Labor Day Sollazzo used his Cadillac to help the Levys move from the Catskills back to the city. Just before the opening of the professional season, the fixers made their move. Sollazzo collared Levy at a party. "Eddie tells me that you're working the Knicks game at the Garden tomorrow night. I've got a big bet on the game. If I win, I'll take good care of you." At first Levy, lightheaded from the drink, refused to take his host seriously. The Knicks won, and over the next few days, the referee received a series of panicky calls. "Tarto's losing a bundle," Gard said. "He wants you to help him out." This was not an exaggeration. Sollazzo had been unable to arrange the outcomes of baseball games and horse races. His extravagant betting had put him deeper in debt, and he now owed more than a million dollars in back taxes. The next time they met, Tarto dropped the indirect approach. "If I had all your games," he promised, "I really would take care of you." Gard stepped in: "Sol, don't be stupid. There's a lot in this for you." Levy held out for several days and then capitulated. He would conspire with the fixers for $1,000 a game.

A few weeks later the college season began. By now Gard had convinced other players and other teams to shave points and dump games. Sometimes it was unnecessary to recruit. Connie Schaff, a New York University man, had waited on tables at Grossinger's alongside Eddie Gard. He wanted to know how much he could earn by following gamblers' instructions. Sollazzo turned his back. He had seen Schaff play in the Borscht circuit and the boy was not yet a star. Salvatore told friends he only bought the great ones.

As the season progressed, the tainted games became increasingly obvious. Bookmakers sometimes refused to cover the point spread. "It was a crazy time," one of them recalled. "There were players dumping, coaches dumping, and referees dumping. But there was one college game that really stood out. One of the refs was doing business, and all game long he didn't even make one call. The other official was running around like a lunatic trying to cover the whole court. The Garden went bananas. Every guy there was screaming at the guy standing next to him."

Until the early fifties Max Kase, sports editor of the *Journal-American*, had expressed only a fleeting interest in college basketball. But he had always loved a good crime story. When the talk of rigged games grew too strident to ignore, he dispatched several reporters to the backroom gambling places and sports hangouts. As they began to trace the rumors to their sources, Kase decided that his paper had stumbled on to something too big for the back pages. This was a matter for the courts. He called the office of District Attorney Frank Hogan and worked out an arrangement. He would turn over the paper's file of names and places; in return, the *Journal-American* would be granted exclusive rights to the story when it broke.

On the morning of January 4, 1951, Salvatore Sollazzo placed a large bet on Western Kentucky in their game against the heavily favored L.I.U. team. The point spread was seven. The Blackbirds were leading by as many as twenty points before one of the players kicked the ball out of bounds. Within minutes his teammates began to miss their foul shots. The performance became so shoddy that some local fans left the stadium, grousing loudly all the way to the exits. In the aisle one of them shouted, "Hey, what's the points tonight? Huh, ya bum?" Seated nearby, reporters and detectives exchanged glances. The final score was L.I.U. 69, Western Kentucky 63. A month later Sol Levy refereed a game in Fort Wayne, Indiana. One of the players from the visiting team had been raised on the Lower East Side. He was astonished to see his boyhood friend Eddie Gard, far from home, sitting in the front row. The player scored fourteen points in the first quarter and his team took the lead. Early in the second period, before his coach could remove him, the player fouled out. He confronted the official: "Sol, what the fuck are you doing to me?" A pair of plainclothes detectives took down every word.

On January 18, the *Journal* printed the first story of a fix by Manhattan College. L.I.U. went untouched. Even so, Sherman White and his teammates were restless. "We couldn't shake the feeling," said one, "that something awful was going to happen." On Saturday night, February 17, his fears were confirmed. After beating Temple University 95–71 in Philadelphia, the C.C.N.Y. team was followed by men from the District Attorney's office. The first arrests were made at Pennsylvania Station, as soon as the team train pulled into New York. The evidence was incomplete and a lot of bluffing was required to obtain confessions. Hogan had recordings of telephone conversations between Eddie Gard and several players haggling about payments. There was talk, in Gard's penetrable code, of "squaring things with the uptown girls," signifying the C.C.N.Y. players, and mentions of "that girl Sally," indicating Sollazzo. Detectives had also observed a long, inaudible conversation between Sollazzo and an L.I.U. athlete. The rest was intimidation and suggestion. The District Attorney and his assistants played back some of the recordings; they isolated the accused and told them, falsely, that two of their colleagues had just admitted everything. One by one the players confessed. Only Sollazzo, arrested during the night, proclaimed his innocence. Indictments were handed down, bail was set, and Sollazzo was taken before a magistrate who had graduated from C.C.N.Y. long ago. The judge denied bail because, he said, the gambler "appears to have corrupted these young men and brought disgrace on a great institution."

That was to be the tone for the rest of the season. As confessions were published, as payoff money was unearthed in cigar boxes and flower pots and jacket linings, university administrators searched for someone or something to blame. They tried not to hear White's heartbroken father: "It would be different if Sherman was raised on the streets. But Sherman had to go to college to learn something he was never taught at home." The head of the FBI angrily agreed. J. Edgar Hoover spoke out against the "hypocrisy and sham" of intercollegiate athletics. "In the name of victory," he said, "college officials will go out and consummate very atrocious crimes."

Some of the players presented reasons for their participation. Roth admitted that he "did it because I wanted to be grown-up. I mean, I was sick and tired of asking my father for money all the time. Whenever I needed a suit or something I always had to go to him. I wanted to be able to do things myself. You know, like a grownup. My father works hard. He's been driving a soda truck for twenty-five years. I knew he didn't have too much money to give me." Many echoed the fixer's line: Everyone was doing it. "I played for St. John's," one of them stated, "and a lot of guys on the team were involved with Sollazzo and Gard. We were no different from anybody else. Some of the guys were sleeping with Sollazzo's wife."

Several journalists found early amusement in the scandal. Jimmy Cannon, the influential columnist of the *New York Post*, offered sarcastic rules for players and schools: "Any discussion of the point spread with strangers should be restricted to vacant lots where a dictaphone can't eavesdrop," and "The intelligent coach doesn't discuss the point spread with his players. If they don't know the odds, they don't belong on the varsity." But his tone changed after the players were suspended from their schools and the entire college basketball season was beyond recovery. "The tall children of basketball have been consumed by the slot machine racket of sports," he wrote. "They are amateurs exploited by a commercial alliance of culture and commerce. . . . It is not because I am a sports writer that I have compassion for the arrested players. They have forfeited honor at an age when the dream of life should be beautiful. We should weep when we come upon a boy who has been fleeced of principles before he is a man. What made them special has destroyed them. Their youth has been slain. The assassin of youth is the most repulsive of animals."

Cannon and his colleagues were aware that there was more than one assassin. Salvatore Sollazzo was sentenced to from eight to sixteen years in state prison. Sherman White received a year's sentence; Gard, Warner, Roth, and Schaff would serve six months. Most of the other players were suspended from their schools. And yet the temptations and the tempters would remain; the children would play again, and the gamblers would be waiting for them.

A lot of resentful athletes blamed the journalists. A C.C.N.Y. felon testified, "It was just to sell newspapers. The newspapers knew that the scandal was partly their own responsibility. With their point spreads and their paper bets they helped make gambling a way of life in New York City. Some of the sportswriters were very close to us. They trusted us and when everything finally blew open, they felt betrayed and carried on a personal vendetta. . . . Virtually all the arrested players were either black or Jews. And almost all of the New York sportswriters were Jewish. They were in a position to help us, but they turned their backs and stepped us into the mud."

Several authorities believed that Madison Square Garden was the real villain. The pressures of the arena, the expectations of the crowd were too much for youth to endure. The Braves of Bradley University voted 11–0 to reject any invitation to play in the National Invitation Tournament scheduled for the Garden. The institution itself, Madison Square Garden, Inc., announced that its executives were thinking seriously about closing the facility to college basketball. But, as Rosen has it, "roundball doubleheaders generated almost as much revenue as the rodeo and the circus and the discussion was very brief."

Phog Allen, the celebrated Kansas coach, studied all the blameworthy candidates—the gamblers, the Garden, the press, the schools—before he decided on the First Cause. It was not men who were to blame, he proclaimed, it was Mountains: "Out here in the Midwest these scandalous conditions do not, of course, exist. But in the East, the boys, particularly those who participate in the resort hotel leagues during the summer months, are thrown into an environment which cannot help but breed the evil which more and more is coming to light." (Allen did not know that a year earlier his team had been the recipient of point-shaving by a team from Bradley, whose home town was Peoria, Illinois. The game had been played not in Madison Square Garden but in the sanctuary of a Midwestern field house.)

Nat Holman, Allen's counterpart at C.C.N.Y., went along with the anti-Catskill mood. Many summers of resort basketball had gone by without a word from him, but now he provided a new version of Captain Louis in *Casablanca*, who was "shocked, shocked to find gambling going on" in Rick's casino. "The hotel teams," he asserted, "are schools of crime. . . . And since playing for these hotel teams may have a bad influence on the boys, we at C.C.N.Y. have decided not to allow their participation. We feel our basketball players represent [the college] throughout the year, not only on the basketball court, but everywhere. If they want to represent someone else, they'll have to seek our permission. I've told the boys that if they disobey this new regulation, they'll be dropped from the squad."

In every state where basketball was a significant sport, newspaper editorials joined the attack. The hotel teams were merely "subterfuges for professionalism." In the Catskills, "the seeds [were] planted by the wily fixers for future harvest." "The softening-up process" began in the Mountains. Toward the end of the year, Milton Kutsher, operator of the resort that bore his name, called a press conference to argue that corruption was not confined to one geographical area. One of the Catskill veterans was there. "It was true, what Milton said," he remembered. "Everybody knew it. There was fixing going on all over. But the Mountains were taller than the Plains. We were what they noticed. After the scandals, the gyms were quiet. The big sport was Simon Says. For entertainment, we went back to singers and dancers and stand-up comics. The only kind of scandal they would ever cause was sexual. That was one problem we could always handle."

CHAPTER 12

ARTHUR MURRAY, CARY GRANT

SOLOMON AND CHARLEY'S AUNT

THE HALL HOUSE, LIBERTY, N. Y.

After the basketball scandal faded from the sports pages, Catskill visitors gazed inward to find amusement in their own habits and beliefs. "It is the test of a good religion," said G. K. Chesterton, "whether you can make a joke about it." By that elastic standard, Judaism in fifties America was an excellent method of worship.

Again the Jewish mother found herself center stage. Sentimentalized, cloaked in blackface in the "Mammy" songs of the twenties, benignly kidded by George Jessel in the thirties and forties ("How was the champagne and caviar, Mama? Oh, the ginger ale was fine but the huckleberries tasted from herring"), she returned in the fifties as more than a purveyor of chicken soup. This time she was a disseminator of guilt. In an affecting memoir of his childhood, Alfred Kazin caught her in the act of berating the young: "What sin have I committed that

God should punish me with you! Eat! What will become of you
if you don't eat! Imp of darkness, may you sink ten fathoms into
the earth if you don't eat! Eat!" The tummlers turned that concern into material. The dialectician Myron Cohen, the brash
young MCs Jan Murray and Jack Carter, the benign schoolteacher Sam Levenson, and scores of other Catskill performers
told their jokes on television. Once again Jewish comedy went
public, this time with a vengeance.

In one routine, Louis Buchalter, shot by police, desperately
claws at the door of his mother's apartment. "Mama!" he cries
as she opens the door. She looks out, horrified at his gaunt
appearance: "Eat first, Lepke. Talk later."

Another mama disputes a newspaper story: "It says here the
world is getting smaller every day. So how come it takes Papa
longer to get home every night?"

Her cuisine became an ideal target. Buddy Hackett spoke
of the first time he failed to get heartburn and thought he was
dying because his fire had gone out. Zero Mostel said that kosher
cooking had killed more Jews than Hitler. When mother jokes
palled, the tummlers decreed that rabbis were in season. At times
the religious leaders connived with criminals:

SINNER: Rabbi, I stole a box of candles.
RABBI: You have to atone. Bring five bottles of sacramental wine to
the synagogue as a gift.
SINNER: I'm broke. How can I possibly get all that wine?
RABBI: The same way you got the candles.

They were crafty in the East European manner:

GOY: Rabbi, how come Jews are so smart?
RABBI: We eat pickled herring. Here, try some. That'll be five dollars.
GOY: But the delicatessen down the street charges only two dollars.
RABBI: See? The herring is working already.

They were exemplars of hubris:

During the Yom Kippur services a cleric tears his garments and cries aloud to the Lord: "I am the lowliest of men, unworthy of the name rabbi. I am a nobody, a no-goodnik. I am nothing!"

Hearing this the shammes (sexton) rips his own clothing and cries, "Forgive me, O Lord. I am an excuse for a man. I am nothing!"

The rabbi looks back at his congregation and sneers: "Look who's nothing!"

Their position was devalued:

FIRST MOTHER: My son the kidney specialist sends me to the Raleigh every summer for a month.

SECOND MOTHER: My son the criminal lawyer sends me to the Concord for the whole summer.

THIRD MOTHER: I come up to Rabinowitz Rest for a weekend in July.

FIRST MOTHER: What a shame. What does your son do?

THIRD MOTHER: He's a rabbi.

SECOND MOTHER: This is an occupation for a nice Jewish boy?

They found solutions for which there were no problems:

Visiting an upstate prison a rabbi hears inmates protesting their innocence. He runs to the mayor to propose that the Catskills have two prisons, one for the guilty and another for the innocent.

And finally they vanished into America:

Mrs. Moscowitz tells her Orthodox rabbi, "My grandchildren are driving me crazy. They want to have a Christmas tree. Could you maybe make some dispensation, a *broche* [Hebrew benediction] over such a tree?"

"Impossible," says the rabbi. "But tell me, what exactly is Christmas?"

She consults a more lenient rabbi, a Conservative.

"No," he says. "I'm sorry. But tell me, what exactly is a Christmas tree?"

She turns to the young new Reform rabbi. "I'll be glad to," he assures her. "Only tell me: what exactly is a *broche*?"

Arthur Murray, Cary Grant . . .

On June 25, 1952, this kind of Catskill comedy received a strained acceptance when *Wish You Were Here* opened on Broadway. The musical, based on Arthur Kober's twenties hit, *Having Wonderful Time*, was full of inside jokes and references to summer vacations in the Mountains. In *The New York Times* Brooks Atkinson expressed the general critical opinion: "Despite a swimming pool, a basketball game, a weeny-roast and some social dancing, there does not seem to be any way of avoiding the blunt fact that a humorous tender romantic comedy has been flattened out to a one-dimensional repetitious Broadway show."

The producers stubbornly refused to put up a closing notice. The show's sole gimmick, a real $15,000 swimming pool in center stage, remained. But after opening night, hundreds of plot and song changes were inserted. Critic Harold Clurman called *Wish You Were Here* the only experimental theater left in New York. Word of mouth improved. When the cast appeared on *The Ed Sullivan Show*, more tickets were sold. Eddie Fisher recorded the title song and it sold a million copies. The musical continued to founder, but it foundered for 597 performances.

The reason for its upstream success was not the plot, the melodies, or the lyrics; it was the audience. By now, thousands had graduated from the resorts as employees or guests. In the Mountains they had gone hunting for food, for mates, for diversion. For them the Old Country no longer signified Eastern Europe or the Lower East Side. It meant the Catskills. Whatever they saw onstage was suffused with nostalgia. "What do they care what Brooks Atkinson said?" asked an organizer of theater parties. "What do the *goyim* know about the Borscht Belt?"

Actually, *Wish* was neither as refreshing as the audiences felt nor as stale as the critics had written. The canny score was by Harold Rome (Harold Rome Rome, as his competitors called him, because of a penchant for repeating lines). When a tummler sang about his origins, the mezzanine rang with the laughter of recognition. He was a combination of

Arthur Murray, Cary Grant
Solomon and Charley's Aunt

An egomaniacal seducer showed that nothing had changed in thirty years:

> *I'm Don José*
> *Of Far Rockaway.*
> *I'm passion's flame*
> *When girls hear my name*
> *They faint from Upper Bronx to Queens.*
> *When you love me, you're loving far beyond your means.*
> *Comes the dawn don't look for me*
> *I'll be gone—on the BMT I'll be . . .*

While Don José performed his Song of Myself, a subtler use of Catskill life was occurring a little farther uptown in the broadcast studios of NBC. On television a comedian's style could still suggest the leer of the streets and the pungency of a delicatessen. But his material had to be accessible to those who had never tasted borscht or heard of chutzpah.

"When we started watching TV," says one Iowan, "and we saw those funny Jews from New York we thought, Well, they read from right to left, that's why they're so different. Still, we immediately got the jokes because the comics never used language we couldn't follow."

The speech of these performers was transformed into approach and body language. They were actually articulating a fluent Yiddish, but it was the Yiddish of the body and the idea, not the word. Sometimes it could be seen in the sad and bewildered look of Ed Wynn or Menasha Skulnik, who seemed to meander through their routines in search of a higher meaning. More often it showed in the staccato gags of younger comics like Jan Murray or Jack Carter or Alan King, whose humor was reminiscent of a neglected child fiercely competing for approval.

Milton Berle displayed it with the tummler's bared teeth and irrepressible ego, insinuating himself into every guest act that appeared on his show, dressing in outrageous drag complete with girdle and lipstick, firing dozens of one-liners at the audience, and then, breathless and covered with sweat, baying for approval until the credits rolled.

In its simplest form, physical Yiddish was spoken by men who played the role of the Eternal Busboy, overweight like Buddy Hackett or too thin like Jerry Lewis, breaking up audiences by making themselves the butt of the joke, dropping dishes, falling down, apologizing, and spilling soup on the patron in the middle of the apology.

On NBC, Sid Caesar's sketch comedy expressed still another brand of physical Yiddish, and it rushed to prominence on a ninety-minute program, *Your Show of Shows*. The critic of the Chicago *Tribune* analyzed the star. "Sid Caesar," he said, "doesn't steal jokes; he doesn't borrow ideas or material. A gag is as useless as a fresh situation is to Milton Berle." The New York *Herald Tribune* reviewer was more effusive: Caesar "has restored the art of pantomime to the high estate it enjoyed before the talkies and radio." Alfred Hitchcock, a director since the silents, concurred: "The young Mr. Caesar best approaches the great Chaplin of the early 1920s."

Caesar had learned that approach at the Avon Lodge, deep in the Mountains. Foreign accents and headlong parodies of middle-class couples came easy to him, and he was not a man to hide his sources. In countless profiles the comedian was voluble about the circumstances of his apprenticeship. In one skit he liked to remember, Caesar played the part of a fly encountering a moth:

FLY: He's crazy, that guy. Eats wool. Blue serge . . . all that dry stuff. Yugh. And then every night he throws himself against an electric light bulb, knocking his brains out. He's crazy. (*Flying downtown, he is happily humming a song when he suddenly sees a sign that depresses him*) Look at that. "Get the powerful DDT. Kills flies instantly." (*He frowns and solemnly remarks*) Oh my, there's a lot of hatred in the world.

"Expanding within this framework," Caesar commented, "this monologue ran for nine minutes when I did it on the air. It worked because houseflies are a fact of everyday life and everyone is familiar with their buzzing and probing. . . .

" 'Familiar,' 'fact of everyday life'—those were the case

words for nearly everything we did. We didn't have to rely on the slapstick and pratfalls everyone else was doing in TV comedy. It was a repetition of my going against the trend in the Catskills."

In Sam Levenson's comedy, the words were in English but the melody was Yiddish, a gentle ironic strain based on exchanges he had overheard in hotel lobbies:

"I don't do exercises. Too old."

"Just for the manager, make a little exercise. How can you go home and tell your friends you didn't make any exercise?"

"All right, one exercise I'll do."

"Good. You see your valises down on the floor? Lean over and touch them without bending your knees. That's the way. Now, while you're down there would you mind opening the valises and *giving back the towels*."

Levenson loved to reminisce about the summer world: "It seemed to me at the time I was immortal. Guests came and went but I stayed on forever. . . . I remember my father wrote me twice a week and as part of the address (he copied it from the ad), he included, 'LG RMS . . . ALL IMPMTS, ALL SPTS, 75 M.N.Y. RSNBLE.'

"I don't think I did much for the Mountains but they did plenty for me. They took me out of the tenements for several summers, provided me with tuition for college and much good subject matter for my unanticipated career in comedy.

"Let's give the little hills a big hand."

Caesar's extempore onslaughts and Levenson's calm, anecdotal approach linked them strongly to the vaudeville Hebrew comic with his mastery of the jape and cringe, mocking with one routine and ingratiating himself with the next. Caesar was aggressive, loud, abusive—and then contrite and smiling, suddenly grateful for the applause of his live audience. Levenson took on the aspect of a waiter, serving customers with obsequious bows and smiles—and doing parodies of them as soon as they left the table. Both comedians were classic instances of psychiatrist Theodor Reik's theory of stand-up comedy. The profession attracted many performers of Eastern European background because it brimmed with "contradictions that characterize the Jewish situation in our civilization."

One of Caesar's writers later made a career of that ambivalence, even ending his letters with the signature "your obedient Jew." Long before *Your Show of Shows*, he had written sketches at a small Ellenville hotel. The first effort, he boasted, "was entitled 'S. and M.,' thirty years before anyone had heard of S. and M. The girl and I walked out from the wings and met in the center of the stage. I said, 'I am a masochist.' She said, 'I am a sadist.' I said, 'Hit me,' and she hit me, very hard, right in the face. And I said, 'Wait a minute, wait a minute, hold it. I think I'm a sadist.' Blackout."

Later he composed his own theme song, with a finishing plea:

> *Hello, hello, hello*
> *I've come to start the show*
> *I'll sing a little, dance a little*
> *I'll do this and I'll do that*
> *And though I'm not much on looks*
> *Please love Mel Brooks*

By the mid-fifties, two electrical devices conspired to change the Catskills forever. Air conditioning was being mass-produced and discounted at less than $200. For the first time, summers in the city would be tolerable to the poor and the lower middle class. The second factor was far more threatening to the Mountains. Television sets went on sale for $500, only $20 down, eighteen months to pay. Guests who spent good money to watch comedians and singers in the resorts could now see them for free in their own bedrooms.

"Used to be, you could use a few good bits for years," complained a former master of ceremonies turned insurance agent. "All of a sudden, you needed fresh material every time you went on a sound stage. God help you if you repeated yourself on *The Ed Sullivan Show*. And if you were on a regular program you needed new stuff every week. Young comedians burned out like cigarettes. A lot of them went into other fields, and plenty of them just disappeared. Nervous breakdowns, even suicide. And don't think the great ones didn't suffer. It was no wonder Sid became an alcoholic."

Two schools remained open for comedians. Nightclubs gave them a place to fail without destroying their reputations. The trouble was that the boites were mainly in San Francisco, Chicago, and Manhattan. Urban audiences tended to be young and impatient with mother jokes. They wanted hip comedy, with its ring of recognition and its use of the absurd and outrageous—material popularized by the new favorite Lenny Bruce. (Few of his enthusiasts knew that Bruce himself had tried to be funny in the Mountains. The only amusement he ever recalled from those failed summers was the words of his mother, Sally. As she watched her son climbing into a car headed west, she thought of the girls in the Catskills. "Make sure my son gets some," she told the driver.) For traditional stand-up comedians that left only one place to learn their craft: the Borscht Belt. In this difficult period, a rabbi turned comedian went to the Mountains and attempted to amuse a convention of *schochets* at the Flagler.

"We have a kosher butcher in my neighborhood," he told them. "You should see. One day a fly landed on his scale when he was weighing a piece of brisket. I never saw a fly that weighed two pounds!"

He was greeted with angry murmurs. Several thick-necked men in the audience made hostile gestures. After a few more jokes Jackie Mason backed into the wings. The owner of the hotel told another comedian, "Get him out of here."

"He's offstage."

"I don't mean off the stage. I mean get him out of the hotel."

The comedian pulled Mason out of the room. "You have to leave."

"All right," came the reply. "I'll just pack."

"I don't think you have time. Forget packing. They are very upset; they want to turn you into chopped liver."

"They really didn't like me?"

"I'll send you your things."

* * *

Arthur Murray, Cary Grant . . .

Woody Allen's 1984 film, *Broadway Danny Rose*, repro-
duces the ethos of the fifties resorts. Danny is a failed comedian
("He worked the Catskills," says a colleague. "Yeah, he did all
the old jokes . . . and stole from everybody. He was exactly the
kind of comic you'd think he'd be"). In his forties he has become
a personal manager representing a set of losers, including a
virtuoso who makes music by rubbing wineglasses, a balloon
folder, a stuttering ventriloquist, and a hypnotist who cannot
revive his subjects. "I promise you if your wife never wakes up,"
Danny assures the husband of one victim, "I will take you to
any restaurant of your choice."

His clients play to indifferent audiences and harsh owners,
and the sense of futility pervades every gesture. Yet they go on
because they have the examples of success before them. Like
Danny, they remain convinced that recognition is only one resort
away:

PHIL: I'd like to help you, Danny. But Weinstein's Majestic Bungalow
　　Colony is a classy place, and I need a classy act.
DANNY: Well, that's why I want to show you this lady. She is the Jascha
　　Heifetz of this instrument.
(*A blond, beehived woman, "the waterglass virtuoso," performs with a
bright, vacuous smile.*)
DANNY: Never took a lesson . . . self-taught. Next year, Philly, my hand
　　to God, she's gonna be at Carnegie Hall. But you, I'll let you have
　　her now at the old price, okay? Which is anything you want to
　　give me. Anything at all, Philly.

The film, like most of Allen's modest comedies, was a small
and artful distortion of the truth. Every honest veteran recognized himself, and perhaps one of his agents, on screen. Joan
Rivers gave the most credible evidence when she recorded her
early years as a comedienne. A wheezing old Buick, she says,
meant more to her career than fresh material: "If the act had a
car, the agent excused a lot of things, because you could take
other acts with you and he kept the transportation money paid
by the hotels. The agent would say, 'On your way to Schwartz's
Bungalows would you mind dropping off Fifi and her talking

parrot at Cass's Cabins?' You would say, 'Absolutely no problem,' but Cass's Cabins would turn out to be forty miles the other
way."

At the Swan Lake Hotel, the young comedienne attempted
to scrape favor with a song:

> *When the soldiers join the sailors and they lick the Jap*
> *When the hero's in a frame-up but he beats the rap*
> *When the maiden greets the villain with a well-timed slap*
> *All you want to do is clap.*
> *Applause, applause, there's nothing like applause.*

She found herself playing to "a field of blank faces, empty
of any emotion beyond boredom and mystification. . . . Only
occasionally, in the oppressive silence, did the pale disk of a face
tilt downward to check a watch and guess when this interminable
thing might be over."

Matters hardly improved when she debuted at Fleischmann's and Kutsher's. "My big song began,

> *"Every bee can make a beeline*
> *every cat can make a feline*
> *but a man's best line may fail."*

All through the showroom, claims Rivers, came the murmurs of "Vas is das?" She lasted two weeks.

For a long stretch, her only assignments came from a small,
stocky Catskill agent whose card read JACK SEGAL, PEP SHOWS,
ominously decorated with masks of comedy and tragedy. Segal
never asked her to audition. She had a car; that was sufficient.
"There were certain places you picked up acts—in front of the
Stage Delicatessen and under the George Washington Bridge.
You could always spot the performers. When you saw a woman
with jet-black hair, eyelashes hitting Jersey, and holding a dry
cleaner's bag of orange crinoline—you figured, 'That's her.' I
taxied men with barking suitcases, ventriloquists whose lips
moved even when they were silent, and a trainer with three tap-
dancing chickens who kept telling me his ambition was to have

a line of chickens equal to the Rockettes. Coming home one night, a guy made out with a singer in the backseat. Every time I had to pay a toll on these trips, I would look around and the entire rest of the car was suddenly sound asleep and snoring."

After three decades of public performing, Rivers concludes that the Catskill hotel audiences were, without question, "the worst in the world. The guests paid a package rate, so everything was free. The Jell-O was free, the shuffleboard was free, the show was free. Nobody in the audience had said, 'Oh, great. Joan Rivers is here. Let's buy tickets.' Joan Rivers was there, just like the shuffleboard. She was something the entertainment department had shoved down their throats, and they thought the peak of sophistication was saying, 'I've seen them all and I've walked out on them all.' "

A good night, she continues, "was half the audience laughing. The worst was the Benz Hotel where nobody spoke English and an interpreter onstage repeated everything I said in Yiddish. It was, 'The beautiful Jane Green.' Silence. Yiddish. Silence. 'How quickly we forget.' Silence. Yiddish. Silence. 'She was married to Lamont Cranston, but he kept disappearing on her.' Silence. Yiddish. Silence. Every line bombed twice."

What did not destroy her made her funnier. Rivers eventually found "a solution to the Catskills. Before the audience could hurt me, I would come out and say, 'Tonight, this is not going to be a comedy act. It is going to be a lecture. I am going to talk about a lot of things. My first topic is that I am single. I have very high standards. If he doesn't have a pulse, forget it. . . .' That made it much easier because a lecture is not supposed to get laughs and sometimes I did better that way. . . . I was also learning a lot of negatives that have helped me tremendously. Never trust an audience. Never think that they are truly your friends. Also I learned always to leave your car behind in the recreation hall, preferably with . . . the engine running. I would get offstage fast and literally climb through a window, jump into the getaway car, and be gone before they realized how much they hated me—but praying that this owner would not telephone the next owner. . . .

"Since then, I have learned that certain kinds of success

can ruin you. If I had been a hit in the Catskills that summer, I would probably not be where I am today. The struggle to make it in the Mountains, the browbeating you suffer, defeats many comics. They wake up at age forty and find they are Catskills comics, locked into that groove of humor, sapped of the talent and the drive they needed to reach the next rung."

The unfortunates locked into that groove of humor were best described by Jackie Mason long after he had made his escape from the Borscht Belt. "Coming back, three o'clock in the morning, we'd all stop at the Red Apple Rest . . . located at the exact halfway mark going and coming to the Mountains. . . . It was Sunday morning by then and the acts were all still high on adrenaline, sitting around, kibitzing with each other— 'I killed 'em! I killed 'em! I killed 'em!' No one committed less than murder. Could have been playing to an audience of deaf and dumb, wouldn't matter, they were killers. And I think that the only thing that impressed them more than who was killing who, who bombed. . . . Doing good was nothing compared to being able to tell everyone who stunk. And they would always say the same thing: 'Isn't it a shame who stunk!' "

One of the men who never emerged from the Mountains was Lou Menschel, a man, according to Mason, "who for twenty years, right up until the moment he died, was preparing his material for Johnny Carson. What should he include? What should he toss out? Not that he ever made it to the Carson show. Not that there was ever a prayer. . . . He had ambition . . . but he didn't know how to express it and he never really got anywhere in his career and he became one of the standard comedians in the Mountains. . . .

"As a person he had the same jealousies about who's making it and he was full of the same rationalizations about why he's not making it; that he doesn't want to make it, that he doesn't need it: 'These successful guys are struggling but they're getting nothing out of it but I have such a great life. I have my own home, I have my own car, you know how much money I got?' Then he would give you facts and figures to prove to himself and to you that he's doing really great, even though you can't tell, and that he doesn't need it because it's a miserable life to be such a success. Failure is really better and flopping is really a hit and this low-class level of show business is more peaceful, more contentment, he doesn't have to be involved in a rat race."

The Catskillian was never more secure than when he learned of a headliner who bombed out of town. "I'll never forget, he always said, 'I'm so happy for people when they do good . . . doesn't hurt me. It does me good. My heart fills with warmth and love and happiness. I'm never so happy as when I see someone else doing good. That's why it hurts me that I just found out that Dick Shawn just bombed in London! You have no idea how terrible I feel. He's such a sweet, wonderful guy and to hear that he bombed in London makes me feel terrible.'

"Menschel takes out an article from a London newspaper that he went to buy special because he felt so terrible that Dick Shawn bombed in London, he wanted to read it himself. And not only that, he felt so terrible that he couldn't stop carrying it around in his pocket . . . as soon as he saw me sitting there he took out this article and showed it to me and he says, 'Isn't it terrible that Dick Shawn bombed in London? It hurts me to see it, look! Look!' "

Through the fifties the O. & W. had suffered a loss of passengers and freight. In 1957, the locomotives of the Ontario and Western, known more familiarly as the Old and Weary, chuffed down the rusting track for the last time. The New York State Thruway had threatened the railroad; Route 17, the refurbished four-lane Quickway through Sullivan County, put it out of business.

The Mountains were now only ninety minutes away from Manhattan by car, without a single toll after the George Washington Bridge. Owners of the large resorts fought the air conditioner and the television set with imaginative dinners, larger rooms, louder music, bigger names. And, of course, air conditioning and television. Milton Berle, George Jessel, Robert Merrill were brought back. Georgia Gibbs, an established recording star, the young and newly famous Sammy Davis, Jr., Tony Martin, Red Buttons, Joey Adams appeared on the resort and hotel circuit. Richard Tucker sang at Saturday-night services. Dialectician Myron Cohen made the rounds; so did many other comedians who had worked their way out of the Mountains, among them Buddy Hackett, Alan King, and Jackie Mason. Jennie Grossinger was upset when Eddie Fisher and Debbie Reynolds announced that their marriage was breaking up. "Two nicer people they don't come," she said. "I hope it'll blow over like little gray clouds." All the same, her resort did a thriving business when Eddie checked in for a weekend with his new amour, Elizabeth Taylor. Guests were especially intrigued to learn that she had pitilessly analyzed herself for reporters: "I've the body of a woman and the emotions of a child."

The agents profited and suffered through this frantic period. "Where else can you rub shoulders with a Marlene Dietrich on a Friday night?" asked Charlie Rapp, "and want to shoot your brains out on a Saturday night when your headliner bombs, or the opening night act doesn't show?"

His worst moment came on Labor Day in 1957: "This was the giant goof of the season. I've got a big work sheet on my wall that tells where everybody is appearing, what car picks up who, which star goes where, how many shows are scheduled for that night—everything.

"The girl in my office read the sheet wrong and accidentally sent three top name acts to a bungalow colony. They played to an audience of sixty surprised *kuchaleyners*, while the major hotel . . . that had paid five thousand dollars for their end-of-season Saturday-night extravaganza, got a harmonica player and a half-assed juggler."

The Concord's old Cordillion Room accommodated 1,500 persons. The new one seated twice as many. Grossinger's advertised a vast indoor pool enclosed by 20-foot glass walls. Kutsher's Country Club hired Morris Lapidus, creator of architecture known in the trade as Miami Beacharama, to design its recreation hall. At the New Windsor in South Fallsburgh, the conversation piece was a $200,000 nightclub with a decor of turquoise, white, gold, and black. The neighboring Pines displayed a whale-shaped $75,000 pool. It was spanned by an Oriental bridge providing a passageway between the cabana area and the hotel's Bamboo Room, designed for dancing. Like most of the large hotels, the Pines offered its patrons two bands, one

American, the other Latin American. Parents were assured that they could mambo until the small hours with equanimity; while they danced, their children would be checked by "night patrols" of the hotel staff, or by telephone operators eavesdropping on the sleepers through room service phones left off the hook.

As luxuries piled upon indulgences, the critics sharpened their knives. Caricatures of the garish and blatant Jew returned in force. *Time* magazine was amused to report that a Catskill waiter "greeted a middle-aged lady by asking her, 'If you wear mink at breakfast how can you top it the rest of the day?' The woman coolly taught him one of the newer ploys of ostentation: 'I save my stone martens for dinner.'"

Dependably, the comedians had far more to say about their hosts. At the Raleigh Hotel, they told audiences, the barber shop was so swanky you had to be shaved before you could enter.

Eddie Fisher spoke of the night he appeared for a charity event. At Grossinger's, "the admission was a one-thousand-dollar purchase of an Israel Bond per person. A man whispered, 'Think of it, it's costing us two thousand dollars for this dinner.' His wife answered, 'See, I'm telling you, Sam, it's costing more and more to eat out these days.'"

At the Nevele, a Wall Street visitor fell into the swimming pool. He was saved by a lifeguard. The man turned to another millionaire and asked, "What do you tip for that?"

If the Concord builds an indoor mountain, Grossinger's warned, it would retaliate by air conditioning the forest. Zero Mostel suggested that the Concord build an indoor jungle for hunting for tigers under glass. George Jessel told the Grossingers to put in wall-to-wall carpeting. "What's unusual about that?" he was asked. Jessel gave them his basilisk stare. "On the beach?"

Several owners refused to go along with the gags. A small but influential group, weary of being caricatured as bagel aristocracy, conceived an ambitious plan. They reasoned that the majority of their patrons, far from being parvenus, were actually intelligent, responsible Jews, just the sort of people who provided the main support for Carnegie Hall and the Metropolitan Opera. It was known that the NBC Symphony had been rootless since its maestro, Arturo Toscanini, had stepped down in April 1954. It was also known that the Berkshires held a music festival in Tanglewood, Massachusetts, and that the Rockies had theirs in Aspen, Colorado. What if the Catskills were to play host to the NBC Symphony? Administrators were found, funds raised, real estate purchased. Some 110 acres were acquired for $12,000, a bargain even in the fifties. Another $110,000 rented bulldozers to hack a concert bowl out of a mountainside, and to create roads, parking lots, and seating areas. On July 1, 1955, the ground breaking began; twenty-nine days later, Eduard Van Beinum, the celebrated Dutch conductor, raised his baton and led the inaugural concert of Beethoven and Brahms.

On opening night there were 4,003 ticket holders, among them the Netherlands Embassy chargé d'affaires, on hand to honor his countryman Mr. Van Beinum, and to salute the memory of the Dutch settlers of old Ulster County, back in the seventeenth century. It was all very serious and ambitious, but New York State's first music festival could not escape the stain of borscht.

"Talk of long-hair music, as the saying goes, is on everyone's lips," reported *The New York Times*, "from the carpeted hotel lobbies to the shops . . . the name of Eduard Van Beinum pops up in local chit-chat almost, but not quite, as often as that of Eddie Fisher, who periodically makes pilgrimages here to sing. Snatches of *La Bohème*, which comprised the second night program, are hummed interestingly by girls in pedal pushers between free cha-cha-cha lessons at the resorts."

This coverage offended the High Catskillians without surprising them. Three generations before, uptown visitors had similarly amused themselves by watching Yiddish audiences as they cheered *King Lear* and called for the author at curtain time. Now the *Times* noted that "hotels are handing out tickets to their guests, some of whom apparently have never before heard a symphony orchestra or seen an opera. (At almost every performance, there has been a burst of applause at the wrong place.)" A hotel executive added to the piece: "It's a big thing! Tremendous! Major! Let me tell you one thing, though. Ellenville will absorb this cultural hubbub precipitated by the festival without missing a meal."

The defenders countered by calling attention to political discussions at Chesters', and popular lectures by sociologists and psychologists. They hailed the success of the Stanley Woolf players, a traveling troupe which had found receptive audiences for its renditions of *Death of a Salesman, The Four Poster, My Three Angels,* and *The Caine Mutiny Court-Martial.* This last was a special favorite because it had been written by one of the Catskills' own, Herman Wouk. Better still, Wouk's fond salute to the Mountains, *Marjorie Morningstar,* had just been made into a hit movie. True, Noel Airman was played by Gene Kelly and Marjorie by Natalie Wood, but that simply proved what the moviemakers had been underlining for thirty years: Jews could be played by goys because now they were just like everybody else. They had stopped their wandering and found a home in the suburbs.

Nevertheless, the journalists who covered cultural activities in the Mountains remained sardonic and unimpressed. It took a different kind of production to arouse their interest. In 1958, the year of *Morningstar,* after six years of planning, Monticello Raceway was constructed on a 245-acre site. It had been the locale of a bungalow colony and a neighboring farm. A consortium of hotelmen served as directors, among them Jennie Grossinger's son Paul; Sidney Sussman of the Windsor, Dave Levenson of Tamarack Lodge, Milton Kutsher of Kutsher's Country Club, and Benjamin Slutsky of the Nevele. "It cost us more than a million but it was a great step for the Catskills," Levenson recalled. "This was not the old kind of Catskill gambling. This was a licensed, state-regulated, important harness track. Opening night we attracted over six thousand patrons, and they kept coming. Nothing in this area ever had such an immediate impact."

Those initial patrons wagered $252,963, and the betting windows did a comparable volume of business for the next eighty-two racing days. In the following season bettors outdid themselves; more than $19 million was spent on the trotters.

Some of the money came back in the form of a glass enclosure and a heated grandstand. A better turf was installed, composed of an eight-inch stone dust base topped by sand and more stone dust. It was impervious to weather and hardened under use, until Monticello became the fastest half-mile harness-racing track in the world. The raceway was such a magnet for patrons that on one spring night they wagered over a million dollars.

A few years later, the Low Catskillians took charge and the raceway became a house of rock concerts and closed-circuit boxing. It was also a stage for the Elephantonian, a race between pachyderms, and the Mammaltonian, a contest of trotting elephant and pacing camel over the length of a mile. Nellie the elephant scored a one-length victory over Koch the camel, covering the furlong in 22.4 seconds.

Monticello suffered through the usual scandal: after two 20-to-1 shots came in, a state investigation was held, fines levied, and jockeys warned. But the greatest uproar occurred off the track, when Andy "Satch" Furman, director of public relations, wrote what he supposed was a comic solicitation of business from the upstate Ku Klux Klan. "I had no idea the KKK had their meetings so close to Monticello Raceway," read his invitation. "Why, you could hop on a bus and come down here and enjoy our racing program. Perhaps you could even have a meeting at the track as well.

"I'm sure Monticello Raceway will be the first harness track in America to invite the KKK for a meeting, as well as for an evening of entertainment."

Furman expressed astonishment when Jewish community leaders voiced their outrage; he told them that the whole thing had been meant as a lark. A few days later, he conceded that perhaps his attempt at black humor "could be a powder keg," and publicly apologized for his indiscretion. The act of contrition was judged to be unacceptable and he was soon employed elsewhere.

Monticello has since forgotten such difficulties, and when the name of Furman comes up in conversation, it is often linked with a happy event. His last great promotion was held in honor of a nineteenth-century inventor and baker, Henry Bauer of Brooklyn. It was a warm event, like the evening itself, and filled with the aroma of edible souvenirs. Even those who objected to the Klan letter admitted that Bagel Night at the raceway was one of the Mountains' most memorable evenings.

CHAPTER 13

DRS. SCHWEITZER AND

STRANGELOVE

Loch Sheldrake, N. Y.

Rabbi Israel Margolies of Manhattan gave notice that he had turned his back on the Mountains. In the early sixties he put his rhetorical question: "How can you expect to have a solemn religious service in a converted nightclub, where the whole congregation was dancing the Watusi just the night before?"

The rabbi seemed most disturbed by the increasing number of Jews who were spending the High Holy Days, Rosh Hashanah and Yom Kippur, in the pleasure domes of the Catskills. The New York Board of Rabbis concurred. "Jewish people go to resorts on other holidays too," their statement said. "But the practice disturbs us most on these days."

Rabbi Benjamin Z. Kreitman of the Brooklyn Jewish Center had no use for the worship offered by the big hotels on *any* holiday. Those elaborate rites, he determined, "reduce religion to the level of entertainment" and create indifference to worship by decreasing respect for it. "I'd rather that people didn't go to any services than go to most of those set up in resorts."

Thanks to suburban migration, the Jewish population of New York City had declined from 2,050,000 to 1,836,000. Synagogue attendance in the five boroughs had diminished in proportion. The long Sunday morning of the Eisenhower years was over; America was entering a new secular age. Rabbi Kreitman and his colleagues knew no other course but resistance, tirelessly speaking and writing against such abominations as the holiday exodus. The rabbi was gratified to note that there was at least one exception to the moral backslide. Only 150 of his 1,500-member congregation traveled across the river for the holidays, as compared with double that number five years before.

Hotel owners were sensitive to the charges of impiety. Religious leaders had been making them for years. Grossinger's own rabbi, Harry Z. Stone, had confessed his difficulties in raising a *minyan*, the ten men necessary for a religious service. "Even those who pray in New York come here to relax," he once told a visiting journalist, to the everlasting embarrassment of his employers. Nevertheless, to Murray Posner, co-owner of the Hotel Brickman, the whole thing came down to the great Jewish tradition of individual choice: "Either you're sincere about your religion or you're not, and the place you're at doesn't change it." Another official was offended by suggestions that worshippers were short-changed in the Mountains. He told *The Wall Street Journal*: "We'll spend more for High Holy Days services than for a regular weekend's entertainment. A cantor can cost up to $15,000 for the holidays, and a choir a couple of thousand more." On questioning he conceded that "if they're famous, they'll pay for themselves in the business they'll draw—and we'll have a beautiful service."

Rabbi Kreitman was unpersuaded. He spoke of the "disgrace of visiting resorts on these sacred days," and added, "I look forward to ten years from now, when no self-respecting Jew would go."

While he looked, a large number of self-respecting Jews continued to visit the Mountains. Mordecai Richler came to the

Catskills in 1965. The Canadian novelist had already spent a large part of his literary career recording and analyzing the vagaries of Montreal Jewish life. The Mountains offered him a new arena for wonder and asperity. He concentrated on the two most promising subjects for self-satire, Grossinger's and the Concord. Richler's piquant style was his own, but his social critique was part of a mainstream begun over half a century before when Abraham Cahan, managing editor of the Yiddish-language *Daily Forward*, first decried the excesses of his fellow immigrants.

Along Route 17 the visitor found himself "assailed by billboards" and noted a few memorable lines: DO A JERRY LEWIS—COME TO BROWN'S. I FOUND A HUSBAND AT THE WALDEMERE. THE RALEIGH IS ICIER, NICIER, AND SPICIER. Grossinger's greeted him with its solipsistic brochure: "On a day in August, 1914, that was to take its place among the red-letter days of all history, a war broke out in Europe. Its fires seared the world. . . . On a summer day of that same year, a small boarding house was opened in the Town of Liberty."

Additional literature notified Richler that among the "typewriter boys" who had served on the staff of the G were the playwright Paddy Chayefsky and the novelist Paul Gallico. Shelley Winters, Betty Garrett, and Robert Alda had spent their formative summers as apprentice entertainers. And among the kitchen help had been hundreds who later became professional men. "Be nice to your busboy" was the Grossinger shibboleth. "Next year when he graduates he may treat your ulcer."

The cultural explosion was duly noted: recently the G had featured the lectures of Max Lerner and Norman Cousins, editor of the *Saturday Review of Literature*. The latest guest speaker, hypnotist Nat Fleischer, offered the theme "Can Love Survive Marriage?"

"I have a degree in psychology," Fleischer boasted, "and am now working on my doctorate."

"Where?"

"I'd rather not say."

The lecture was heavily attended, and the listeners leaned forward to catch Fleischer's bromides. In a few years the Beatles

The original Grossinger farmhouse as it stood ready to receive boarders in 1914. *Inset:* The Founding Mother and Father: Selig and Malke Grossinger in the Old Country. *Below:* An aerial view of Grossinger's after it became the G, with its own airfield and post office, c. 1950.

Above, left: Max Brender (right), owner of the largest poultry breeding farm in New York State, helps prepare 1,000 fertile eggs to found chicken dynasties in the Middle East. *Above, right:* Loading the cargo for flight from Grossinger's to LaGuardia Airport, and then to Palestine under the supervision of Major Aubrey, later Abba Eban. (Not one egg was broken en route.)

Opposite, center: The Two Eddies. Eddie Cantor embraces Eddie Fisher in 1949, after one of the most meticulously planned and orchestrated "discoveries" in show business history. *Below:* Fisher with his failed Grossinger romances: wife number one, Debbie Reynolds, and wife number two, Elizabeth Taylor. *Above, top:* Nelson Rockefeller, on the campaign trail, makes a stop-off to court the Jewish vote at Grossinger's, carefully seating Jennie on his left; *below:* The two Rockies compare fists as Nelson Rockefeller returns to the Mountains to grin alongside former heavyweight champion Rocky Marciano. The champ also liked to do his training at the G.

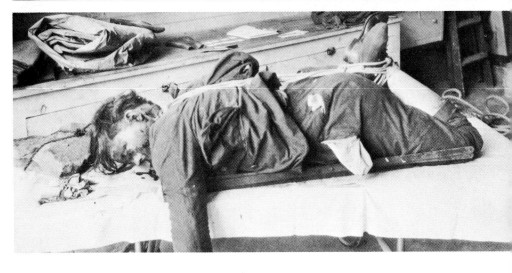

Lawless times in upstate New York. *Opposite, top:* Izzy Einstein and Moe Smith, prohibition detectives extraordinaire, in their civilian attire and (center) in disguise as thieves, a favorite role in the Mountains. *Opposite, below:* In 1937 Walter Sage, a Brooklyn gangster, was stabbed thirty-seven times with an ice pick, then tied to a pinball-machine rack and deposited in Swan Lake. *Right:* A Wanted poster for Louis Buchalter, alias Lepke, who treated his mother to weekends in the Catskill resorts, and who liked to go there himself when he was not fulfilling a contract for Murder, Inc. *Below:* The college basketball scandal erupts in 1951 as three of the brightest stars of the Long Island University team are booked on charges of bribery. From left are high-scoring Leroy Smith, two detectives, Adolf Bigos, the LIU captain, a detective, and Sherman White, All-American.

$25,000 REWARD
DEAD OR ALIVE

TWENTY-FIVE THOUSAND DOLLARS will be paid by the City of New York for Information leading to the capture of "LEPKE" BUCHALTER, aliases LOUIS BUCHALTER, LOUIS BUCKHOUSE, LOUIS KAWAR, LOUIS KAUVAR, LOUIS COHEN, LOUIS SAFFER, LOUIS BRODSKY.

WANTED FOR CONSPIRACY AND EXTORTION

The Person or Persons who give Information Leading to the Arrest of "LEPKE" will be fully protected, his or her identity will never be revealed. The Information will be received in absolute confidence.

RIGHT HAND

LEFT HAND

DESCRIPTION — Age, 42 years; white; Jewish; height, 5 feet, 5½ inches; weight, 170 pounds; build, medium; black hair; brown eyes; complexion dark; married, one son Harold, age about 18 years.

PECULIARITIES—Eyes, piercing and shifting; nose, large, somewhat blunt at nostrils; ears, prominent and close to head; mouth, large, slight dimple left side; right-handed; suffering from kidney ailment.

Frequents baseball games.

Is wealthy; has connections with all important mobs in the United States. Involved in racketeering in Unions and Fur Industry, uses Strong-arm methods. Influential.

This Department holds indictment warrant charging Conspiracy and Extortion, issued by the Supreme Court, Extraordinary Special and Trial Terms, New York County.

Kindly search your Prison Records as this man may be serving a Prison sentence for some minor offense.

If located, arrest and hold as a fugitive and advise the THE DETECTIVE DIVISION, POLICE DEPARTMENT, NEW YORK CITY, by wire.

Information may be communicated in Person or by Telephone or Telegraph, Collect to the undersigned, or may be forwarded direct to the DETECTIVE DIVISION, POLICE DEPARTMENT, NEW YORK CITY.

Tummlers and talents. *Above, left:* Danny Kaye as he appeared at White Roe in the summer of 1935 and (right) in an art nouveau version of "Brother, Can You Spare a Dime?" Five years later he was Hollywood's hottest property. *Center:* Sophie Tucker, the Last of the Red Hot Mamas, who switched from "My Yiddishe Momme" to "God Bless America" for her wartime Mountain finale. *Below:* Two of television's most popular and influential comedians learned their trade and made their first reputations on the stages of the Catskill resorts: (left) Milton Berle, (right) Sid Caesar.

Above, left: Jerry Lewis, a clown at Brown's when he was still a teenager; *right:* George Jessel, America's Toastmaster General and fixture at all the major resorts; *inset:* A rare meeting of the incoming and outgoing generations of tummlers. *Below, left:* Robert Merrill, né Merrill Miller, whose baritone was a favorite of Catskill patrons; *right:* Jan Peerce, né Pincus Perelmuth, a tenor who continued to sing at Saturday-night services in the Mountains long after he and Merrill were established stars of the Metropolitan Opera.

Even today, young comedians regard the Catskills as a prime training ground for the Big Time because of those who went before. *Above, left:* Henny Youngman, master of the one-liner. *Right:* Alan King, who went from stand-up comedy to film actor and producer. *Center:* Buddy Hackett, at home in the Borscht Belt or Las Vegas. *Below, left:* The most unlikely Broadway superstar, Jackie Mason. *Right:* Joan Rivers, who considered resort audiences "the toughest in the world."

would be earning royalties for espousing identical thoughts. "In order to remain sane," the hypnotist told them, "what do we need? ALL OF US. Even at sixty and seventy. LOVE. If you've been married for twenty-five years you shouldn't take your wife for granted. Be considerate."

Richler watched a woman under a tangle of curlers. "I've been married twenty-nine years," she boasted, "and my husband doesn't take me for granted."

This seemed to alarm a sunken-bellied man in the back row who stood up to get a better look at the lady. "I'd like to meet her husband," he muttered, and sat down. "The shmuck."

Later in the day, Richler entered the Grossinger bar. He mistook the man on the next stool for a physical culturist. "I swim this morning," the guest said. "I swim this afternoon—indoors, outdoors." Then he added, "My God, what a collection! When are all the beauties checking in?"

By evening, the complainer had been taken aside by a staff member and informed, "You can't sit down at a table and say to a lady you've just met that she's, um, well stacked. It's not refined." He was told that he would have to change his table again.

"All right," the swimmer grumbled. "Okay. I like women. So that makes me a louse."

Richler's dining companions "included a teenager with a flirtatious aunt, and a bejeweled and wizened widow in her sixties. 'I hate to waste all this food,' the widow said, 'it's such a crime. My dog should be here, he'd have a wonderful time.'

" 'Where is he?'

" 'Dead,' she said, false eyelashes fluttering, just as the loud-speaker crackled and the get-together for singles was announced. 'Single people *only*, please.' "

As Richler prepared to leave the G, a hostess offered him cookies. They were to sustain him for the fifteen-minute drive to " 'over there'—*dorten*, as they say in Yiddish—the Concord."

If Jennie Grossinger was "the Dr. Schweitzer of the Catskills," Richler decided, "Arthur Winarick must be counted as its Dr. Strangelove." The owner of the Concord, now in his seventies, was asked if he had ever been to any of Europe's luxury resorts. The disdain was palpable. "Garages with drapes," he boomed. "Warehouses."

There would be no warehouses on his property. The Concord maintained a Big Name nightclub policy (Judy Garland, Jimmy Durante), a resident graphologist, a former Tarzan as Director of Water Activities ("This magnificent outdoor pool," Buster Crabbe told his customers, "makes all other pools look like the swimming hole I used to take Jane and the chimps to"), and a shopping arcade known as Little Fifth Avenue. Unfortunately, the famous pastel snowdrifts were no longer a Concord feature. "We had to cut out the colored stuff," Winarick sadly confided. "Some people were allergic to it."

Perhaps they were the customers mentioned on a sign in the arcade:

MAKE AN OIL PAINTING IN AN HOUR
EVERYBODY A REMBRANDT
The Spin Art Shop
50 cents
5 × 7 oil painting
Only Non Allergic Paints Used

A Concord employee reminisced: "In the old days, you know, we used to go in for calisthenics, but no more. People are older. Golf, okay, but—well, I'll tell you something—in these hotels we cater to what I call foodcoholics. Anyway, I used to run it—the calisthenics—one day I'm illustrating the pump, the bicycle pump exercises for fat people—you know, in-out, in-out—zoom—her guts come spilling out. A fat lady. Right out. There went one year's profits, no more calisthenics."

During his tour of the Mountains Richler looked in on smaller places, among them Itzik's Rooms, the Bon-Repos, and Altman's Cottages. Altman's was run by Ephraim Weisse, a refugee who had been in four concentration camps. He sounded the first truly sour note. Maybe the big hotels were doing well, he said, but the little places were being squeezed out. They could not offer nightclubs or heated pools, their old customers were dying off or retiring to Miami, Los Angeles, or—could you be-

Drs. Schweitzer and Strangelove

lieve it?—Tel Aviv. There was no longer a future in playing host. "The air is the only thing that's good," Weisse complained. "Business? It's murder." He shrugged. "I survived Hitler. I'll outlast the Catskills."

As Richler completed the swing, he remarked on a strange phenomenon. Wherever possible, nature, the very thing that had attracted the immigrants long ago, was kept at bay. Outlying lodges were linked to the main buildings "through a system of glassed-in and sometimes even subterranean passages, all in the costly cause of protecting people from the not notoriously fierce Catskills outdoors." On a sunny day at the Laurels he found a young couple lying under an ultraviolet lamp by the heated indoor pool. And at Brown's, where guests were promised MORE OF EVERYTHING, a considerable number of guests ignored the endless run of facilities to sit on the balcony overlooking Route 17. From that vantage point they could watch the cars and the people coming and going. "Obviously," the tourist concluded, "there's still nothing like the front-door stoop as long as pass-ersby know that you don't have to sit there, that you can afford everything inside."

And yet all through this rich material, Richler's satire seems uncertain of where to come down. This was the middle of the sixties and there were vague stirrings of social revolution. Borscht Belt guitarists, asked to sing the Hebrew song "Tzena Tzena," were slipping in new lyrics written by members of the Congress of Racial Equality. Philip Roth was beginning to publish his furious tragicomedies of Jewish middle-class life. Self-criticism, the Hebraic trait that Freud had so artfully dissected, was in the air.

"By a none too cunning process of selected detail," Richler acknowledged, "one can make Grossinger's, the Catskills, and the people who go there appear totally grotesque." The trouble was that the archetypal Grossinger guest already belonged to the most frequently fired-at class of American Jews. "Even as *Commentary* sends out another patrol of short story writers *Partisan Review* irregulars are waiting in the bushes, bayonets drawn. Saul Bellow is watching, Alfred Kazin is ruminating, Norman Mailer is ready with his flick-knife, and who knows what manner of tripwires the next generation of Jewish writers is laying out at this very moment."

He wonders, "Was there ever a group so pursued by such an unsentimental platoon of chroniclers? So plagued by moralists? So blamed for making money? . . . In a Clifford Odets play they were the rotters. The rent collectors. Next Jerome Weidman carved them up and then along came Budd Schulberg and Irwin Shaw. In fact, in all this time only Herman Wouk, armed with but a slingshot of clichés, has come to their defense. More of an embarrassment, I'd say, than a shield."

And here they were at Grossinger's et al., "sitting ducks for satire. Manna for sociologists." Here they were "breathless, but at play, so to speak, suffering sour stomach and cancer scares, one Israeli bond drive after another, unmarriageable daughters and sons gone off to help the Negroes overcome in Mississippi."

With all its grossness, the land of the resorts was their dream of plenty realized. Richler felt compelled to warn the reader, "If you find it funny, larger than life, then so do the regulars. In fact, there is no deflating remark I could make about minks or matchmaking that has not already been made by visiting comedians or guests. Furthermore for an innocent goy to even think of some of the things said at Grossinger's would be to invite the wrath of the B'nai B'rith Anti-Defamation League."

On the afternoon of July 22, 1964, seventy-six-year-old Harry Grossinger suffered a fatal coronary thrombosis at Maimonides Hospital, the institution that had received so many contributions from his family. Harry, Jennie's publicity-shy husband, had been a familiar figure at the Washington Market in Manhattan for more than forty years. Twice a week a chauffeur-driven Lincoln Continental had taken him to the stands, where he approved all the vegetables and meat destined for Grossinger's tables. Others would do it now, and the cuisine would never be quite the same. Harry was ecumenically mourned; Jennie received consolatory telegrams from thousands of her guests, including "The Padre of Guadalcanal," the Reverend Fred Gehring of Philadelphia; Francis Cardinal Spellman; Nelson Rockefeller, governor of New York State.

Drs. Schweitzer and Strangelove

On November 21 of that year, Arthur Winarick also succumbed to a heart attack. He was seventy-five. Most obituaries retailed the old stories: the time he played host to a trio of Catskill veterans, singers Harry Richman and Sophie Tucker and comedian Joe E. Lewis, lamenting because Tucker's original pianist—Beethoven—could not be there that night. Newspapers recalled Winarick's desire for a 50-hole golf course and the boasting about his place to an unidentified guest, only to find that it was a busboy he had hired the week before. And they added a few new tales: ladies without their own could rent a mink at the Concord from the mobile racks of Irving Shavelson, who ran Abet Rent-A-Fur in New York. The maître d' checked seat assignments by inserting a colored peg into a large board showing all the tables. White pegs stood for married guests, blue for single men, pink for single women. It was Winarick's dream that one night there would be a blue peg and a pink peg at every table, in a dining room so large that a waiter could refuse to serve a guest because "your table isn't in my state." The New York *Herald Tribune* ended its tribute by labeling Winarick's dream "Miami-in-the-Catskills."

That was the way most politicians thought of the Concord, and of the Catskills in general. To them Miami meant unlimited sunshine, glitter, and, most important, registered Jewish voters. Seizing on the happy notion of a relaxed, internationalist audience, Richard Nixon's running mate Henry Cabot Lodge campaigned in the Mountains at the beginning of the sixties. "Even on this beautiful day, in this wonderful country," he said, "I cannot but think we live in a world full of dangers . . . some obvious, others mysterious."

He received a mixed reaction. "Such a personality," said a woman in tight-fitting pants and plastic shoes, "such an approach." Her friend agreed: "The way he words his words." Milton Blackstone was not so sure. No doubt thinking of his client Eddie Fisher, he decided that the candidate lacked "something in the voice that says 'I love you.' "

At the conclusion of Lodge's speech a guest hissed, "He gave Suez back to the Arabs." Her husband was more disconcerted because Lodge and the Republican governor had dined gratis at Grossinger's. "To a Rockefeller," he grumbled, "they give free."

John Lindsay, making his first run for mayor of New York City on the Republican–Liberal ticket, came up to the Catskills in the summer of 1965 searching for support. He did not begin well. Before his appearance, local Democrats had torn down every blue-and-white *Vote for Lindsay* poster in Monticello and Liberty. The candidate's volunteers had been up until 3 a.m. replacing them. It was worth the effort. Some 100,000 New York City residents were stopping in the region that weekend, and Lindsay tirelessly worked the Windsor Hotel, the Pines, the Nemerson, the Flagler, Kutsher's, the Laurels, and the Concord. Gradually guests left their softball games, their shuffleboard courts, and sometimes their meals to get a look at the lanky *goyische* candidate. They were unmoved until he spiced his talks with a little Yiddish. A few listeners addressed him prematurely as Mr. Mayor. When he spoke about coming up here on Shabbos (the Sabbath), he was greeted with scattered applause. And after the candidate called himself a lunatic who was running for office "like a *meshugenah*," he received a standing ovation. A listener at the Concord poolside made his mind up then and there: "It might be that Lindsay really is nuts. But he's *our meshugenah*."

In August 1966, a congressional election year, President Lyndon Johnson came by to dedicate the Ellenville Community Hospital, to salute two Jewish legislators, Senator Jacob Javits and local congressman Joseph Resnik, and to put in a word for the new Medicare program. "Standing in this place today," proclaimed L.B.J., "I almost want to echo the words which Moses heard from the burning bush: 'Take off thy shoes, for this is holy ground.' " En route he was heard to say, "I love the Catskill region. I don't think I've ever seen such a beautiful sight as the Shawangunk Valley." Protestors bearing signs proclaiming VIETNAM MURDERER and NO MORE ESCALATION repeatedly chanted their slogans. They were drowned out by the Fallsburgh Central School band playing "Hello, Lyndon" to the tune of "Hello, Dolly."

* * *

Drs. Schweitzer and Strangelove

No matter what was happening in New York City, circa 1967, the Mountains were almost impervious to the doctrine of Liberation. As far as single women were concerned, the year might have been 1916 or 1936 or 1946. Little had changed since the Talmud commented: "More than man desires to marry, woman desires to be married."

In the resorts success stories were trumpeted, and failures forgotten. "I was running Simon Says," testified Grossinger's unofficial matchmaker Lou Goldstein. "And a very nice fellow was standing next to an attractive girl, and he wasn't even listening to the game. So I worked out where they were among the last six in the game and I said, 'Simon Says face each other.' Then I said, 'Simon Says walk toward each other.' And there they were standing face to face. And then I said, 'Give her a hug.' Which he did! He was so excited. And I shouted, 'You're out. Simon didn't say to hug her.' He shouted back, 'The hell with you and the game—I'm happy!' One month later they came back and she was wearing an engagement ring."

That sort of rainbow finale was the goal of sixties' Singles Week in August. The event, according to Milton Blackstone, was "the absolute latest concept in Catskill tradition." For seven days the voices were reminiscent of insects rasping their most persuasive mating calls at the approach of autumn.

The first day was always the most uncomfortable. It started with merciless appraisals of one's fellow guests as they registered according to the initials of their last name: Adler through Feinstein, Gruber through Moscowitz, Oser through Zimmerman. "Standing in line waiting is a good way to start meeting people," said Morton Sunshine, general manager of Grossinger's. "Of course if your name begins with B you'll only meet people with names A through F, in the beginning. But it's a start."

It was not unusual for women to change clothes seven times a day. Outfits included slacks and blouse for breakfast, a bikini for the pool, white tennis garb for the courts, a summer dress for lunch, a different bathing suit for an afternoon dip, a fresh dress for dinner. The wardrobe was completed with party dress and mink stole for an evening of shows, dances, and "mixer parties." The expense was terrific, but most of the participants regarded clothing as an investment to be amortized over the years of marriage.

"I come here because it's sort of like a department store sale," said a forty-year-old divorcee, ratifying the libretto of *Wish You Were Here*. "A lot of potential mates you find are a little shopworn or damaged, but there are a lot of bargains, too. It all depends on luck and getting to the counter first. I hate it, but what are you going to do?"

At another resort, a young woman named Elsie remembered a happy occasion long ago. "My parents met here," she recalled. "Maybe the same magic will work for me."

A second divorcee showed her stepdaughter how to get along and go along: "I shouldn't give away trade secrets, but you've got to connive constantly at the resorts if you want to succeed. You can't afford to settle at one table or one deck chair at the swimming pool; you have to keep moving. I've been up here often, and I know how to do it."

Two sisters found a different method of working the hotels. The older one was married; she regarded herself as bait. "I was wearing my wedding ring when I arrived," she whispered, "but I took it off when I found I was having trouble at the singles parties and things. Lots of men seemed to like to talk to me. When they start to get interested I steer them toward my sister. It's kind of like teamwork. My husband hates my being here without him, but it's all for a good cause."

A teacher from the Midwest defected after one day. "I came to New York City for a couple of weeks to stay with cousins," she complained. "But they shipped me up here as soon as I arrived. I don't like the long lines or the mechanical atmosphere, and I'm leaving tomorrow. Why is it that every family has to push its girls so hard to find husbands?"

A friend concurred: "I know what you mean. For the boys, the question always is 'Harvey's son is twenty-eight and he's already earning $15,000. What's wrong with you?' For us it's 'Your cousin Helen is married to that nice salesman, and already has two beautiful children. When are you going to settle down?' "

Drs. Schweitzer and Strangelove

Besides, the teacher continued, "most of the boys here are from the Eastern states. When they find out where I'm from, I get labeled GU—Geographically Undesirable." It was no comfort for her to learn that a girl who came from the far reaches of the Bronx or Brooklyn was also labeled GU. In the Borscht Belt the women outnumbered the men by almost two to one, and she wanted out.

Older women had fewer options; hardly any of them left before closing time. One candid fifty-five-year-old lived alone in midtown Manhattan. She traveled widely and had many acquaintances. "But I'm lonely, all the same," she grimly admitted, and signed up for the singles mixer at the Concord. No one asked her to dance. At the sidelines, many women her age or younger sat in small groups, chatting idly with each other. Occasionally a lonely woman could stand it no longer and flagged a passing male. When she asked for a whirl around the floor, he agreed, holding his partner tentatively, talking in monosyllables until the music stopped. Then he would smile, excuse himself, and disappear.

In order to spare the guests such discomforts, some of the more luxurious hotels introduced computer dating in the late sixties. Guests were required to fill out elaborate questionnaires. These concerned sex, income, education, religious inclinations. Some included a brief Rorschach ink-blot test. A few hours later the computer would print out a list of potential mates. The recipient then filled out Date Grams addressed to the most likely prospects and waited for the strains of Mendelssohn.

The world of artificial intelligence could provoke as much angst as it soothed. A thirty-five-year-old woman became hysterical when she lost her computerized list of potential husbands. She insisted that Grossinger's search its garbage pail by pail, and she was not mollified until Stephen Milgrim, president of Operation Math Inc., irritatedly printed out a duplicate.

"A lot of people like to sneer at the computer," Milgrim said, once his customer quieted down. "But you'll notice that the ones who sneer loudest are the first to check their mailboxes for Date Grams. They all believe in it, although we've never been able to get it going in the poorer classes. The hotel guests are middle class, with some money and some sophistication." Milgrim theorized that "the computer relieves people of responsibility, and tells them it's all right to do things they wouldn't normally have courage to do. For instance, the computer tells girls it's all right for them to leave notes asking boys on their lists for dates. Everyone's socially insecure and this is a prop."

He gestured to an attractive assistant working her way through a file of papers. "Can you beat that? She's a good-looking gal. And she's paying forty bucks a day to stay here, and what does she do? She works for me, free. I think they feel if they're somehow closer to the system that will help them—maybe like temple priestesses. I actually had to turn volunteers away."

At the end of one frantic period, a *New York Times* reporter took stock: "Seven days after it all began, they ended their week on the public marriage block—most of them were broke and exhausted, but still hungry-eyed. Most were ready to return as many more times as necessary." It was convincing proof of Oscar Wilde's aphorism that the basis of optimism is sheer terror. "Everywhere there appeared to be a certain air of tension and a feeling of yearning," said the *Times*. "For some, the hours of waiting and worrying paid off in new friendships. For others, there seemed to be little hope, but the spark remained alive."

A refugee from Nazi Germany had come to the United States with her sister a year before: "She still has trouble with English. She is charming but, at fifty-four, she is often discouraged in her search for a husband or even a good friend. . . .

" 'My sister went back to France,' she sighed, 'but I know some of the crowd that comes. . . . I'm going to keep trying. I'm lonely. But you've got to try. When you stop trying you're dead. Every time I go somewhere, my sister writes me, *nu* [well]? I have to tell her, not yet.

" 'But one of these days . . .' "

A special flavor attended the productions of drama companies serving resorts in the sixties. For *Fair Game*, a play about a young divorcee, the word "virgin" was excised for fear of offense. In *The Marriage-Go-Round*, a blond visitor announced that since she was "younger, prettier, and more intelligent" she would have no difficulty stealing the husband of an older woman. Middle-aged ladies greeted her speech with boos. In the next act their husbands jeered when the temptress was thrown out of the house.

One of the Mountains' most durable traditions was an overreaction to performances—to tragedians and jugglers, to dancers, animal acts, singers, skaters, to magicians, comics, hypnotists, symphony orchestras, jazz combos, water shows. In this they were often encouraged by the owners. Grossinger's management, for example, found that the noise of approval could be increased by issuing little wooden mallets. Guests were instructed to beat them vehemently on chairs and tables instead of applauding. "You never heard such cacophony," said one musician. "It sounded as if they had opened up on us with loaded Uzis. I don't know whether it was the entertainers or the audiences who complained, but the next year everybody went back to clapping their hands together. In the Catskills, you *can* stop progress."

When they were not attending musicals and dramas, the ticket holders participated in seminars on modern drama from O'Neill to Brecht, and symposiums on subjects as diverse as contemporary American fiction and how to do the cha-cha in six lessons. In a 180-seat theater that was once a Mountaindale church, presentations of *Guys and Dolls, Call Me Madam,* and *Wish You Were Here* were sold out. At the playhouse of the Mount Cathalia Hotel in Ellenville, the repertoire included *Under the Yum-Yum Tree* and *The Marriage-Go-Round.* In White Lake, the Sunlight Playhouse put on *Born Yesterday* and *Come Back, Little Sheba.* On the other side of the lake the Laurel Playhouse offered jazz and folk-song festivals. After a darkness of almost ten years the Kiamesha Playhouse reopened with *The World of Sholem Aleichem* and *The Diary of Anne Frank.* As before, there was a mix of stars, amateurs, and acolytes with good references. The prominent character actors Joseph Buloff and Morris Carnovsky came to the Catskills directly from Broadway and Hollywood. They were assisted by Andrea Miller, the daughter of orchestra leader Mitch Miller, and Marcia Levant, daughter of pianist Oscar Levant.

Forestburg emphasized the works of major playwrights. The town's summer theater offered *Candida* and *Much Ado about Nothing*. South Fallsburgh emphasized a somewhat lighter program: the Gaiety Burlesque Theater. Its owner, Danny Klein, had received periodic visits from representatives of the village board, the sheriff's office, and the state police. He got the message. "The accent is on comedy," Klein assured his examiners. "The girls are—I hate to say it—secondary."

Soundouts was the grandiose title used by promoters. To the knowledgeable it simply meant small festivals of folk and pop and rock music held on the rolling hillsides near Woodstock in Ulster County. In 1969 some sponsors decided to stage their "Great Mother Soundout" in the town of Wallkill in southern Ulster County. The Woodstock Festival rang all the sixties chords of peace—uncontaminated air, workshops for making music, pottery, and verse. It also offered the biggest names in contemporary popular music: Joan Baez, Creedence Clearwater Revival, Jefferson Airplane, Janis Joplin, The Who, Joe Cocker, Ravi Shankar. The logo of the Woodstock Festival's "Aquarian Exposition" was a dove of peace sitting on the neck of a guitar. As Alf Evers observed, "Never had any appeal to the rebellious young managed to offer so artful a bag of lures."

Nevertheless, they failed to persuade the officials of Wallkill. A Woodstock paper editorialized long and hard against "the undesirable element," represented by long-haired loud rock musicians and their followers, and after considerable work had been done on the site, permission to hold the festival was abruptly withdrawn.

The promoters knew there would be little point in protesting. Time was short; money was tight. They packed up their belongings, along with the name of the festival, and crossed the border into Sullivan County. In the town of Bethel—Hebrew for consecrated spot—they found a Jewish dairy farmer who entertained their offer. For $50,000, Max Yasgur agreed to make his alfafa and corn fields the ground floor of their folk spectacle.

The difference in counties was palpable. The Woodstock art colony had been developed back in 1902 by Ralph Whitehead, an artist who insisted that his town be "entirely without

Drs. Schweitzer and Strangelove

Jewish landowners, Jewish shopkeepers, and Jewish boarding houses." The residue of his bias was still manifest in Ulster's suspicion of odd-looking and strange-sounding newcomers. Sullivan County was entirely different. Foreigners, after all, had brought prosperity to the region. So had entertainers.

And there was something more. These guitarists with their Choctaw outerwear and their amplified guitars were caterwauling about the Vietnam War, racism, and the inequities of American society. A great many of the town fathers were the descendants of immigrants to the Lower East Side. They had long since abandoned the debate of their socialist grandfathers, but they retained strong beliefs in equality and justice. The musicians seemed to be addressing those issues. Of course, not all officials welcomed what was already being billed as the "impending youthquake." A sign appeared in Bethel: STOP MAX'S HIPPIE MUSIC FESTIVAL. NO 150,000 HIPPIES HERE. BUY NO MILK. But it vanished as rapidly as it had appeared. And at town meetings, the conservatives who voiced objections to the "hippie invasion" were swiftly overruled.

As the Woodstock Festival gained velocity, the unworldly Max Yasgur expressed his philosophy: "I wish I was retired. I'd spend the rest of my life gratis just working among these kids, and I'd find out what the problem is. Listen, legalizing marijuana may not be a good thing, but to make a whole generation criminals is a worse thing." That kind of expression gained him a new respect. *The New York Times* called Yasgur "a Farmer with Soul," and rock fans decorated his alfalfa fields with signs: DO NOT DESTROY THESE. THEY ARE THE PROVIDER'S CROPS. Someone printed bumper stickers overnight: MAX YASGUR FOR PRESIDENT.

The success of the festival was also its curse. Some 500,000 attendees clotted every road to Bethel with cars, motorcycles, and buses. During the long intervals when nothing moved, drivers and passengers sat on the hoods and roofs of their vehicles, or at the bases of roadside billboards advertising good times at the Concord and the Raleigh. Alf Evers found that "even older and more conventional people bound for nothing more startling than a weekend at a Sullivan hotel or a bet at the Monticello

Raceway and now caught in the jam shared in the pervasive feeling of good-humored tolerance."

Summer boarders stood before their roadside hotels and returned the peace sign given with uplifted fingers by the young people. Elderly Hasids in black hats and coats had no notion of what the slow parade to Bethel was all about. Still, they smiled and waved back. At the festival, when water ran out, Catskill neighbors came by with overflowing cans and bottles. In nearby Monticello, an ecumenical gesture exemplified the spirit of the age: the ladies of the Jewish Community Center made thirty thousand free sandwiches for the hungry attendees. The food was distributed by the sisters of the Convent of St. Thomas.

Eight months later, Yasgur was still receiving mail addressed only to the Groovy Farmer at the Festival. He wandered through the places where for seventy-two hours music and the haze of pot smoke and declarations of Love had filled the hills. "Spring is coming," the Groovy Farmer observed, "and we're ready to start the plowing and planting. I don't see much difference this spring from last spring." He paused and corrected himself. In the process he set the tone for the decade to come. "However, nobody could get involved with half a million youngsters and be the same afterward as he was before."

CHAPTER 14

A MORE ECUMENICAL

APPROACH

No one can stare at the sun or death, says a Yiddish proverb. That may be why, all through the early sixties, the owners of *kuchaleyns* and bungalow colonies looked the other way as their aging clientele slowly diminished. Some of the longtime guests had passed away, some were too ill or infirm to travel. Others had retired to more benign climates. They were all irreplaceable. By the middle of the decade the children and grandchildren of the reliable summer folk had immersed themselves in New York professional and business life. When these young people thought of the little cabins it was with embarrassment or condescension. To them the Catskills were superannuated. Singles bars supplied more than enough candidates for the evening or the altar. Route 17 had no place in their plans. They were growing more familiar with the roads around Miami, Disneyland, Las Vegas, the Hamptons, the Jersey Shore.

By the end of the decade larger places started to go under, and in the early 1970s managers pointed to the headlines and openly argued that the great resorts must change or die. The evidence supported them. Picket lines had briefly but loudly ringed Grossinger's and the Concord in separate labor disputes with Local 343 of the Hotel, Restaurant and Bartenders Union. And in 1973, a catastrophic decision was handed down in New York State Supreme Court. The plaintiff was Antonio Morales; the defendant, the Concord Hotel. Morales had been the sparring partner of Doug Jones, then in training to fight Ernie Terrell for the World Boxing Association heavyweight title. The two men had sparred for three rounds before Morales retired to a hotel dressing room to change his clothes.

Fifteen minutes later the boxer was found lying on the floor unconscious. Apparently he had tripped over a outdoor bench that, according to his counsel, had no place in a dressing room. Morales had allegedly suffered a brain injury as a result of the fall. The jury of six men was told that he was presently confined to a wheelchair with no control over his bodily functions and no ability to testify. After only two days of deliberation they awarded the accident victim $1.75 million. The Court of Appeals upheld them. It was one of the most generous judgments in the history of New York State.

After that, fashions seemed to run against the Borscht Belt. Underweight was in, and the famous Catskill menus came to be regarded as unhealthy. The cinema replaced stage comedy and drama as the entertainment of choice. Recorded British groups, led by the Beatles, the Rolling Stones, and the Bee Gees, exerted a profound influence on style. Suddenly the old ethnic entertainers looked dowdy and irrelevant. Stand-up comedians grew as obsolete as radio. The country laughed at a different kind of humor. The sexual skirmishes of *Who's Afraid of Virginia Woolf?* and *Bob & Carol & Ted & Alice* earned record grosses. When guests hummed American songs, they were numbers composed in Nashville, Tennessee, instead of New York, New York. Hoteliers were forced to scramble for a diminishing vacation dollar, recalling the frantic days before World War I when owners gathered at the railroad station to shout their wares and revile their competitors.

Several solutions were put forward: a more ecumenical approach, special rates for business conventions, and the one that received the most heated debate, legalized gambling. "Look what it did for Las Vegas," argued one of the smaller and more impecunious owners. "It could turn the Mountains around overnight." One of his guests demurred: "We don't need the Catskills pointing upside down."

Alf Evers observes that although environmentalists and religious leaders opposed gambling casinos, "owners of the large Sullivan County hotels . . . testified to the effect that the old rural image of the Catskills was no longer valid and that a more modern one was needed for the region's economic salvation." Word was passed, funds were allocated, lobbying was initiated in Albany. The Flagler, its clientele severely diminished, was sold to a shady group of investors. They planned to call their place The Fountains of Rome and turn it into the Caesars Palace of the Mountains.

Less than two years later, anti-gambling organizations proved that they had some powerful connections of their own. Every time the issue of big-league casinos came up for a vote the legislation was blocked. The owners of The Fountains panicked and sold out, the place so abruptly abandoned that soiled dishes were left uncollected on the tables. In 1973, the Crystal Run School, which had been operating a center for the retarded in Middletown, New York, took over The Fountains of Rome and twenty-five acres of grounds.

Just outside of Livingstone Manor word went out that a temple would soon rise on a 1,400-acre site. This, it developed, was not a synagogue but a retreat for the Zen Studies Society. The Buddhists regarded their natural surroundings as something other than a place for romantic walks. William P. Johnstone, the treasurer, remarked, "We have a lot of wood on the land. Millions of trees badly need thinning out so that more sun and air can produce a really great forest for the next generation. Fifty acres a year of such thinning will provide our energy." Although the monastery had legally qualified for tax-free status, it remained on the local tax rolls. The spiritual leader, Eido Roshi, explained: "As newcomers to this small village we would like to establish good public relations." That they did. At first, local residents were wary and resentful; then the postmaster announced that upon consideration he found the Zen society "choice neighbors." His fellow citizens told a reporter that next to the summer home of Irving Berlin, the new monastery was the area's most important landmark.

Five miles away, two signs misled tourists. Atop a red-and-white guardhouse at the end of a back road, block letters told passersby: THIS IS IT! WELCOME. A few yards away, a contradictory placard warned, THESE PREMISES ARE FOR THE USE OF WALDEMERE GUESTS ONLY. ALL OTHERS ARE TRESPASSING AND SUBJECT TO ARREST.

Neither message was valid. Visitors were unwelcome, and the Waldemere did not exist. For fifty-two seasons the resort (I FOUND A HUSBAND AT THE WALDEMERE) had been operated by the Rosenthal family. After its close, Milton Cohen, a surviving relative, quietly sold the buildings and twenty-five surrounding acres to the Students International Meditation Society. A spokesman for the center said it would be used to promulgate the teachings of the Maharishi Mahesh Yogi, meditation counselor to the Beatles. Out of curiosity, Cohen took the society's orientation course. "So far," he testified, "it's relaxed and taken the tension out of me."

Tom Hust, of the Joseph Gersten Realty Company in Monticello, attributed the decline of the hotel industry to the increase of land values. Properties of one hundred or more acres were selling for $1,500 per acre, compared with $300 five years before. The land boom had been triggered by second-home developers, tapping the new money of young New York professionals. Few of them had Jewish affiliations.

Dan Berkowicz, director of New Hope, yet another facility for the retarded built on the grounds of an abandoned Liberty hotel, offered a realistic appraisal of the current real-estate situation. "If I were building," he said, "I wouldn't build a nightclub."

A More Ecumenical Approach

Irma Glass, of Landmark Real Estate in Monticello, grimly foresaw the end of the Borscht Belt. In addition to rising land values, she pointed out, concern with diets "had hurt the hotels because they traditionally catered to people who enjoyed gourmet foods, which are now an obsolete pastime." Just how obsolete could be seen in the scores of small places that had quietly gone bankrupt, their buildings left to fall apart in the sun. Some of those that had survived had strange new uses: Paul's in Swan Lake and Young's Gap in Liberty were places where narcotics addicts were sent to beat the heroin habit. As Glass saw it, "The old hotels are simply obsolete and lower rates for air travel have lessened the area's attractiveness, especially for young people." To her, the evidence clearly demonstrated that the Catskill resort business was "sick and decadent."

Early in the seventies two very different Catskill celebrities were laid to rest. In November 1972, after a long series of illnesses, Jennie Grossinger died of a stroke. The eighty-year-old had been recuperating in a ranch house called Joy Cottage, at the place that bore her name. She was buried beside the founding mother, Malke, who had died at about the same age back in 1952.

Jennie was recalled as the principal benefactor of a medical center in Tel Aviv and another in Liberty, New York, as a fundraiser for scores of local charities, as the classic Jewish mother figure, as a nonpareil hostess and lodestar of the resorts. In an unusually warm obituary, *The New York Times* said that she had brought a little farm "to the rank of flagship of the fleet of landlocked luxury liners anchored in the Catskills. . . . She ruled, with regal dignity, a domain larger than Princess Grace's Monaco. . . . For the guests, as many as 150,000 a year, Mrs. Grossinger was the voice of the recreational plantation. On Saturdays, after the lavish entertainment had bedazzled the viewers in the 1,700-seat auditorium, she would often take the stage and, in her quiet voice, thank the visitors for taking the trouble to come.

"Whether she was greeting guests who had endured the long trip up with the 'hackie' who had picked them up between Brooklyn and the Bronx, or such dignitaries as Governor Rockefeller or Senator Robert F. Kennedy, who came by chauffeured car, Mrs. Grossinger was the symbol that they were visiting a family, not merely an impersonal hostelry."

It was not true, as her competitors alleged, that Milton Blackstone had invented Jennie. He had simply merchandised the genuine article. Quentin Reynolds noted Mrs. Grossinger's unique amalgam of awe and confusion in the presence of the famous. One morning, said the journalist, she received a call from her son Paul, then general manager of the hotel. "Rocky just phoned," he informed her. "He's speaking at the Pines Hotel this afternoon and is landing at the airport in about an hour. He asked if he could stop in and see you. Remember how he liked those egg rolls last time he was here?"

"Egg rolls?" Jennie asked. "Rocky has been to my house a dozen times, and he never asked for egg rolls. And what do you mean he's landing at the airport in an hour? Where has he been? I saw him in the dining room last night."

Paul realized what was wrong. "I don't mean Rocky Marciano. I mean Nelson Rockefeller."

In a *New York Post* column, Jackie Robinson, a guest at the G since his days on the Brooklyn Dodgers, provided a glimpse of an uncommon gesture made in the fifties: "I was fortunate enough to be included among those greeting her on Ralph Edwards' 'This Is Your Life' television show. . . . As I stood in the wings awaiting my turn to be brought on, I watched the others before me as they were introduced. Each walked up to Jennie and embraced her to the applause of the studio audience.

"Now, this posed a special problem for me, as a Negro man appearing on a show honoring a white woman. I was well aware that the program was being viewed by millions of people all over the country, and though Jennie and I were friends, I wasn't at all certain of what her reaction would be. I knew that people sometimes felt and acted differently in public than they ordinarily would in private. So I was faced with a dilemma: should I continue in the pattern and greet Jennie with a kiss, or should I instead merely speak my piece, offer my hand and dispense with any embrace?

"I decided on the latter course. But as I walked out on the

stage, Jennie—not waiting for me to make the first gesture—turned to me, smiled delightedly and opened her arms wide. As I came to her, she threw her arms about me, and we embraced to thunderous applause from the studio audience."

At a town meeting, a rival owner asked, "What's going to happen to the G now that the J is gone?" Not a thing, he was told. People die. A legend endures. One of her friends unfolded a statement she had made a few years before. No public-relations adviser could have provided her phrasing: "You know, when I die, wherever I go, I hope there's a hotel there. And I hope they'll let me run it. I know I'll find a lot of my former guests and I'll remember what they liked to eat. And my mother will be there to do the cooking . . . and Papa . . . and Harry."

The following April, Max Yasgur, the gentle farmer who had become patron saint of the counterculture, died of a heart attack. The fifty-three-year-old had been on vacation in Florida, far from the mountainside where Aquarius came of age.

A wealth of symbols appeared in the seventies to represent the Catskill decline. None was more disturbing than the story of Milton Blackstone. In 1973, the great engineer of public consent was found in a seedy hotel on the West Side of Manhattan. Friends said that Blackstone had undergone a dramatic personality change. He was increasingly withdrawn, occasionally paranoid, and, at times, severely emaciated.

They had first remarked on his eccentric behavior some ten years before, when their "usually sharp-witted and intelligent colleague" began to converse in an irrational manner. The cause of deterioration was traced to a Dr. Max Jacobson. A friend had once sat in the physician's East Side waiting room while Blackstone received an injection. After the shot, he said, "you couldn't shut Milton up. He would rant and rave incessantly, jumping from one subject to another. It was impossible to discern any real information from his speech. Even when you could understand the topic he would go off into the ethereal.

"Then, a couple of hours later, we would go back to the hotel and all of a sudden he was like a man dying. He would shake from head to toe, lie in bed almost in a state of inertia, terribly depressed. I've heard Blackstone call this doctor at all hours and plead with him to let him come for a shot. He would plead like a baby pleads for milk. Sometimes he would visit the doctor twice a day."

The provider of injections was known to his list of celebrity clients as "Dr. Feelgood." Max Jacobson's treatments consisted of a combination of vitamins, hormones, and amphetamines, and the results were dramatic for a short period and catastrophic afterward. Eddie Fisher had been a patient, and on Blackstone's advice Jennie Grossinger had submitted to Dr. Feelgood's ministrations until her personal physician, William M. Hitzig, intervened. Dr. Hitzig had been wary since the day he was called in to treat Blackstone. "I found him in a state of collapse," said Hitzig. "He couldn't stand up. He had no blood pressure. I tried to convince him to give up the injections. I succeeded in convincing Jennie . . . but Milton Blackstone was very frightened about not getting the stuff."

Fisher refers to himself in his memoirs as Dr. Feelgood's "Pavlovian dog." At the time Blackstone was being so heavily drugged, the singer said, "Max was giving me as many as three or four shots to keep me going during the day and a massive dose of tranquillizers to help me sleep at night." Debbie Reynolds, Fisher's wife during that period, remembered that the pockets of Jacobson's "dirty, rumpled old dark suit were always bulging with little vials and needles. . . . If you had an earache, he'd give you a shot in the ear. If you had a cold in your nose, he'd give you a shot in the nose. Wherever it hurt, he'd stick the needle.

"Thirty years ago few if any people knew that amphetamines were addictive and dangerous. Nor did anyone question why a twenty-six-year-old man needed a shot every time he went onstage.

"Everybody swore by [Jacobson]. His New York waiting room was filled with Broadway stars, politicians, and socialites who had become dependent on his 'miracle' drugs. President John F. Kennedy took him to the Summit with Khrushchev in Vienna in 1961." Not until Milton Blackstone had landed on the Bowery did Fisher try to end his years of drug dependency.

Drs. Schweitzer and Strangelove

"Where that kind of will power came from I don't know," he says. "Maybe it was left over from the days when I let nothing stand in the way of my becoming a successful singer. Maybe it came from that part of my personality that knuckled under to authority and I obeyed without question the commands of men like Max Jacobson and Milton Blackstone." Fisher backslid several times before he was clean of substance abuse. There were always pushers, he says, "happy, for the right price, to supply my needs. But some instinct, some lucky intuition, warned me to be careful of the formula I got from one of them. I had a sample analyzed not once but twice and then called Max Jacobson to ask his advice. He came to my bungalow at the Beverly Hills Hotel and I showed him the analysis. A look of horror crossed his face. 'There's enough cyanide in there to kill a horse,' he said. Then, his head lowered and his hands covering his face, he murmured, 'Oh, God, what have I done?'

"Those were Max Jacobson's last words to me. I never saw him again. In 1975, a two-and-a-half-year investigation by New York State medical authorities culminated in the loss of his license to practice medicine on the grounds of 'unprofessional conduct.' A broken and humiliated man, he died three years later."

Several months after Jacobson was prosecuted, Fisher prepared to make a comeback at the Concord. On the afternoon of his first performance Fisher went for a dip in the hotel pool. Only a few of the guests recognized the frail figure with dyed hair and a new face-lift. A member of the audience reported that opening-night ticket holders "watched the fifties pop star as if he were a tightrope walker with vertigo—fascinated, waiting for the fall. It never came. Instead, after he had belted out a few songs in a strong baritone, the older patrons leaped to their feet applauding."

One of the younger attendees also got to her feet. Fisher's daughter Carrie, three years away from her role as Princess Leia in the *Star Wars* films, had not seen her father in seven months. She appeared in the audience unannounced, and when he saw her, Fisher pulled Carrie onstage for a duet. He held the microphone close, toned down his voice, and crooned the Rodgers and Hammerstein tune "If I Loved You." Afterward a Concord patron asked for his autograph and offered him empathy. "I've been married four times myself," she said. Another looked at the father and daughter and said, "I feel like crying." Some of the tears were for the damaged man; some were for herself and for a time and place that were rapidly slipping by.

If there was to be no official gambling in the Catskills, if real-estate speculators were once again wandering the Mountains, if Jews were finding fewer and fewer reasons to come to Sullivan County, the resorts still had one more resource to draw upon. "It's remarkable the vistas that are open to us with business conventions," maintained Charles Slutsky, owner of the Nevele. Howard L. Bern, director of sales at Grossinger's, readily allowed that "we would not be in business today without conventions."

Emptied of vacationers, the immense auditoriums and accommodations enticed a new kind of visitor: the salesmen and managers of such *goyische* concerns as General Electric, Eastman Kodak, Buick, Hunt Foods, and the Macmillan Company. James Murray, director of Grossinger's convention sales, worked out a routine: "We give these groups a complimentary cocktail party, a full daytime program, and a holiday with a real resort spirit. And since the group is isolated here, the entertainment is geared to complement the business situation, not compete with it." In short, executives and employees were likely to see an industrial show centered around the product, not a Vegas singer or an insult comedian.

Some aspects were unchanged. Hotels catering to business and industry continued to stress the unlimited quantities of food, the free meeting rooms (the Grossinger playhouse was renamed Convention Hall), the golf courses and swimming pools. To avoid discomfort, tipping was calculated beforehand and presented in the company's master bill. Until the inflation of the late seventies, gratuities totaled some $2.40 per person: $1 for the waiter, 50 cents for the busboy, 50 cents for the chambermaid, 25 cents for the captain, and 15 cents for the maître d'.

Reduced group rates gave the hotels a smaller income, but the loss was supplemented with a lively bar business; Jewish

clientele had always been better feeders than drinkers. The owners were further gratified to learn that a great deal of money was
being spent at the gift and sundry shops by conventioneers, many
of them from out of state.

The main difficulty came in enticing major companies to
the Catskills. Jewish dietary restrictions forbade the serving of
pork and the mixing of milk with meat. Borscht Belt resorts
circumvented the law by offering a hideous substitute for bacon
made with deep-fried and highly spiced calves' liver; ersatz milk
was concocted of soy beans and chemicals. The Gentile wariness
of kosher cuisine was "an added hurdle," Murray conceded.
"But when we point out the variety of our meals and the fact
that we can serve such foods as ravioli and Irish stew within the
dietary laws, we rarely have any objections to the cuisine." Slutsky agreed: "People are cosmopolitan enough nowadays so that
they're used to buying food in a delicatessen. And with the substitutes now for cream, there is little we cannot provide them in
the way of food."

A *Times* financial reporter was assigned to cover the conventions. As he watched a typical meeting, Norge dealers were
given lectures and literature about their company's new refrigerators. They were then released to sport in the March air. It
seemed a perfect locale, and yet, the *Times* was compelled to
say, "with all the gains being made in attracting conventions to
the Catskill hotels, there is still one item that is offered to many
of their regular weekend guests but eliminated from the facilities
for midweek business groups."

No host could provide it, no resort would have dared. Not
to an assemblage of staid conventioneers. The absent item was
romance. Once upon a summer, the account went on, "it was a
staple at these resorts where group tables in the dining rooms
and a variety of social activities bring boy and girl in constant
contact. For businessmen, however, the purpose of the trip is
the meeting or convention." The writer added wistfully, "Especially when the little woman is nearby at the pool or playing
bridge."

In fact, with all the celebrated facilities, ten-course meals
and unending list of entertainers, the most urgent appeal of the

Mountains had always been romance. It sustained the hotels during depressions and wars, it attracted new generations and gave the resorts their reputations as forecourts of sexual adventure and familial happiness. When romance vanished from the Mountains, the Catskills faded from the public mind.

The mainstay of resort labor, college students, grew increasingly scarce in the seventies. The war in Vietnam, the rise in social conscience, a heightened awareness of black and Hispanic demands—all contributed to a new disdain for the typical guest. Contemporary accounts show that the students who accepted jobs in the Mountains did so with discomfort and resentment. Rose Meadoff, a Monticello employment agent, had studied the styles of summer employees for forty years. There was a time, she said, when an employer could expect gratitude if not subservience. That was before the youthquake of the seventies. Now Mrs. Meadoff noticed several bothersome changes. For one thing, job seekers drove up in their own cars; for another, the boys wore their hair at shoulder length. "I ask them," she said, "what is more important, your hair or the possibility of making good money to pay for your education? And I tell them about the thousands of kids I placed who went on to become doctors, lawyers, and teachers."

In most instances, the applicants grudgingly compromised their political statements and their aesthetics for eight weeks of work. They trimmed their hair and shaved off their beards. That was as much as they were willing to yield. Marijuana was smoked openly and bookshelves in the staff rooms customarily housed Tom Wolfe's *The Electric Kool-Aid Acid Test* and R. D. Laing's *The Politics of Experience.* Below-stairs discussions revealed a withering contempt for guests. It far exceeded the usual irreverence of waiters who feel above their stations.

Gretchen Reise, a graduate of Bucknell University, earned graduate-school tuition at Grossinger's. The work made her feel "queasy," she claimed, because "by and large, the [people] I serve represent everything that my generation is against."

In most hotels the dishwashers and laborers were black or

Drs. Schweitzer and Strangelove

Hispanic. Owners referred to them generically as "bimmies," a word of disputed lineage. Milton Kutsher believes that it once referred to Bimini Island, from which many of the black helpers emigrated in the twenties. Catskill historian Dorothy Shapiro feels that it may be a Yiddishization of the English word "bums." In any case, the bimmies were housed apart from the temporary summer staff. It was not a tactic designed to win the hearts of young progressives. Nevertheless, service still meant money, and money came from tips. To get them, undergraduates not only avoided confrontations, they invented new selves.

David Greenburg, who had a full scholarship at Williams College, liked to convey the impression of a poor Jewish boy in search of tuition. Others invented stories of deceased fathers and hospitalized mothers, or made much of their ethnicity. George Turbow, a busboy from Jacksonville, Florida, bought a religious pendant. "I never wore a mezuzah before," he said. "I got it just for the job."

Energy and ingenuity were no guarantees of success. The resorts were struggling and most of the older guests were retirees on fixed incomes. A waitress at Grossinger's complained, "One woman took me aside and handed me something, saying, 'This is for you, darling.' You know what she gave me for a week's meals? Two inflatable clothes hangers." Richard Lewis, who was on his way to the University of Virginia Medical School, spoke about Delmar's suffocating atmosphere. It was true that no one asked him to dance with the homely girls. That was because there were no homely girls. There were no girls at all. Some one hundred Delmar guests, most of them in their sixties and seventies, rarely appeared on the dance floor or at poolside. They were served by three waiters and three busboys. Once the dinner meal was cleared away, there was nothing to do. "We've bought a cribbage set," one of the waiters griped. "That's how bad things are."

Those in search of livelier diversions went off to the little towns along with their fellow students. "You've got to get away," said a waitress from Stevensville. She and her friends usually headed for the Monticello Raceway. After the last race they haunted the bars. Most got to sleep at 4 a.m., and they were up at seven in time to serve breakfast. "We do our sleeping in shifts between meals," said a Grossinger's bellhop.

A waiter from Cornell confessed that most evenings he and his colleagues would smoke some grass, then "get drunk and rap all night long." A young feminist, in her junior year at the University of Buffalo, showed how far the Catskills had come since the randy days of Don José from Far Rockaway. The waitress was attracted to the coeducational facilities because "girls live with boys like friends and not like sexual objects." Maddie Kutsher had grown up at her parents' resort. The University of Pennsylvania junior offered a brief autobiography that summarized it all: "A few years ago my mother was always encouraging me to go out with this or that employee. Now she wants me to go away."

All four elements are part of Catskill history: earth, water, air, and fire. Since the end of World War II, more than one hundred hotels, motels, boardinghouses, camps, and private homes nearby have been destroyed by conflagrations, frequently under suspicious circumstances. The fires may have resulted from carelessness, from the mischief of vandals, from spite toward a neighbor or the desire to collect on an insurance policy. In each instance, said the *Times*, the flames were "wrapped in the enigma of lonely forests where no one can see and in small towns where no one will tell."

Whoever profited from the burning of buildings, the towns themselves sustained heavy losses. Fleischmanns was a depressing example. Every summer the community's population used to rise from 500 to 10,000, mostly German, Austrian, and Hungarian Jews. By the late seventies, the hotels they had patronized were dismantled or demoralized. Plaster was cracked and grounds flecked with paint peeling off the exterior walls. In the seventies, fewer than 1,000 vacationers patronized the area. The permanent residents of Fleischmanns—particularly the young— were bored and restless. Some of them were said to set fire to buildings simply to watch the red sparks against the night sky.

Drs. Schweitzer and Strangelove

A few volunteer firemen were rumored to ignite old structures in order to have something to do on a slow weekend.

"It is a peculiar thing about rural areas," said Alton M. Weiss, editor of *The Catskill Mountain News* in Margaretville. "You'll get a teenager with a couple of beers in him on a Saturday night, maybe he's not too sharp to begin with, maybe his parents don't really know as much about him as they should. And so he does it. It's a kind of expression of rural hell-raising and boredom and it just sort of happens in remote areas."

One of the hotel owners watched a competitor's place burn to the ground. "In the crowd of onlookers," he said, "I heard people whispering a phrase I hadn't heard in years: 'Jewish lightning.' All the years we put money in the locals' pockets because of the business we brought in, all the good times—they were forgotten now that the resorts were in trouble. Every time the sirens started, the thought was, The Jews are playing with matches in order to collect money from the insurers, even when they knew some delinquent had set the blaze. I had a feeling we were going back to the anti-Hebrew crusade. Except that there were fewer and fewer Hebrew businesses to crusade against."

There were fewer businesses of all kinds. John Hocko, who had grown up in Fleischmanns, spoke of the time "when there were four butchers, three barber shops, a bowling alley, three produce markets, three bakeries, an A&P, three doctors and as many dentists." He calculated the differences as the seventies ended: "We've got no butchers, no barbers, no bowling alley, just one bakery, no A&P, no dentists and only one doctor."

More remarkable contrasts could be seen a few towns south. In Kerhonkson, a one-legged tap dancer named Peg Leg Bates had built a place he advertised as "one of the finest black resorts in the country." Thirty years before, white hotels had allowed him to entertain but not to stay overnight. The Peg Leg Bates Country Club was his answer. He greeted his guests with a message every Saturday morning: "While you're here you are secure, you are protected. You will not be robbed; you will not be mugged." Posted signs read: WE HAVE KARATE EXPERTS ON

THE PREMISES. Bates counted the variety of patrons on his fingers: "I get nurses, cooks, maids, chauffeurs, the working people. The food is good, the show is good; it's nice and quiet and they get respect."

At the Pines a comedian named Mal Z. Lawrence wrought a few laughs out of changing times. "Years ago," he recalled, "you used to sit down for dinner, your waiter was Mendel, Yankel, Yussel, Moishe. Now it's Pablo, Xavier, Chico, Julio. Julio says to you, 'Hey, man, you want a kipper, man? You want some horseradish, man?' " He did not point out that Hispanics were increasingly on the receiving end, although most of them bypassed the Jewish hotels for the "Spanish Alps" in Plattekill, not far from Ellenville. A roadside billboard listed some twenty villas catering to Spanish-speaking customers.

They were proof that the Catskills could still conform to any ethnic ideal. To the early settlers the Mountains had signified primal wilderness before the predations of mankind; to nineteenth- and early-twentieth-century immigrants they were Europe redivivus; to modern Hispanics, the sunny slopes and fields magically evoked the Caribbean. Ismael (Shorty) Martínez, owner of the Sunny Acres Hotel-Motel, voiced the philosophy of his visitors: "Why do we have to go back to Puerto Rico when we have the island right here?" A guest of Las Villas, Ralph Jiminez, said the scene "reminds me of Puerto Rico with its easygoing life, friendly people, and good treatment. And we don't get gypped like in the Latin clubs in the city."

Villas ranged in size from the San Juan, little more than an oversized candy store, to the Villa Nueva, a baronial manor that would not have been out of place in Madrid. The Hispanic patrons seemed to bear no resemblance to the Jews who had preceded them. They ate an entirely different cuisine, dressed in more vibrant colors, and kept unaccustomed hours. On weekends they slept in until early afternoon. At about 2 p.m. Latin bands filled the dance halls and the fields with merengues, chachas, and rumbas. The musicians took a break for dinner and then returned until the 3 a.m. closing. One summer evening as Pedro Guardarramas watched fifty couples dancing to the music of El Chino and his Tropical Combo in his resort, he observed,

"I don't try to make money off these people. They are mostly so very poor. But look, they are having a good time and that's what counts." At that moment it was as if nothing had changed in three generations. Selig Grossinger, contemplating the weary refugees from city sweatshops, had said almost exactly the same thing back in 1915.

CHAPTER 15

VICHYSSOISE IN CATSKILLAND

Part of Liberty's Business Section, Liberty, N. Y.

The anecdotes differ; the morals are identical. Having changed his name and his religion, a former Jew finds himself at dinner with old-line *goyim*. All goes well until the hostess serves baked ham. Horrified, he blurts out the name of forbidden pig meat in Yiddish: "*Hozzer! Oy, vay—*" As the other guests glare at him, he attempts to recoup: "—whatever *that* means."

A sinner sobs the truth to his rabbi: he has just eaten shrimps wrapped in bacon. "Very well," the rabbi tells him. "Just don't do it again. And stop feeling so bad. After all, it was just this once." The confessor keeps on weeping. "You don't understand, rabbi. I'm crying because I liked it."

In the eighties life imitated lampoon. The undesirable sobriquets Borscht Belt, Derma Road, and Sour Cream Sierras clung to the resorts like bills glued to the sides of abandoned buildings. Some of the owners argued for a full embrace of the nicknames. "What's wrong with Borscht Belt?" inquired one. "Okay, so it's not flattering, but at least people know where it is." He was told to look at the calendar. This was not 1950, a colleague informed him. The world had changed and so had the guests. "And in this day and age the last thing they want are reminders of gluttons and greenhorns."

An owner of the Raleigh got the message. Asked about the Catskills' most famous dish, George Gilbert loftily replied, "Between you and me, I've never tasted it." Jerry Erhlich, president of the Pines Hotel, took an assimilationist approach: "We don't even use the word 'borscht' on our menu. We just call it beet soup, because otherwise people wouldn't know what it was." Elaine Etess, Jennie Grossinger's granddaughter, assured her patrons that although "blintzes and borscht are most popular, our cuisine is not just Jewish. We have the most incredible Chinese food."

For his part, Milton Kutsher, of Kutsher's Country Club, termed borscht "a relic of the antediluvian age." A guest at his table agreed. Selma Glickburg said that she ordered beet soup only because iced tea and coffee are "too dull." By her reckoning, "borscht went out about twenty-five years ago. We're into vichyssoise and pasta primavera."

The Nevele had operated a strictly kosher kitchen for more than seventy years. In the eighties, substitutes gave way to the real *treyf*—such forbidden foods as bacon in the morning and shrimp cocktails at dinner. The Concord adhered to its kosher cuisine, but accommodated its newest group of tourists by providing Japanese translations of the menu.

And profits still receded. Faced with the unthinkable, competitors declared a truce and pooled their resources for a television commercial. The thirty-second spot exhibited the requisite waterfall, bathing beauty, and couple strolling in the woods. It also offered an eighties name and orthography for the Mountains, concocted by a New York City publicity agency. "Come to the country," a voice purled, "where the greens are greener.

Where the blues are bluer. The country that has fresh air and fresh food. Whose stars are really big stars. That's not far, and not foreign. CatskilLand."

Ehrlich contributed $200,000 to broadcast the advertisement. His critics were given a terse rationale: "We're trying to break an image problem. We're not 100 percent catering to just a Jewish clientele anymore. It's more international. There are Chinese, Japanese, Polish, Irish. We do keep a kosher hotel. But that's about it."

The strategy was effective. At the staid Stevensville, where a sign forbade smoking on the Sabbath, conventions of Irish, Polish, and black groups called for reservations, along with members of the Women's Christian Temperance Union. To head off complaints about Jewish strictures against the mixing of meat and milk, the maître d' prepared a new policy: Ignorance is kosher. "I tell them to hide the butter under the plate," he said. "If I don't see it, I can't do or say anything, right?"

A Canadian poet named Abraham Klein composed some doggerel on this phenomenon:

> Now we will suffer loss of memory;
> We will forget the tongue our mothers knew;
> We will munch ham, and guzzle milk thereto,
> And this on hallowed fast-days, purposely. . . .
> To Gentile parties we will proudly go;
> And Christians, anecdoting us, will say:
> "Mr. and Mrs. Klein—the Jews, you know. . . ."

Some culinary traditions were permanent in CatskilLand: breakfast at the Concord still offered a choice of five herring styles, shmaltz, baked, fried, pickled with cream sauce, and pickled with onion rings. If a waiter saw any indecision over the three dinner entrees, he understood it as a signal to bring all of them. Milton Kutsher was sanguine about the current Catskill situation. "You'll see," he predicted. "Borscht will recede. This will just be a nice place to vacation. When they talk of the area, they'll talk with respect. When they pay enough, people have respect."

That kind of confidence was growing rare. Only twelve large resorts lasted into the eighties, and some of them were secretly troubled. The smaller places were in even deeper waters. In the fall of 1983, a food inspector found shocking evidence in the kitchen of Tessler's Resort Hotel: six packages of boneless pork loin and five packages of pork loin slices. Rabbi Scholem Rubin, director of kosher law enforcement for the New York State Agriculture Department, judged the case particularly heinous because it had occurred during the Jewish High Holy Days. "We've never had a case like this in sixty years," he testified. Then again, there had been no times like these in sixty years.

The news that everyone had been dreading was confirmed in 1985. Grossinger's was to be sold to developers. Hidden details began to emerge. The centerpiece of the Jewish resorts had been losing money—a projected $1.8 million in 1985. Occupancy rates had fallen below 50 percent. Family members distributed a memo assuring employees that their jobs were secure. A twenty-year veteran threw it in the wastebasket. "A nice gesture," he said, "but it doesn't fool me. All you have to do is take a look at the blueprint for the new place. Right away a death warrant." The reborn Grossinger's, a folder promised, would have as many as 2,000 town houses, condominiums to be built alongside the 25-acre lake and the 27-hole golf course. Favorite buildings, among them the Grossinger playhouse, were superfluous. They would be razed. Staffers needed no more facts; they started typing up their resumés.

When the buildings tumbled down in October 1986, Eddie Fisher was the only headliner in attendance. He had gone far since the Eddie Cantor night, too far, and something drew him back to the place where it had all begun some thirty years before. The former pride of the Catskills was to recall that his son Todd "had become a Born Again Christian, and, very sincere and earnest in his beliefs, he tried to convert me. I admired the change they had brought to his life. I was proud of his spirit and strength of character. But I was born a Jew and a Jew I would die."

Others were called upon to reminisce about the G, and they

conjured up an amalgam of Valhalla and the Stage Delicatessen. To Geri Simon of Brooklyn, "going to Grossinger's was the height, the epitome of everything. There were swingers here in those days. My girlfriend and I used to close the bar at 3 a.m." For her the good times had reached their peak in 1962, when the apotheosis of Catskill hospitality issued a private invitation. Imagine, said Ms. Simon, "here was Jennie Grossinger, a world-renowned, asking me to a cocktail party."

Jules Fischer, a Manhattan dentist, thought back to the fifties, when romances began on the Olympic-size outdoor ice-skating rink. "I used to come up eighteen weekends in a row during the skating season," he said. "I used to skate all day and dance all night. The dining room was seven-eighths singles. I had some beautiful times here."

Employees were overcome with sentiment. The entertainment director, Jerry Weiss, had started as a night clerk in 1943. "I feel I'm losing part of my family," he said, gazing at photographs of himself with hundreds of headliners, from Jayne Mansfield in a leopard-skin bikini to Lena Horne in a fur-trimmed gown.

Ida Sherrin had already retired once as an elementary-school teacher. She was about to bow out again, this time as Grossinger's last mistress of Guest Relations. The place had been sold, but the *shadchen* was still on assignment. "You can meet people anywhere, even in the subway," she advised a lonely visitor. "When you're waiting for the subway, try to stand near a man who appeals to you."

Only Bill Goldwasser, who had risen from busboy in 1943 to head of the dining room in the eighties, refused to look back. "People want everything to remain the status quo, exactly as it was," he commented. "They say, 'Can I sit with Georgia the waitress?' I say, 'I'm sorry. Georgia passed away. She has a right to die.' "

In October 1986, a small crowd watched Grossinger's exercise the same right. A seventy-six-year-old woman, up for the day to pay her last respects to Jennie, picked over the wreckage of the resort's cherished old playhouse. She shook her head. "That I should live to see this day. Yuppies at Grossinger's. Well, nothing lasts forever." She made a grand gesture to the surrounding hills. "Pretty soon, we'll all be gone, one by one, the people and the places."

Less than two years later, Jerry Lewis received a $50,000 payment for entertaining at Brown's, the place where he and his father had tummeled, the resort that for thirty years had used his profile on their billboards. The check was returned for insufficient funds. On July 19 Brown's filed for bankruptcy under the provisions of Chapter 11. Once more, end-of-an-era conversations could be heard all over the Mountains.

There would always be a few holdouts who refused to join the mourning line. Historian Alf Evers had lived in the area for most of the century, and he often amused himself by imagining a latter-day Rip Van Winkle closing his eyes in 1940 and awakening in 1980. To be sure, Rip "might well have been shocked to see that the once great Catskill Mountain Hotels . . . had been torn down or burned. He would have noticed smaller hotels and boarding houses standing empty and uncared for while they awaited collapse or destruction by vandals." But it would not have made the sleeper despair, not if he knew the territory. "The Catskills have taken much punishment from land speculators, absentee landlords, tanlords, quarry men, charcoal makers, and others. After each assault the mountains have had enough vitality left to bounce back and become covered again with healthy living things."

And in the mid-eighties the Jews did make one last effort to bounce back. They started by turning bungalow colonies into cooperatives. Some of the new owners were in their sixties and seventies, bored with summers in the Sun Belt. CatskilLand had no appeal for them; they were out to recapture the past. They did everything they could to restore the reassuring composition of cottages set around a common yard and shaded by stately maples and pines. They refurbished the casinos and tried to bring back the old music and games. In the late eighties visitors could hear the familiar click of mah-jongg tiles and the shuffle of pinochle cards. On sunny afternoons, long shadows fell across the repainted signs of Green Acres, Breezy Corners, Sunshine Cottages. No yuppies could be found here, no squash courts, no sounds of Johnny Mathis or computer-dating services. Gray power had summoned up the aura of the forties: early Sinatra records, salamis hanging from the ceiling, married couples, and family jokes. On certain nights one could almost hear President Roosevelt giving a fireside speech.

For most buyers, said Paula Yeager, a Liberty real-estate agent, "there's a sentimental value besides the land value. They all seem to feel like they're coming back home." Henry Dyzenhaus was illustrative. He and eighteen friends had bought the Green Acres bungalow colony near Liberty in 1981. By turning it into a series of co-ops, they solved the dilemma of where to stay for July and August.

"We used to come to the Catskills with our children," he said. "And we rented a bungalow. Then we went to the Raleigh and Grossinger's and Brown's. Then we decided to come for a little longer—the whole summer."

To maintain Green Acres, a five-member committee oversaw the operation of the bungalow colony and set annual maintenance fees, usually less than $500. Some owners renovated bathrooms or added mirrored closets, but no one had the heart to replace the pine wainscoting on the walls. Flowers decorated every yard; Dyzenhaus himself grew marigolds, petunias, and dill in a white-painted rowboat set in the grass near his front door. Green Acres' swimming pool went unused. Nearly all the residents were retirees, content to sit and chat in lawn chairs.

Their conversations were flavored with Yiddish, another reminder of vanished times and places. At Green Acres, as in other resuscitated colonies, the majority of investors were Polish survivors of the Holocaust. Under the tan and freckles their arms bore the blue identification numbers tattooed in concentration camps. This common grief, said Dyzenhaus, somehow "makes it easier." The Germans had taken their relations, said Israel Korman, another co-op owner, "so this became a family."

Some ten miles away, at Lansman's Bungalow Colony in Woodbourne, a different generation was at play. Eighty-five families were summering on its ninety-seven acres. Little boys and girls ran across the grounds and a line of players waited for their allotted hours on the tennis courts. Gas-fired grills were incorporated into the landscape; a dozen living rooms were lit with the fluorescent glow of videogames. Martin Friedman, president of the co-op's board of directors, advised a visitor to disregard the incorporated title. We're Lansman's, he said, but "we don't consider ourselves a bungalow colony anymore. We call ourselves a summer resort."

In reliable Catskill fashion, comedians sent the first signals of a Jewish return. "You can't miss Woodbourne," said Mal Z. Lawrence. "There's a giant crocheted yarmulke hovering over it with a giant bobby pin in the back. You get great reception on your Walkman." Woodbourne was a central source for comedians. At 9 p.m., before the end of the Saturday-night Sabbath, the main street was silent and empty. One hour later, hundreds of the modern Orthodox and Hasidim crowded into the town's small business center. Every shop was open, hawking religious articles, yarmulkes, fringes, and T-shirt iron-ons that said "Torah—It's the Real Thing." One weekend at the Woodbourne, theater patrons were offered a first-run Hollywood feature on Saturday evening, followed by a midnight show of Jewish singers. On Sunday the center held a rally for Shmuel Pressburger, rival of Teddy Kollek for the mayoralty of Jerusalem.

In Loch Sheldrake, the site of the Hotel Evans was renamed Vacation Village, a complex of attached town houses and separate homes. Rozzi and George Bornstein owned one of the three-story A-frames, and each summer they came east from Chicago to revive memories of their Bronx childhoods. "You go into South Fallsburgh," said Rozzi, "challah bread from Williamsburg, cakes from Borough Park, appetizers from Coney Island. And each year it gets bigger. Where else in the world can you buy Jewish *sfarim* [books] at four o'clock in the morning, and charge it on MasterCard?"

At the Hasidic bungalow colony of Camp Tiferes, time seemed to flow in two directions, like the Hudson River. Although the conveniences of cars and color television sets were in evidence, the husbands wearily arrived from the city on Thursday night and returned to work on Sunday, keeping the ancient hours of the Sabbath. For four hours every day Rabbi Mordechai Perl drilled seventeen children in the lessons of the Talmud.

The ceiling fan was inadequate and the conditions were crowded, not at all what Perl was used to in Brooklyn. But he was philosophical in the manner of countless predecessors: "Life in the bungalow—we do it for the kids."

Terry Fuchs, the mother of five small children, was the eternal Catskill wife as she explained that "the husbands, most of them, don't like it here. There's two rooms, when they're used to five or six or seven. For the wives it's an easier life. There is less housekeeping, and when you don't have your husband here, you don't have to cook as much."

Within the sound of her voice, a blue bookmobile was making its rounds, driven by a librarian named Avram Chaim Young. He followed a ten-year-old trying to pounce on a frog. Young offered the boy a copy of *Naughty Yitzchak Saul*, the story of a rabbi's son who learns to appreciate his fellow creatures. "From then on," read the moral, Yitzchak Saul "spent all his time learning Torah and doing mitzvahs, and, what is more, he loved learning Torah out in the courtyard surrounded by the animals."

At the Moonlight colony, run by Orthodox families, a salesman whose vanity plates read KINGSHOE unloaded a van of child-size Keds sneakers. He assured his young customers that he would make weekly stops through Labor Day. Dave the Pickle Man was the next to drive up.

Older residents found that the new Jews were still coming from the East but moving directly to the right. Morris and Ruth Franzel of Brooklyn had spent twenty-five of the last thirty summers at Kaufman's Bungalow Colony, increasingly occupied by the elderly. The seventy-seven-year-old Morris sat on his porch and reminisced: "When the religious people came along, they kicked us out, in a manner of speaking. They told us they were religious and if we could abide by their rules we could stay, but we're in the Reform movement." He gestured to his graying neighbors and added sardonically, "So, we looked around until we found this home of the aged."

The conservative tide rose with the increasing presence of Hasids. The roots of their belief, like their wardrobes, reached back to the mysticism that had swept Polish Jewry in the nineteenth century. These unworldly Jews were in the Catskills but not of them, fenced off in their own colonies. On any day but the Sabbath they could be observed, talking among themselves, using the public telephones, shopping at the kosher butcher shops, driving their buses to jobs in Manhattan, where they owned discount appliance stores and worked in the jewelry district. The one place they could not be found was on the tax rolls. To visitors the Hasids' Old World characteristics, the beards, high black hats, and alpaca coats, made them seem charming ghosts materialized from the stories of Isaac Bashevis Singer. The natives had less romantic notions. Members of the sect were as hermetic as any shtetl dweller, and despite their piety and tidiness, they were regarded even by other Jews as an unwelcome sight. "It hurts us as year-round residents," complained Walter Klein, a baker at Katz's bakery in Liberty. "They should have to pay their fair share of fire and police costs. . . . There's a lot of resentment about this among year-round residents. They put a school in, call it a yeshiva, and it's off the tax roll."

"The trouble with the Hasids," agreed one of his colleagues, "is that there's no way of knowing who they really are. To them, we're the outsiders. We resent them and they resent us. This is not the way of the Jews, not in the Mountains."

This was a simple denial of history. Dislike of newcomers was part of the great Catskill tradition. The Ashkenazi—the German Jews—had resentfully watched the arrival of their Eastern European brethren during the epoch of the pogroms. Those people of the Pale, once they were acclimated, looked down at the new arrivals, dizzy from steerage and sweatshops and the city itself. And they in turn persuaded themselves that they were superior to fugitives from the Holocaust. In time each found a place in the community. The Hasids seemed the least miscible Jews of all, and yet there was hope. Each weekend some of them contrived to meet with their neighbors, not at the synagogue, but, of all places, on the athletic fields.

Every Sunday, bungalow colonies sent out teams to face each other. The OBBL (Orthodox Bungalow Baseball League— even though the game played was softball) had grown from five teams in the seventies to five divisions in the eighties. Each division had thirty-eight teams and five hundred members, among them some forty Hasidim. Players ranged in age from sixteen to over sixty, and they came from as far away as California and Australia. The sunshine athletes, mostly from New York City, included a Catskill radio personality who called himself Country Yossi; William Rapfogel, a director of the American Jewish Congress; Democratic New York State Assemblyman Sheldon Silver from the Lower East Side; and Samuel Friedman, an insurance executive and author of scholarly books on the Talmud.

The Hasidic players, religious fringes tucked into their pockets, *payes* bulging under their baseball caps, slid into second base and pursued ground balls with the same vigor they applied to their religious studies and their vocations. "To them," observed the league commissioner, Jerry Schreck, "sports are both a form of relaxation and a form of competition." The same could have been said of any softball competitors in any state on any Sunday afternoon. The assimilation of American style was further emphasized by Silver's happy recollection of the league's first summer, when he played on the championship team. For over a decade the politician had vainly tried to repeat the performance. "It's been the same problem as the Mets," he said. "No hitting."

Yet certain aspects and events belonged exclusively to the people of CatskilLand. Shreck remembered that one former player was also a member of the American Arbitration Association. "He served as an arbitrator for some knotty softball questions, and they are sometimes more knotty than Talmudic thought." In one contest, when a mentally handicapped player hit a pop-up, the infielders exchanged glances and let the ball drop. As they scrambled for it in a great display of ineptitude, the runner puffed around third and came home. The players later said that they often allowed the handicapped player a home run in order to bolster his spirits.

What kind of baseball is that? someone asked. The pitcher's definition was soon repeated all over the Catskills. "It's Jewish baseball," he said.

A   C H A N G E   O F   S E A S O N

Of all nineteenth-century prophets, Heinrich Heine had the clearest vision of what would happen to his fellow *Juden*. "If Europe were to become a prison," he said, "America would still present a loophole of escape . . . then may the Jews take their harps down from the willows and sit close by the Hudson to sing their sweet songs of praise and chant the lays of Zion."

The escapees did come in wave upon wave, generation after generation, first from Europe's walled ghettos, then from its shtetls and minimum-security prisons, and ultimately from its death rows and gulags, to sit close by the river. Their haven was called the Catskills, a region that worked its way into the Jewish experience before the Jews took it into the American mainstream. Each generation shared two traits with its predecessors: a religion and a desire for something more than sanctuary. Above all else the immigrants wanted acceptance. The price was a piece of themselves, and of Eden.

It is the nation's oldest story. Pioneers find a territory congenial to their beliefs. In time, the land and the people change each other. In the end, neither would be recognizable to the original settlers. Today remnants of Old World Jewry can still be found in the rapidly developing Mountain communities, a Hasidic organization here, a resuscitated bungalow colony there. At least for now it is possible to stay at the Concord and visit the synagogue just off the main lobby. Kosher sections are in many Catskill supermarkets; Jewish charities continue unabated; the Shapiros and Levines and Resniks are leaders and legislators in the townships. But the old ethos is dispersed, swept away by the demands and ironies of success. What survives is what always endures in the history of the Jews anywhere in the world: memory.

When witnesses speak of the Mountains today it is never with indifference. The remembrance is always tinged with enchantment or acrimony. Woody Allen has his bitter fun with guests in a sendup of Hasidic tales and their commentaries.

"A man visited Rabbi Shimmel of Cracow. 'My heart is heavy,' he told the Reb, 'because God has given me an ugly daughter.'

" 'How ugly?' the Seer asked.

" 'If she were lying on a plate with herring, you wouldn't be able to tell the difference.'

"The Seer of Cracow thought for a long time and finally asked, 'What kind of herring?'

"The man, taken aback by the query, thought quickly and said, 'Er—Bismarck.'

" 'Too bad,' the Rabbi said. 'If it was matjes, she'd have a better chance.'

"Here is a tale that illustrates the tragedy of transient qualities such as beauty. Does the girl actually resemble a herring? Why not? Have you seen some of the things walking around these days, particularly at resort areas?"

The anecdote of critic Diana Trilling is loftier but just as damaging. She was asked what she once saw in Lillian Hellman, later to become a social and political foe. "All my life," she explained, "I had wanted to know a large-sized woman, a woman with dimension, daring and imaginative, with boldness of vision, and I thought that I would find her in Lillian."

"Well, did you?"

"No, what I found was a woman sitting around in a rocker in a hotel in the Catskills saying, 'He didn't remember my birthday; she didn't send me a card at Christmas; he didn't bring me a flower.' She was always checking up on people, chalking up. That's what she was always talking about."

Others view the Borscht Belt with mistier eyes. The late Leo Steiner, owner of the Carnegie Deli in New York City, had been a busboy and kitchen helper in the Catskills. His voice grew young as he told customers about the legendary repasts where "they used to put tons and tons of food on the table. You name it, it was put there. Every day it was the same thing. It was a different menu every day, but every Monday it was the same thing; every Tuesday it was the same thing, and so on. Friday night's dinner, I don't know how you could ever walk away from that table. You got everything on God's green earth."

"Remember *Mr. Hulot's Holiday*?" asks journalist Joyce Wadler, who grew up in Fleischmanns. "I wondered when I saw it if all summer resorts were melancholy because people go with such tremendous expectations. But Fleischmanns was particularly melancholy, because when I was born it was a resort that already had had its wonderful time. They were nostalgic about a Europe that really didn't exist anymore—with the little scraps of the Viennese stuff. But that Europe was gone."

Despite—or perhaps because of—that pervasive sadness, Wadler's Catskill childhood was suffused with light. "When my uncle died," she says, "he died very unexpectedly: heart attack in the office. The cemetery was tiny and there was a little hill and the immediate family was in a horseshoe around the grave. But when I looked up, there was all of Fleischmanns stretched out for my uncle. It was very lovely. The Methodist minister and everybody were there. . . . He knew everyone. Even though the rabbi who said the eulogy didn't know him, it was to me what being an upstate Jew was. The family was around, Jews were a little closer, and the Gentiles were all there. . . .

"I went through the whole thing with the 1960s and people saying I hate America; I never felt that. I still felt that America was where you didn't turn into a lampshade. You could have anything if you worked for it. And where people didn't discriminate, because in Fleischmanns . . . we were Jewish farmers and they were Gentile farmers, but we were all farmers and we were all connected."

Alvin Fertel, a junior-high-school administrator, thinks of the *kuchaleyn* where he spent his early summers. "I went back about twenty-five or thirty years later to show it to my children. The building was still standing, even though it was abandoned. They couldn't get over the smallness of it, I mean the actual tininess of it. The entire bungalow wouldn't fit into a normal-size living room. The bedrooms were just big enough to accommodate two double beds with a space for one person to stand between them. The living room—there was no living room. There was just a very tiny kitchen, a three-burner stove, a wooden icebox, cold water. No shower. You took your shower in a community shower. The women washed their clothing in a community washtub."

This overcrowding is not what stays in Fertel's mind. He prefers to talk about a "tremendous spirit of camaraderie. Plenty of kids my age. We had enough to have a baseball team and every kind of team. . . . I learned to swim up there.

"My mother keeps telling a story about me: she was always chasing after me trying to feed me and I would never eat and I came running into the house one day and I said, 'Ma, quick, get me some bread! Get me some bread!' So she cut a big piece of pumpernickel, brought up from the Bronx, and buttered it, and I ran outside and fed it to the chickens."

A doctor who spent several years playing basketball in the Mountains once thought of becoming a professional athlete. "I was good enough," he believes. "There were offers. And then came the scandals, the disgrace to the Jewish ballplayers. I might have been caught, I dumped a few games in the resorts.

"Madison Square Garden was another matter. I wasn't in with the big boys, and I got scared. I stopped playing. I got serious about my studies and I went to medical school. Now I go occasionally to the Catskills and my adolescence comes back, without any of the bad things. You forget that you were poor and scared, that a good tip meant you could buy another book, and a bad game could ruin your life. You only remember the girls in the canoes and the laughter in the casinos, and the guests who were happy with a joke, a song, a meal. Who would be satisfied with such simple pleasures in our times? And you remember the hundreds of talented people who passed through. Industrialists, *goniffs* (thieves), characters, athletes, legislators, doctors, clowns. I think about them constantly. Once there was a kingdom up here. If you missed it, you missed all the highs and all the lows, the comedy and tragedy. You missed life."

Alan Gelb, a lawyer, remembers his days as a waiter at the New Alpine Hotel. "One woman at breakfast . . . 'Vaiter, I want a ricekrips mitot milk,' she said. 'Ricekrips,' I understood. 'Mitot milk' threw me. So I said, 'Lady, do you mean hot milk or without milk?' and she says, 'That's right, mitot milk.' So I brought the milk on the side. These were the people who liked to drink very hot beverages. I don't know why, but people who come from some parts of the world appear to enjoy very hot things. I remember the one who asked for tea. I put boiling water in the little carafe and brought the carafe and a cup and saucer and teabag and she said, 'Not hot.' 'Lady, I just took it out of the cauldron.' 'It's not hot enough.' I pick it up. I go back into the kitchen. I leave the carafe as it is, but I open the spigot and run the steaming water over the handle of the cup. I bring it back. It's the same water. She pours it in. 'That's hot.'

"They were wonderful. The accented English. . . . The lady who wanted a 'linkesveal.' 'Excuse me?' 'A linkesveal.' I don't wish to be rude. I go into the kitchen. I shout out to the Chinese chef, 'One linkesveal,' and out it comes—a lean piece of veal."

Like so many others, Gelb finds that waiting on tables was "marvelous training for practicing law. . . . Great discipline. You had to bite your tongue with guests. The same thing with clients; adversaries you can lose your temper with."

With all this affectionate regard, how could the Catskills fade so completely from the Jewish view? The answer is in Gelb's final, confessional sentence: "While the people were interesting to talk to because they had business and real world experience, it wasn't where any of us was hoping to go. We were hoping never to have to go back there as a guest. We were trying to use that as a platform to go elsewhere."

After World War II the Mountains were recalled in novels. In the eighties a similar nostalgia was expressed on film. *Sweet Lorraine*, a modest feature about the last days of a Catskill resort, was shot on location at the empty Weiden Hotel in South Falls-burgh. Its frantic atmosphere, at once warm and suffocating, is authentic, its tone autumnal. The owner wryly recalls her parents' "improvements" after the war. "All the hotels were modernizing, so they cut off the porch." The cook watches some real-estate men leaving the premises. "The Hasids made you their standard offer," he surmises. "Well, it wouldn't be summer without them." He salutes a better era when "everybody dressed for dinner . . . classy times." The day the owner is forced to sell her hotel she can only look back at it helplessly, as if the Lorraine were a failing old lady en route to a nursing home: "No matter what went wrong, she always *looked* beautiful."

By merchandising its choreography and an infectious sixties score, *Dirty Dancing* became a hit with virtually the same material. Here, too, a girl comes of age at a Mountain hotel, this time called Kellerman's. Archetypes are everywhere. A balloon-faced tummler runs through his oedipal routine: "I finally met a girl exactly like my mother. Dresses like her, acts like her. So I brought her home. My *father* doesn't like her." A loudspeaker announces the latest cultural event: "On the west porch we have a symposium by Rabbi Morris Sherman on the psychology of insult comedians." The owner catalogues the past: "Bubba and Zeyda serving the first pasteurized milk to the boarders . . . through the war years, when we didn't have any meat . . . through the Depression, when we didn't have anything."

The orchestra leader nods. "Lots of changes, Max. Lots of changes."

A Change of Season

"It isn't the changes so much. It's that it all seems to be ending. You think kids want to come with their parents to take fox trot lessons? Trips to Europe, that's what the kids want. Twenty-two countries in three days." His coda, "Seems like it's all slipping away," is swallowed by the words of the staff, singing a tribute at the farewell dinner:

> Join hands and hearts and voices
> Voices hearts and hands
> At Kellerman's the friendships last long
> As the Mountain stands.

If there had been the slightest memory of *Wish You Were Here* or *Marjorie Morningstar*, it was expunged by these films. From here on, audiences who heard the word "Catskills" understood that it referred to the Jewish version of *Heartbreak House*.

That was a familiar address for Jackie Mason. The comedian had graduated from the Mountains to become a promising headliner twenty years before. But one Sunday evening on *The Ed Sullivan Show* his monologue ran late. To indicate the minutes left, Sullivan held up two fingers off-screen. Mason held up one finger, on camera. This gesture was interpreted as obscene, and his host, an influential columnist as well as a TV master of ceremonies, angrily pushed the comedian into obscurity. Then, in October 1986, Mason abruptly became famous when he performed in the most unlikely of places, the Brooks Atkinson Theatre. For fifty years social directors had fantasized about having their names in lights; a few of them actually went on to realize that dream. But they had acted in roles, not as themselves. Mason made no attempt to hide behind a character. He was simply presenting what he called "the ultimate tummel," the untrammeled resort comic par excellence complete with dentalized Ts, hunched shoulders, singsong delivery, and familiar material. It was as if a Catskill ice floe had been melted down to reveal a frozen comedian perfectly preserved along with his routines. The smirking old anti-Semitism of the thirties was back: Mason showed a diamond ring and labeled it "a Jewish name tag." Ethnic slurs, once outré on the legitimate stage, were repeated and amplified:

"My best friend is a guy, half-Italian, half-Jewish. If he can't buy it wholesale, he steals it.

"I got another friend, he's half-Polish and half-Jewish. He's the janitor, but he owns the building.

"I got another friend, he's half-German and half-Polish. Hates Jews, can't remember why."

Prostitutes, psychiatrists, children, the Catskill scene ("Did you ever notice that Gentiles on vacation are always running and jumping and leaping around? A Jew on vacation is just looking for a place to sit. A Jew sees a chair, it's a successful vacation")—all were there, indistinguishable from their previous appearances in the Mountains. Without changing his attitude or compromising his approach, the *badkhn*, the clown of Eastern Europe, had made it all the way to Broadway.

To his own astonishment, Mason was an immediate sensation. Frank Rich, chief drama critic of *The New York Times*, had avoided the one-man show, but after it received a Tony Award, he was induced to attend. Rich reported that the performance "turned out to be exactly what I feared it would be: Borscht Belt comedy spooned out as if it were so much chicken fat at Sammy's Rumanian. Yet for all the familiarity of his attack, Mr. Mason was very, very funny." The comedian later acknowledged that "it's basically the same stuff that I've been doing for thirty years. Nothing's changed. Maybe it's a little more structured but essentially it's the same."

Belated success was accompanied by a strange malaise. Mason "asked everyone, 'Why now? Why did it take so long?' I couldn't get an answer. I don't know if there is an answer.

"Well, there is an answer—a Jew always assumes that every question has an answer, he's just not smart enough to know what it is. I couldn't figure it out. It made me crazy. To this day, I still go out and stop people in the street. 'Excuse me, mister, do you happen to know why?' "

If the puzzle had an obvious solution, Mason could hardly be blamed for ignoring it. But the fact was that in the New York City of the eighties, when neither buildings nor institutions were allowed to grow old, discards turned into antiques overnight and yesterday's vulgarity was today's treasure. It hardly mattered whether the object was a piece of furniture, a toy soldier, or a stand-up comic. When the resort circuit was active, no working MC would have been allowed through a Broadway stage door except to visit friends in the cast. Now that the Borscht Belt was safely moribund, the once-embarrassing clown could be saluted as an emblem of all that had been lost. Not that the ticket holders wanted to return to the Jewish playground; they thought it was better to be seen in the orchestra of the Atkinson than the casinos of Liberty and Monticello. Like Mason, they had gone legit.

Today their places in the Mountains have been taken by different and unrecognizable faces and names. In the remaining temples of Sullivan County, the words of Ecclesiastes have a special significance: "A time to get, and a time to lose; a time to keep, and a time to cast away." What is cast away is an obsolete idea, and the land itself. What is obtained is employment and money. At least that is the dream of those who welcome the developers of Parc Europe—advertised as "a large-scale dramatization of history."

In the spring of 1989 the mayor of Ellenville, Pauline Venezia, burbled, "I get excited every time I think about it. Imagine having buildings . . . old castles, old monasteries, people in costumes. Think how a theme park will stimulate interest in this area and how land values will increase."

An area resident, Angelina Poppo, endorsed the notion of "having Europe in my back yard. I can walk there. I won't even have to fight the traffic or the airlines." Her friend Rosalie Sherry predicted that "every state in the nation will be envious. You can't imagine the amount of people it will attract." Or the number it would repel. Tom Minor, director of the Catskill Center, an environmental group, spoke for a large and outraged constituency. He found the Parc "an atrocious idea and the phoniest thing I ever heard of. What we already have here is a rural slice of America that people are hungry for—not phony touches of Europe where people can spend their money."

But even as he spoke, the rural slice was growing smaller. Tax dollars were noticeably scarce for town and amenities. So scarce that while plans were being drawn for Parc Europe, the Sullivan County Board of Supervisors proposed the unthinkable: a hotel room tax of 2 percent. "There has never been a hotel tax before because no one had the guts to do it," said proponent Dennis Greenwald, supervisor of Mamakating. "The resort industry used to be a dominant political influence in the county, and it would have been political suicide."

No longer. The complaints of Wilbur Parks, an automobile-parts salesman in Grahamsville, were met with overpowering indifference. "There aren't many hotels left, and what few we have we should try to keep, not drive out," he said. "Without hotels, what are you going to have?" Silence greeted his question, and he went on: "You're going to have zilch."

Andrew Boyar, supervisor of Highland, opposed the tax because he believed it would injure an already wounded industry. "A lot of people look at the resorts as the rich uncle," he said. "They think, 'They've got the money, so let's nail them.' Maybe they were rich in their heyday, but not in 1989. They're dying, and I don't want to speed their death."

Milton Kutsher pointed out that Catskill visitors are "very strange. They'll spend hundreds of dollars in a few days, but if they have to spend another $20 that they're not getting anything in return for, they might say 'Why are we here?' We don't know how they'll react to this."

One owner was not waiting around to find out. He spent the time packing up for Florida, forced into premature retirement. "Is this all?" he demanded as he clicked suitcases shut. "After two hundred years of history, is this what things come to? That a few stubborn Jews stay on? That the rest move out and leave the Mountains the way they left the Bronx? That the Hispanics and the blacks and the foreigners move in?"

He knew the answer. That is exactly what things come to. They must; it is the region's immutable history. First came the Indians, and then in varying order the Dutch, the Yankees, the tanners, the loggers, the railroaders, the aesthetes, the reactionaries. Into the wilderness came Jacob the Jew; those who followed him nourished dreams of freedom, worshipped as they chose, pursued careers and pleasures, displaced others, and built a way of life in a world of summers. To every thing there is a season, and a time to every purpose under the heaven. The season has changed, the Catskills remain, and now it is another people's turn.

SOURCE NOTES

BIBLIOGRAPHY

ACKNOWLEDGMENTS

INDEX

SOURCE NOTES

INTRODUCTION

Indian and Dutch names: *The Catskills: Land in the Sky*, by John G. Mitchell and Charles D. Winter (Viking, 1977).

Plattekill saying: *The Catskills: From Wilderness to Woodstock*, by Alf Evers (Overlook Press, 1982).

CHAPTER 1

Lou Goldstein recollections: Interview, October 1986. Servico plans: *The New York Times*, October 21, 1985; *Servico Annual Report*, 1985; "American Scene," *Time* magazine, October 27, 1986.

Tummlers and their audiences: *The Borscht Belt*, by Joey Adams, with Henry Tobias (Bobbs-Merrill, 1966).

Grossinger's history: *Waldorf-in-the-Catskills: The Grossinger Legend*, by Harold Jaediker Taub (Sterling, 1952); Jennie Grossinger obituary, *The New York Times*, November 11, 1972; *The Borscht Belt*, op. cit.

Mal Z. Lawrence: Interview, October 1986; Fisher speech and anecdota: *Time*, op. cit.

CHAPTER 2

Jacob the Jew: Hardenbergh Patent Memoranda in Clermont account book of the Livingstons.

Jacob Brink, Longyear, Chambers, Middah, Hardenbergh: *The Catskills* (Evers), op. cit.

Lord Cornbury: "The Cornbury Legend," in *Proceedings, New York Historical Association*, Vol. 13, 1914.

Washington, the Stirling Lottery: *Lord Stirling*, by Alan Chester Valentine (Oxford University Press, 1969).

Correspondence of the Jews of Newport, R.I., and President Washington: *Adventure in Freedom: Three Hundred Years of Jewish Life in America*, by Oscar Handlin (McGraw-Hill, 1954).

Jacob De La Motta: *The Jews of the United States 1790–1840*, Joseph L. Blau and Salo W. Baron, eds. (Jewish Publication Society, N.D.)

Source Notes

Mordecai Noah: *Jacksonian Jew: The Two Worlds of Mordecai Noah*, by Jonathan D. Sarna (Holmes & Meier Inc., 1981); *This Land I Show You: Three Hundred Years of Jewish Life in America*, by Stanley Feldstein (Doubleday, 1978); *American Jewish Landmarks*, by Bernard Postal and Lionel Koppman (Fleet Press, 1986); *Steeled by Adversity: Essays and Addresses on American Jewish Life*, by Salo W. Baron, ed. by Jeanette M. Baron (Jewish Publication Society, 1971).

"You know the Cattskills, lad": from *The Pioneers*, by James Fenimore Cooper (Library of America, 1985).

Van Winkle's "pestilent ground": from *The Sketch Book of Geoffrey Crayon, Gent.*, by Washington Irving (Library of America, 1983).

Edens and the New Jerusalems: from *The Dyer's Hand*, by W. H. Auden (Random House, 1962).

Ararat: *A History of the Jews in the United States*, by Lee J. Levinger (Union of American Hebrew Congregations, 1949); Address by Mordecai M. Noah, *Publications of the American Jewish Historical Society*, Vol. XXI; the Tender Sheep: *This Land I Show You*, op. cit.

Sholem, its origins and end: "The Jewish Colony at Sholem, Ulster County," *Olde Ulster*, Vol. VIII, June 12, 1912; "Establishing a New Jerusalem at Sholem," *Olde Ulster*, August 1931; Supplement, *Our Jewish Farmers*, by Gabriel Davidson (L. B. Fisher, 1934); "Before Today's Headlines," by Katherine T. Terwilliger, *The Ellenville Journal*, July 31, August 7, August 14, 1969; "The Sholem Colony; The First American Jewish Rural Settlement," by H. David Rutman, *The Ellenville Journal*, January 1973; Deeds, Mortgages, Mortgage Sale Defaults in Ulster County Clerk's Office, Ulster County, N.Y.

CHAPTER 3

"Children of the devil": *The History of Anti-Semitism: From the Time of Christ to the Court Jews*, by Leon Poliakov (Vanguard Press, 1965).

Israelische Annalen and Abraham Kohn: *This Land I Show You*, op. cit.

Gimbel, Bloomingdale, Seligman: *Our Crowd: The Great Jewish Families of New York*, by Stephen Birmingham (Harper & Row, 1966).

"On ev'ry path": *This Land I Show You*, op. cit.

Franklin legend: *The Pennsylvania Gazette*, March 13, 1753.

Theodore Griesinger: "Source Material on Jewish Immigration," *Yivo Annual of Jewish Social Science*, Vol. VI, 1951.

Cole and the Hudson River School: *The Hudson River and Its Painters*, by John Kowat (Viking, 1972); *Nature and Culture: American Landscape and Painting 1825–1875*, by Barbara Novak (Oxford University Press, 1980).

"Between 1840 and 1880, two hundred thousand German Jews settled": *This Land I Show You*, op. cit.

Source Notes

Fleischmann estate: *The Catskills* (Evers), op. cit.

Gould statements: *The Life and Legend of Jay Gould*, by Maury Klein (Johns Hopkins University Press, 1986).

Origin of Vilna: *Vilna*, by Israel Cohen (Jewish Publication Society of America, 1943).

"One-third conversion": *The Jews in America: The Roots, History and Destiny of American Jews*, by Max Dimont (Touchstone, 1979).

The Rise of David Levinsky, by Abraham Cahan (Harper & Bros., 1917).

Background of Eastern European Jewry: *World of Our Fathers: The Journey of the Eastern European Jews to America and the Life They Found and Made*, by Irving Howe (Harcourt Brace Jovanovich, 1976); *Europe and the New World*, by Bernard Martin, *A History of Judaism*, Vol. II (Basic Books, 1974).

Immigration statistics: *The Promised City: New York's Jews 1870–1914*, by Moses Rischin (Corinth Books, 1964).

"The eyesore of New York": *Portal To America: The Lower East Side 1870–1925*, edited by Allon Schoener (Holt, Rinehart and Winston, 1967).

Rosenfeld poem: *The Penguin Book of Modern Yiddish Verse*, ed. by Irving Howe, Ruth R. Wisse, and Khone Shmeruk (Viking, 1987).

Statements of United Hebrew Charities and Jewish Alliance of America: *This Land I Show You*, op. cit.

Statements of Baron de Hirsch: *Steeled by Adversity*, op. cit.; *Poor Cousins*, by Ande Manners (Coward, McCann & Geoghegan, 1972).

A "mixed and rapidly moving summer population": *Illustrated Guide to the Hudson River and Catskill Mountains*, by Ernest Ingersoll (1893).

"Summer Homes": *To the Mountains by Rail*, by Manville B. Wakefield (Wakefair Press, 1970).

Hilton-Seligman affair: *Our Crowd*, op. cit.

Harte poem: *Poor Cousins*, op. cit.

Mark Twain: *Harper's Monthly*, September 1899.

Anti-Hebrew Crusade: Kingston *Argus*, May 7, 1879; Saugerties *Evening Post*, May 5, 1879.

Twenty hotels "entered into an agreement": Pine Hill *Sentinel*, April 17, 1889.

"Race Prejudice at Summer Resorts," by Alice H. Rhine, *The Forum*, Vol. 3 (1887).

"Criminals and Officers of the New York Society for the Prevention of Crime," *The Catskills* (Evers), op. cit.; *Gangs of New York*, by Herbert Asbury (Alfred A. Knopf, 1928).

"New Israel: A Modern School of Crime": *The American Metropolis from Knickerbocker Days to the Present Time*, by Frank Moss (Collier, 1897).

Yellowstone Cowboys: *The Catskills* (Evers), op. cit.

"Jews or Gentiles?": Pine Hill *Sentinel*, May 15, 1889.

Nichols's prediction: Pine Hill *Sentinel*, August 16, 1899.

Gerson ad: *To the Mountains by Rail*, op. cit.

Source Notes

CHAPTER 4

"a gray stone world": *World of Our Fathers*, op. cit.

"worker's disease": *A Bintel Brief*, Vol. 1, ed. by Isaac Metzker (Doubleday, 1971).

"off to the hospital": *The Battle with the Slums*, by Jacob Riis (reprint of 1902 edition, Patterson Smith, 1969); Dr. George Price: *This Land I Show You*, op. cit.; overcrowding: *World of Our Fathers*, op. cit.; *The Promised City*, op. cit.

"Join the Cloakmakers Union": *A Bintel Brief*, op. cit.

"added muscle": *The Catskills* (Evers), op. cit.

"Go to the Mountains": New York *Evening Post*, June 1, 1901.

Farms sold to Jews: *The Ellenville Journal*, August 10, 1906.

Jewish Agricultural Society: *World of Our Fathers*, op. cit.

"900 steerage passengers": *On the Trail of the Immigrant*, by Edward Steiner (Revill, 1906).

"no swarming like that of Israel": *The American Scene*, by Henry James (Indiana University Press, 1968); *Henry James: The Master*, 1901–1906, by Leon Edel (Lippincott, 1972).

Adams quote: *The Letters of Henry Adams*, ed. by J. C. Levenson and Ernest Samuels (Harvard University Press, 1983).

"almost a Jew": *The Autobiography of Lincoln Steffens* (Harcourt Brace, 1981).

The Spirit of the Ghetto, by Hutchins Hapgood (Funk & Wagnalls, 1965).

Boris Thomashevsky: *The Book of My Life*, by Boris Thomashevsky (Trio Press, 1937); *Vagabond Stars: A World History of Yiddish Theater*, by Nahma Sandrow (Harper & Row, 1975); *Bright Star of Exile: Jacob Adler and the Yiddish Theater*, by Lulla Rosenfeld (Thomas Y. Crowell, 1977); *The Yiddish Theater in America*, by David S. Lifson (Thomas Yoseloff, 1965).

Thomashevsky at Hunter: *My Father and I*, by Joseph Schildkraut (Viking, 1959); reminiscences of Teddy and Harry Thomas, interviews with author, July 1986.

"In the Catskills," by Z. Libin, *The Jewish Daily Forward*, August 9, 1903.

"Little Shlomo": *Little Did I Know*, by Maurice Samuel (Alfred A. Knopf, 1963).

Cahan's advice: *World of Our Fathers*, op. cit.; *This Land I Show You*, op. cit.

Rigi Kulm: *The Rise of David Levinsky*, op. cit.

CHAPTER 5

"Country Cousins," by Morris Rosenfeld, *The Jewish Daily Forward*, August 9, 1911.

Yente's letters: *Yente un andere shtiferayen (Yente and Other Mischief)*, by B. Kovner (Y. Adler) (Moses Gurewitz Publishers, 1914).

Source Notes

"establish a beachhead": *The Borscht Belt*, op. cit.

"Sheeny Mountains": *The Jewish Daily Forward*, August 10, 1907.

Fallsburgh incident: *To the Mountains by Rail*, op. cit.

Whitehead on Woodstock: *The Catskills* (Evers), op. cit.

uneasy relations . . .: *The Catskills*, by T. Morris Longstreth (The Century Co., 1921).

Lerner family: Interview with Max Lerner.

Flagler advertisements: *Summer Homes*, 1895 and 1909.

Selig and Malke Grossinger: *Waldorf-in-the-Catskills*, op. cit.

Jewish Agricultural Society, *Annual Reports*, 1909, 1910, 1920.

"the room renters . . .": "Catskills Playground of the Masses," *The American Hebrew*, August 31, 1928.

Adams: *The Borscht Belt*, op. cit.

Free ice: Interview with Irving Shapiro, February 1989.

Jewish Working Girls Vacation Society: *Annual Report*, 1901.

Triangle fire: *The Fate of the Jews: A People Torn*, by Roberta Strauss Fuerlicht (Times Books, 1983); *Portal to America*, op. cit.; *The Promised City*, op. cit.

Unity House: *The Message*, June 8–September 14, 1917.

History of the *badkhn*: "Merrymakers and Jesters Among Jews (Materials for a Lexicon)," by Ezekiel Lifschutz, *YIVO Annual of Jewish Social Services*, Vol. VIII (1952); *The History of Jewish Marriage*, by Philip and Hannah Goodman (Jewish Publication Society, 1965).

Flagler description: *The Catskills* (Evers), op. cit.

Joseph Gold: Interview with David Gold, August 1986.

"in the lounge . . .": *The Joys of Yiddish*, by Leo Rosten (McGraw-Hill, 1968).

Izzy and Moe: *The Liberty Register*, January 27, 1922; *Ardent Spirits: The Rise and Fall of Prohibition*, by John Kobler (Putnam, 1973); *On and Off the Wagon*, by Donald Barr Chidsey (Cowles, 1969). *To the Mountains by Rail*, op. cit.

CHAPTER 6

"A Modern Rip Van Winkle": *The Liberty Register*, January 20, 1920.

Albert reminiscence: *50 Golden Years*, by Mrs. Ben Miller and Daniel S. Roher (The Ellenville Hebrew Aid Society, 1959).

Co-op history: *The Answer—A Co-operative* (Federation of Jewish Farmers, 1960); "black pages": Interview with executive, July 1987.

"value of a vacation": "Going to the Mountains: A Social History," by Betsy Blackmar, in *Resorts of the Catskills* (St. Martin's Press, 1979).

Levinson memoirs: Conversation with David Levinson, August 1987.

Spring Glen ecumenism: "Our Corner of Ulster," by Katherine T. Terwilliger (Rondoot Valley Publishing Co., 1977).

Source Notes

Ford anti-Semitism: *Henry Ford and the Jews*, by Albert Lee (Stein and Day, 1980); *The Last Billionaire: Henry Ford*, by William C. Richards (Scribner's, 1948); *The Catskills* (Evers), op. cit.

Klan meetings and Communist Party founding: *Charlie's Days*, by Charlie Crist (Catskill-Delaware Publications, 1983); *Woodstock: History of an American Town*, by Alf Evers (Overlook Press, 1987).

Immigrant vulgarity: *World of Our Fathers*, op. cit.

bitter apprenticeship and Hart's weekly schedule: *Act One*, by Moss Hart (Random House, 1959); *The Borscht Belt*, op. cit.

"pocket an extra ten . . .": *Scandals of '51*, by Charles Rosen (Holt, Rinehart & Winston, 1978).

The girls on Forsythe Street: *Tageblatt*, September 12, 1912, et. seq.

Father's complaint: *The Jewish Daily Forward*, June 21, 1909, et. seq.

Vaudeville history and Keith backstage sign: *Once Upon a Stage*, by Charles and Louise Samuels (Dodd, Mead, 1974).

Robenstein: "The Alien Corn," from *The Complete Stories of Somerset Maugham* (Doubleday, 1952).

A people's humor: *Jokes and Their Relation to the Unconscious*, by Sigmund Freud; translated by James Strachey (Norton, 1960).

The Jokes of Sigmund Freud: A Study in Humor and Jewish Identity, by Elliott Loring (University of Pennsylvania Press, 1984).

Jewish Wit, by Theodor Reik (Gamut Press, 1962).

Daemonic individuals: *The Seven Lively Arts*, by Gilbert Seldes (Harper & Bros., 1924).

Morris Weiner: *Pep Op De Peepul.* Unpublished memoir by Dr. Saul Gladstone, 1981.

Schedule: *Resorts of the Catskills*, op. cit.

Meyer Wolfsheim: *The Great Gatsby*, by F. Scott Fitzgerald (Scribner's, 1953).

Robert Cohn: *The Sun Also Rises*, by Ernest Hemingway (Scribner's, 1954).

"beware of folks": *Collected Poems*, by e. e. cummings (Harcourt Brace, 1938).

"The Jew is everywhere": *The Thirty-nine Steps*, by John Buchan (Pan, 1947).

Sir Marcus: *This Gun for Hire*, by Graham Greene (Viking, 1982).

CHAPTER 7

Reinetz: Interview with Elie Wiesel, November 1987.

Crime as marginal phenomenon: *World of Our Fathers*, op. cit.

Lepke and his milieu: *Murder, Inc.: The Inside Story of the Mob*, by Burton Turkus and Sid Feder (Farrar, Straus & Young, 1951); *The Big Bankroll: The Life and Times of Arnold Rothstein*, by Leo Katcher (Harper & Row, 1959); *Meyer Lansky: Mogul of the Mob*, by Dennis Eisenberg, Uri Dan, Eli Landau (Paddington Press, 1956); *Line Up Tough Guys*, by Ron Goulart (Sherbourne Press, 1966); *From Gags to Riches*, by Joey Adams (Fred-

erick Fell, 1946); *The Borscht Belt*, op. cit.; *Legs*, by William Kennedy
(Penguin Books, 1985); interviews with Catskill residents who requested
anonymity, 1987.

Silvers's reminiscence: *This Laugh Is on Me*, by Phil Silvers, with Robert Saffron
(Prentice-Hall, 1973); "In the beginning": Interview with veteran entertainer, December 1986.

Holdup men and jewelry robbery, et. seq.: *To the Mountains by Rail*, op. cit.

"A fellow jailbird": "Memories of West Street and Lepke," from *Life Studies*,
by Robert Lowell (Vintage, 1959).

White Roe: *Pep Op De Peepul*, op. cit.

The Mountain Hotelman: B. Kovner columns, 1930–1932. Private collection,
Dorothy Shapiro, Liberty, N.Y.

Maurice Samuel poem: "Al Harei Catskill," *The Menorah Treasury*, edited by
Leo Schwarz (Jewish Publication Society, 1964).

"Child from its beginnings": "Kochalein: Poor Man's Shangri-La," by Harry
Gersh. From *Commentary on the American Scene*, ed. by Elliot E. Cohen
(Alfred A. Knopf, 1953).

Pride of the Catskills: *Act One*, op. cit.; *The Borscht Belt*, op cit.; "The Jew in
Stand-up Comedy," by Anthony Lewis, in *From Hester Street to Holly-
wood*, ed. by Sarah Blacher Cohen (University of Indiana Press, 1983);
"Shylock's Mispoche": "Anti-Semitism on the American Stage," by Ellen
Schiff, from *Anti-Semitism in American History*, ed. by David A. Gerber
(University of Illinois Press, 1987); *The Fabulous Fanny*, by Norman Kat-
kov (Alfred A. Knopf, 1963); *So Help Me*, by George Jessel (Random
House, 1943).

Reservoir of Jewish phrases: *The Joys of Yiddish*, op. cit.

"In the thirties": Interview with owner, April 1988.

"Arrival" meant recognition: *The Rise and Fall of the Borscht Belt*. Film by
Peter Davis, 1985.

CHAPTER 8

Shadchen stories: *The Joys of Yiddish*, op. cit.

"Up there": Interview, May 1986.

"I went up": Interview, August 1986.

"One of the girls": *The Borscht Belt*, op. cit.

Connelly: Introduction to *Having Wonderful Time*, by Arthur Kober (Dramatists Play Service, 1948).

Bungalow colony veteran: *The Rise and Fall of the Borscht Belt*, op. cit.

Camping Out, Hebrew Education Society, Theater of Mating: "Jewish Summer
Camps and Cultural Transformation," by Phyllis Deutsch, *American Jewish History*, Vol. LXXV, No. 3 (March 1986).

Katz, Dr. Max Wolff: *The Borscht Belt*, op. cit.

Source Notes

White Roe: *Pep Op De Peepul*, op. cit.

Noel Airman: *Marjorie Morningstar*, by Herman Wouk (Pocket Books, 1955).

"many boys and some girls did it": *Journal of American Jewish History*, op. cit.

Grossinger history: *Waldorf-in-the-Catskills*, op. cit.; *Jennie and the Story of Grossinger's*, by Joel Pomerantz (Grosset & Dunlap, 1968); *Growing Up at Grossinger's*, by Tania Grossinger (McKay, 1975).

Howard Fast: Interview, September 1987; Michael Gold: *Writers on the Left: Episodes in American Literary Communism*, by Daniel Aaron (Hippocrene, 1974); *This Land I Show You*, op. cit.

City College: *The Course of Modern Jewish History*, by Howard Morley Sachar (Delta, 1977).

"absence of its Jewishness": *The Literature of American Jews*, ed. by Theodore L. Gross (The Free Press, 1973); "The Vanishing Jew of Popular Culture," by Henry Popkin, *Commentary*, July 1952.

Jews and the cinema: *King Cohn*, by Bob Thomas (Putnam, 1967); *A History of the Jews*, by Paul Johnson (Harper & Row, 1987); *Merely Colossal: The Story of the Movies from the Long Chase to the Chaise Longue* by Arthur Mayer (Simon & Schuster, 1963).

CHAPTER 9

Danny Kaye: Interview with Richard Diamond, February 1987; Recollections, Kaye sketch: *Pep Op De Peepul*, op. cit.

Caesar in the Catskills: *Where Have I Been?*, by Sid Caesar, with Bill Davidson (Crown, 1982).

Eighteenth-century assimilation: *Selected Essays*, by Ahad Ha-Am (Jewish Publication Society, 1912).

Jewry in Music, et. seq.: *Richard Wagner: The Man, His Mind, and His Music*, by Robert W. Gutman (Harcourt, Brace & World, 1968).

"no mother tongue": *The Jews*, by Chaim Bermant (Times Books, 1977).

Concord history: Interview with Gordon Winarick, November 1988; "The Concord: Eat, Swim, Eat, Rest, Eat," by Alan Levy, *The New York Times*, October 8, 1974; "Pleasure Dome in the Catskills," by Gilbert Burck, *Fortune*, June 1955; Arthur Winarick obituary, New York *Herald Tribune*, November 22, 1964.

Jacob Kaminsky: *This Land I Show You*, op. cit.

Identity jokes: *Encyclopedia of Jewish Humor*, compiled and ed. by Henry D. Spalding (Jonathan David, 1969); *A Treasury of Jewish Folklore*, ed. by Nathan Ausubel (Crown, 1948).

Sophie Tucker: *Some of These Days*, by Sophie Tucker (Doubleday, Doran, 1945).

"Hollywood Conventions: The Disappearing Jew of Popular Culture," by Henry Popkin, *Commentary*, July 1952, op. cit.

Source Notes

Evasions: *Dusk in the Catskills*, by Reuben Wallenrod (The Reconstructionist Press, 1957).

Still-active owner: Interview, January 1988.

Herzl: *A History of Zionism*, by Walter Laqueur (Holt, Rinehart & Winston, 1972).

Grossinger charity work: *Jennie*, op. cit.

"Lack of further action": *Jewish Life in Twentieth Century America: Challenge and Accommodation*, by Milton Plesur (Nelson-Hall, 1982).

Roosevelt and the Jews: *World of Our Fathers*, op. cit.; *The Future of American Politics*, by Samuel Lubell (Greenwood, 1983); *The Politics of Rescue*, by Henry Feingold (Holocaust Library, 1980).

Sergeant Seeger: "Act of Faith," in *Short Stories: Five Decades*, by Irwin Shaw (Delacorte, 1978).

War Bonds, *Jennie*, op. cit.

Men were in short supply: Interview with Catskill veteran, January 11, 1988.

"He sang the whole day long": *Sam Clemens of Hannibal*, by Dixon Wecter (Houghton Mifflin, 1952).

CHAPTER 10

Rationing, et al.: *Don't You Know There's a War On?*, by Richard Lingeman (Putnam, 1970); *Washington Goes to War*, by David Brinkley (Alfred A. Knopf, 1988).

Remaining in the ghetto: *Men and Politics*, by Louis Fisher (Duell, Sloane & Pearce, 1943).

Gene De Paris at Livingston Manor: *PM*, August 1941 et seq.

Entertainers: *Between Acts* by Robert Merrill with Robert Saffron (McGraw-Hill, 1973); interview with Johnny Pransky, April 1988.

Pincus Perelmuth: *The Bluebird of Happiness: The Memoirs of Jan Peerce*, by Alan Levy (Harper & Row, 1976).

Chesters' Zumbarg: "The People I Lived Off Of." Unpublished paper by Ann Chester; interviews with Ann Chester, March, April 1988.

"IRV SHAPIRO IS A HERO": *Grossinger Bugle*, February 26, 1945.

Mock wedding: *The Decline and Fall of the Borscht Belt*, op. cit.

Joseph Levitch: *Jerry Lewis: In Person*, by Jerry Lewis, with Herb Gluck (Atheneum, 1982).

Fund-raising: *A Child of the Century*, by Ben Hecht (Simon and Schuster, 1954); *World of Our Fathers*, op. cit.

"We did what we could": Interview with Catskill veteran, February 6, 1988.

Neglected novels: *Summer on a Mountain of Spices*, by Harvey Jacobs (Harper & Row, 1975); *Woodridge, 1946*, by Martin Boris (Ace, 1981).

Peekskill riots: *A Journal of the Plague Years*, by Stefan Kanfer (Atheneum,

Source Notes

1973); *Paul Robeson, All-American,* by Dorothy Butler Gilliam (New Republic Books, 1976); interviews with Ann Chester, op. cit.

CHAPTER 11

Rep. Rankin: *A Journal of the Plague Years,* op. cit.
Investigations: *The Committee,* by Walter Goodman (Farrar, Straus & Giroux, 1968).
"It was a very difficult time": Interview with resort owner, September 11, 1987.
The Holy Land: *Jewish Life in Twentieth Century America,* op. cit.; *The Jews in America,* op. cit.
Memories of Brickman's: Murray Posner in *The Rise and Fall of the Borscht Belt,* op. cit.
Grossinger accounts: *Jennie,* op. cit.; *Waldorf-in-the-Catskills,* op. cit.
Eddie Fisher memoirs: *Growing Up at Grossinger's,* op. cit.; *My Life and Loves,* by Eddie Fisher (Harper & Row, 1981); *New York Journal-American,* August 16, 1952.
Basketball fever, et. seq.: *Scandals of '51,* op. cit.; *The Game They Played,* by Stanley Cohen (Farrar, Straus & Giroux, 1977); *Who Struck John?* by Jimmy Cannon (Dial, 1956); "Annals of Crime: The Bewildered Fixer," by Robert Rice, *The New Yorker,* March 5, 1955; *New York Journal-American, New York Post, The New York Times,* February 11 through May 31, 1951; Interviews with players and owners, July, August 1986.

CHAPTER 12

Childhood Memoir: *A Walker in the City,* by Alfred Kazin (Harcourt, Brace, 1951).
Wish You Were Here references: *You Must Remember This . . . Popular Song-writers 1900–1980,* by Mark White (Scribner's, 1985); *The World of Musical Comedy,* by Stanley Green (Grosset & Dunlap, 1960); *The New York Times,* June 26, 1952; Original Cast Album, RCA Camden Records, 1960.
Your Show of Shows: Where Have I Been?, op. cit.
Levenson: *Meet the Folks,* by Sam Levenson (Citadel, 1949).
"Used to be, you could use a few good bits . . .": Interview with former comedian, August 2, 1988.
Mel Brooks, Lenny Bruce: *The Last Laugh: The World of the Stand-Up Comics,* by Phil Berger (Morrow, 1987); *The Life of Kenneth Tynan,* by Kathleen Tynan (Morrow, 1987).
Mason: *Jackie Oy!: The Birth and Rebirth of Jackie Mason,* by Jackie Mason, with Ken Gross (Little, Brown, 1988); interview with Mason, January 1987.
Woody Allen: *Three Films of Woody Allen* (Vintage, 1987).

Source Notes

"If the act had a car": *Enter Talking*, by Joan Rivers, with Richard Merryman (Delacorte, 1986).

"Comedians Crisis": paper by Samuel Janus, 1978; *Time* magazine, October 2, 1978.

CHAPTER 13

Rabbis against resorts: *The Wall Street Journal*, September 23, 1965; "The Catskills in the Wry," by Alan Levy, *Cavalier*, September 1965.

Richler on the Catskills: from *Notes on an Endangered Species and Others*, by Mordecai Richler (Alfred A. Knopf, 1974).

Harry Grossinger: Obituary, *The New York Times*, July 23, 1964; *Jennie*, op. cit.

Arthur Winarick: *The New York Times*, September 3, 1963; Obituary, *The New York Times*, November 22, 1964.

Lodge campaign: New York *Herald Tribune*, September 4, 1960; Interview with George Gilbert, July 13, 1986.

Lindsay campaign: *The New York Times*, August 1, 1965.

Lyndon Johnson visit: The Middletown *Times Herald Record*, August 20, 1966; *The Ellenville Press*, August 25, 1966.

Singles week: "The Sour Cream Sierras of New York," *Sports Illustrated*, July 2, 1962; "Only a Few Win Catskills Mating Game," *The New York Times*, August 28, 1967; *The Rise and Fall of the Borscht Belt*, op. cit.; *Waldorf-in-the-Catskills*, op. cit.; "Special Flavor": *The New York Times*, July 11, 1962.

Woodstock and Max Yasgur: *The Catskills* (Evers), op. cit.; *Woodstock*, op. cit.; *The New York Times*, July 23, 1969, August 18, 1969; New York *Daily News*, September 22, 1969, April 5, 1970; *New York Post*, August 23, 1969.

CHAPTER 14

Strikes: *The New York Times*, March 9, 1973.

Morales: *New York Post*, *The New York Times*, April 4, 1973.

"old rural image": *The Catskills* (Evers), op. cit.

Fountains of Rome, Crystal Run School: *The New York Times*, May 27, 1979; interviews with Liberty residents, July, August 1986.

Buddhist center: *The New York Times*, August 24, 1975.

Waldemere: *The New York Times*, November 25, 1973; interviews with Monticello residents, August 1987.

Jennie Grossinger: *Jennie*, op. cit.; *Waldorf-in-the-Catskills*, op. cit.; *Growing Up at Grossinger's*, op. cit.; *The New York Times* obituary, November 21, 1972.

Source Notes

Jackie Robinson: *New York Post*, January 8, 1960.

"when I die": New York *Daily News*, April 7, 1968.

Yasgur: *Time* magazine, February 19, 1973.

Blackstone decline: Interview with Johnny Pransky, August 15, 1987; *The New York Times*, January 16, 1973; *My Life and Loves*, op. cit.; *Debbie: My Life*, by Debbie Reynolds, with David Patrick Columbia (Morrow, 1988); *People* magazine, August 18, 1975.

Business conventions: Interviews with hotel owners, July, August, 1987; *The New York Times*, March 5, 13, 1966; *Growing Up at Grossinger's*, op. cit.

Interviews, former waiters, busboys, September 1988; *The New York Times*, July 20, 1970.

History of fires: *The Liberty Register*, May 28, 1920; *To the Mountains by Rail*, op. cit.; *The New York Times*, July 27, 1976.

Peg Leg Bates: Interviews with former guests, April 1986; *The New York Times*, July 15, 1985.

Spanish Alps: *Gentlemen's Quarterly*, August 1985; Interviews with former guests, June 1986; *The New York Times*, August 7, 1965.

CHAPTER 15

Borscht Belt arguments: Interview with George Gilbert, June 1986.

Catskill cuisine: *The New York Times*, July 26, 1986; August 11, 1988.

CatskilLand: Sullivan County Chamber of Commerce.

Poem: "Hath Not a Jew," by Abraham Moses Klein, *A Treasury of Jewish Quotations*, ed. by Joseph L. Baron (Crown, 1956).

Tessler's scandal: *The New York Times*, October 12, 1983.

Grossinger's sale: Interviews with Grossinger veterans; *Time* magazine, October 27, 1986; *The New York Times*, October 19, 21, 1985; *My Life and Loves*, op. cit.

Brown's in Chapter 11: New York *Daily News*, September 13, 1988.

Rip Van Winkle: *The Catskills*, op. cit.

New bungalow colonies: Interviews, *Jewish World*, August 19–25, 1988; *The New York Times*, August 24, 1987.

Hasids and softball: Interviews, *Jewish World*, op. cit.

CHAPTER 16

Heine quote: *Justice to the Jew*, by Madison Peters (McClure, 1908).

Send-up of Hasidic tales: *Getting Even*, by Woody Allen (Random House, 1971).

Trilling: *Lillian Hellman: Her Legend and Her Legacy*, by Carl Rollyson (St. Martin's Press, 1987).

Source Notes

"Tons of food": Interview with Steiner; *Jewish Times*, by Howard Simons (Houghton Mifflin, 1988).

Wadler, Fertel, Gelb: *Jewish Times*, op. cit.

"There were offers": Interview with doctor, March 1988.

Sweet Lorraine: Angelika Productions.

Dirty Dancing: Vestron Productions.

Mason: *The World According to Me!* by Jackie Mason (Simon and Schuster, 1987); *Jackie Oy!*; op. cit.; interview with Mason, August 1986.

Parc Europe: Interviews with Catskill residents, April 1989; *The New York Times*, May 1, 1989.

Room tax: Interviews with resort owners, April 1989; *The New York Times*, April 3, 1989.

"Is this all?": Interview with former owner, April 1988.

BIBLIOGRAPHY

As is evident from the text, many more books (to say nothing of periodicals and newspapers) were consulted than the ones listed below. These are here because I believe them basic to an understanding of the Mountains and of the people who worked and lived there. Those wishing to plow further in the Catskill fields are urged to consult Dr. Kenneth Libo at the National Museum of Jewish History in Philadelphia, to whose library I have donated most of the following works.

THE BACKGROUND

Ausubel, Nathan, ed. *A Treasure of Jewish Folklore*. Crown, 1948.

Baron, Joseph L., ed. *A Treasury of Jewish Quotations*. Crown, 1956.

Ben-Sasson, H. H., ed. *A History of the Jewish People*. Harvard, 1976.

Bermant, Chaim. *The Jews*. Times Books, 1977.

Cohen, Israel. *Vilna*. Jewish Publication Society, 1943.

Davidowicz, Lucy. *The Jewish Presence*. Harvest, 1978.

Feingold, Henry L. *The Politics of Rescue*. Holocaust Library, 1980.

Feinsilver, Lillian M. *The Taste of Yiddish*. Yoseloff, 1970.

Fuerlicht, Roberta S. *The Fate of the Jews*. Times Books, 1983.

Fussell, Paul. *Abroad*. Oxford, 1980.

Goldberg, M. Hirsch. *The Jewish Connection*. Stein and Day, 1976.

Goodman, Philip and Hannah. *The History of Jewish Marriage*. Jewish Publication Society, 1965.

Grayzel, Solomon. *A History of the Jews*. Jewish Publication Society, 1959.

Gross, David C. *The Jewish People's Almanac*. Doubleday, 1981.

Ha-Am, Ahad. *Selected Essays*. Jewish Publication Society, 1912.

Howe, Irving, and Eliezer Greenberg, eds. *A Treasure of Yiddish Stories*. Schocken, 1973.

Howe, Irving, et al. *The Penguin Book of Modern Yiddish Verse*. Viking, 1987.

Johnson, Paul. *A History of the Jews*. Harper & Row, 1987.

Landau, Ron. *The Book of Jewish Lists*. Stein and Day, 1982.

Laqueur, Walter. *A History of Zionism*. Holt, Rinehart & Winston, 1972.

Martin, Bernard. *A History of Judaism*. Basic Books, 1974.

Postal, Bernard, and Lionel Koppman. *American Jewish Landmarks*. Fleet, 1986.

Rosten, Leo. *The Joys of Yiddish*. McGraw-Hill, 1968.

Sachar, Abraham L. *A History of the Jews*. Alfred A. Knopf, 1967.

Bibliography

Sacher, Howard M. *The Course of Modern Jewish History*. Delta, 1977.
Schweitzer, Frederick M. *A History of the Jews*. Macmillan, 1971.

ANTI-SEMITISM

Gaber, John G. *The Origins of Anti-Semitism*. Oxford, 1983.
Gerber, David A., ed. *Anti-Semitism in American History*. University of Illinois Press, 1986.
Gilliam, Dorothy Butler. *Paul Robeson, All-American*. New Republic Books, 1976.
Goodman, Walter. *The Committee*. Farrar, Straus & Giroux, 1968.
Kanfer, Stefan. *A Journal of the Plague Years*. Atheneum, 1973.
Lee, Albert. *Henry Ford and the Jews*. Stein and Day, 1980.
Perlmutter, Nathan and Ruth Ann. *Anti-Semitism in America*. Arbor House, 1982.
Poliakov, Leon. *The History of Anti-Semitism*. Vanguard, 1965.
Richards, William C. *The Last Billionaire: Henry Ford*. Scribner's, 1948.

JEWISH-AMERICAN HISTORY

Baron, Salo W. *Steeled by Adversity*. Jewish Publication Society, 1971.
Benton, Barbara. *Ellis Island*. Facts on File, 1987.
Birmingham, Stephen. *The Grandees*. Harper & Row, 1970.
———. *Our Crowd*. Harper & Row, 1966.
———. *The Rest of Us*. Harper & Row, 1984.
Brandes, Joseph. *Immigrants to Freedom*. University of Pennsylvania, 1971.
Brinkley, David. *Washington Goes to War*. Alfred A. Knopf, 1988.
Cahan, Abraham. *The Rise of David Levinsky*. Harper & Bros., 1917.
———. *The Education of Abraham Cahan*. Jewish Publication Society, 1969.
Cohen, Elliot, ed. *Commentary on the American Scene*. Alfred A. Knopf, 1953.
Comay, Joan. *The Diaspora Story*. Steimatzky, 1982.
Congdon, Don, ed. *The Thirties*. Simon & Schuster, 1962.
Davidson, Gabriel. *Our Jewish Farmers*. L. B. Fisher, 1934.
De La Motta, Jacob. *Jews of the United States, 1790–1840*, Joseph L. Blau and Salo W. Baron, eds. Jewish Publication Society, no date.
Dimont, Max. *The Jews in America*. Touchstone, 1979.
Feldstein, Stanley. *This Land I Show You*. Doubleday, 1978.
Fisher, Louis. *Men and Politics*. Duell, Sloan & Pearce, 1943.
Gold, Michael. *Jews Without Money*. Liveright, 1935.
Gross, Theodore, ed. *The Literature of American Jews*. The Free Press, 1973.
Handlin, Oscar. *Adventure in Freedom*. McGraw-Hill, 1954.
———. *The Uprooted*. Little, Brown, 1952.

Bibliography

Hapgood, Hutchins. *The Spirit of the Ghetto*. Funk & Wagnalls, 1965.

Howe, Irving. *World of Our Fathers*. Harcourt Brace Jovanovich, 1976.

Janowsky, Oscar I., ed. *American Jew*. Harper & Bros., 1942.

Koppman, Lionel, and Bernard Postal. *Guess Who's Jewish in American History*. Shapolsky, 1986.

Kurtz, Seymour. *Jewish America*. McGraw-Hill, 1985.

Lebeson, Anita L. *Pilgrim People*. Minerva, 1975.

Levinger, Lee J. *A History of the Jews in the United States*. Union of American Hebrew Congregations, 1949.

Lewisohn, Ludwig. *The American Jew*. Farrar, Straus, 1950.

Libo, Kenneth, and Irving Howe. *We Lived There Too*. St. Martin's Press, 1984.

Lingeman, Richard. *Don't You Know There's a War On?* Putnam, 1970.

Manners, Ande. *Poor Cousins*. Coward, McCann and Geoghegan, 1972.

Marcus, Jacob R. *Memoirs of American Jews*. Jewish Publication Society, 1955.

Metzker, Isaac, ed. *A Bintel Brief*. Volume 1. Doubleday, 1971. Volume 2, Viking, 1981.

North, Joseph. *New Masses*. International, 1969.

Peters, Madison. *Justice to the Jew*. McClure, 1908.

Plesur, Milton. *Jewish Life in Twentieth-Century America*. Nelson-Hall, 1982.

Postal, Bernard, and Lionel Koppman. *American Jewish Landmarks*. Fleet, 1986.

Rischin, Moses. *The Promised City*. Corinth Books, 1964.

Sanders, Ronald. *The Downtown Jews*. Harper & Row, 1969.

————. *Shores of Refuge*. Holt, 1988.

Sarna, Jonathan D. *Jacksonian Jew*. Holmes & Meier Inc., 1981.

Schoener, Allon, ed. *Portal to America*. Holt, Rinehart and Winston, 1967.

Schwartz, Leo W., ed. *The Menorah Treasury*. Jewish Publication Society, 1964.

Simons, Howard. *Jewish Times*. Houghton Mifflin, 1988.

Sowell, Thomas. *Ethnic America*. Basic Books, 1981.

Steiner, Edward. *On the Trail of the Immigrant*. Revill, 1906.

REGIONAL

Blackmar, Betsy. *Resorts of the Catskills*. St. Martin's Press, 1979.

Carmer, Carl. *The Hudson*. Farrar and Rinehart, 1939.

Crist, Charlie. *Charlie's Days*. Catskill-Delaware Publications, 1983.

Ellenville Hebrew Aid Society. *50 Golden Years*. 1959.

Evers, Alf. *The Catskills*. Overlook Press, 1982.

————. *Woodstock*. Overlook Press, 1987.

Flexner, James Thomas. *The Hudson River and the Highlands*. Aperture, 1985.

Bibliography

Irving, Washington. *The Sketch Book of Geoffrey Crayon, Gent.* Library of America, 1983.

Kowat, John. *The Hudson River.* Viking, 1972.

Mitchell, John G., and Charles D. Winter. *The Catskills.* Viking, 1977.

Myers, Kenneth. *The Catskills.* University Press of New England, 1988.

Novak, Barbara. *Nature and Culture.* Oxford, 1980.

Simpson, Jeffrey. *An American Treasure.* Sleepy Hollow Press, 1980.

Valentine, Alan Chester. *Lord Stirling.* Oxford, 1969.

Wakefield, Manville B. *To the Mountains by Rail.* Wakefair Press, 1970.

Winters, William. *Years of the People.* Clay-Lor, 1977.

RESORTS AND ENTERTAINMENT

Adams, Joey, with Henry Tobias. *The Borscht Belt.* Bobbs-Merrill, 1966.

Allen, Woody. *Getting Even.* Random House, 1971.

Cohen, John, ed. *The Essential Lenny Bruce.* Bell, 1977.

Cohen, Sarah B., ed. *From Hester Street to Hollywood.* University of Indiana Press, 1983.

Ewen, David. *American Musical Theater.* Holt, 1959.

Friedman, Lester D. *Hollywood's Image of the Jew.* Ungar, 1982.

Green, Stanley. *The World of Musical Comedy.* Grosset & Dunlap, 1960.

Grossinger, Tania. *Growing Up at Grossinger's.* McKay, 1975.

Kober, Arthur. *Having Wonderful Time.* Dramatists Play Service, 1948.

Kofsky, Frank. *Lenny Bruce.* Monad Press, 1974.

Levenson, Sam. *Meet the Folks.* Citadel, 1949.

Lifson, David S. *The Yiddish Theater in America.* Yoseloff, 1965.

Lipsky, Louis. *Tales of the Yiddish Rialto.* Yoseloff, 1962.

Liptzin, Sol. *The Flowering of Yiddish Theater.* Yoseloff, 1963.

Mostel, Kate, and Madeline Gilford. *170 Years of Show Business.* Random House, 1978.

Pomerantz, Joel. *Jennie and the Story of Grossinger's.* Grosset & Dunlap, 1968.

Richler, Mordecai. *Notes on an Endangered Species and Others.* Alfred A. Knopf, 1974.

Rosenfeld, Lulla. *Bright Star of Exile.* Crowell, 1977.

Sandrow, Nahma. *Vagabond Stars.* Harper & Row, 1975.

Seldes, Gilbert. *The Seven Lively Arts.* Harper & Bros., 1924.

Taub, Harold J. *Waldorf-in-the-Catskills.* Sterling, 1952.

Tobias, Henry. *Music in My Heart and Borscht in My Blood.* Hippocrene, 1987.

White, Mark. *You Must Remember This.* Scribner's, 1985.

Wilson, Earl. *Let 'Em Eat Cheesecake.* Doubleday, 1949.

Bibliography

BIOGRAPHY AND AUTOBIOGRAPHY

Berle, Milton, with Haskel Frankel. *Milton Berle*. Delacorte, 1974.

Caesar, Sid, with Bill Davidson. *Where Have I Been?* Crown, 1982.

Cantor, Eddie. *As I Remember Them*. Duell, Sloan and Pearce, 1963.

———. *The Way I See It*. Prentice-Hall, 1959.

Edel, Leon. *Henry James: The Master*. Lippincott, 1972.

Fisher, Eddie. *My Life and Loves*. Harper & Row, 1981.

Gabler, Neal. *An Empire of Their Own*. Crown, 1988.

Gutman, Robert W. *Richard Wagner*. Harcourt, Brace & World, 1968.

Hart, Moss. *Act One*. Random House, 1959.

Hecht, Ben. *A Child of the Century*. Simon and Schuster, 1954.

Jessel, George. *So Help Me*. Random House, 1943.

Katkov, Norman. *The Fabulous Fanny*. Alfred A. Knopf, 1963.

Kazin, Alfred. *A Walker in the City*. Harcourt, Brace, 1951.

Klein, Maury. *The Life and Legend of Jay Gould*. Johns Hopkins Press, 1986.

Levy, Alan, and Jan Peerce. *The Bluebird of Happiness*. Harper & Row, 1976:

Lewis, Jerry, with Herb Gluck. *Jerry Lewis: In Person*. Atheneum, 1982.

Mason, Jackie. *The World According to Me!* Simon and Schuster, 1987.

Mason, Jackie, with Ken Gross. *Jackie, Oy!* Little, Brown, 1988.

Merrill, Robert, with Robert Saffron. *Between Acts*. McGraw-Hill, 1973.

Reynolds, Debbie. *Debbie*. Morrow, 1988.

Rivers, Joan, with Richard Merryman. *Enter Talking*. Delacorte, 1986.

Rollyson, Carl. *Lillian Hellman*. St. Martin's Press, 1987.

Samuel, Maurice. *Little Did I Know*. Alfred A. Knopf, 1963.

Schary, Dore. *Heyday*. Little, Brown, 1979.

Schildkraut, Joseph. *My Father and I*. Viking, 1959.

Silvers, Phil, with Robert Saffron. *This Laugh Is on Me*. Prentice-Hall, 1973.

Steffens, Lincoln. *The Autobiography of Lincoln Steffens*. Harcourt Brace, 1981.

Thomashevsky, Boris. *The Book of My Life*. Trio Press, 1937.

Tucker, Sophie. *Some of These Days*. Doubleday, Doran, 1945.

Tynan, Kathleen. *The Life of Kenneth Tynan*. Morrow, 1987.

CRIME

Asbury, Herbert. *Gangs of New York*. Alfred A. Knopf, 1928.

Cannon, Jimmy. *Who Struck John?* Dial, 1956.

Chidsey, Donald B. *On and Off the Wagon*. Cowles, 1969.

Cohen, Stanley, *The Game They Played*. Farrar, Straus & Giroux, 1977.

Eisenberg, Dennis, et al. *Meyer Lansky*. Paddington Press, 1956.

Katcher, Leo. *The Big Bankroll*. Harper & Row, 1959.

Kobler, John. *Ardent Spirits*. Putnam, 1973.

Moss, Frank. *The American Metropolis*. Collier, 1897.

Bibliography

Rosen, Charles. *Scandals of '51*. Holt, Rinehart & Winston, 1978.
Turkus, Burton, and Sid Feder. *Murder, Inc.* Farrar, Straus & Young, 1951.

JEWISH HUMOR

Adams, Joey. *From Gags to Riches*. Frederick Fell, 1946.
Allen, Woody. *Three Films*. Vintage, 1987.
Berger, Phil. *The Last Laugh*. Morrow, 1987.
Blumenfeld, Gerry. *Some of My Best Jokes Are Jewish*. Kanroy, 1965.
Eichhorn, David M. *Joys of Jewish Folklore*. Jonathan David, 1981.
Freud, Sigmund. *Jokes and Their Relation to the Unconscious*. Norton, 1960.
Learsi, Rufus. *The Book of Jewish Humor*. Bloch, 1941.
Levenson, Sam. *In One Era and Out the Other*. Pocket, 1973.
Loring, Elliott. *The Jokes of Sigmund Freud*. University of Pennsylvania Press, 1983.
Oliver, Donald, ed. *The Greatest Revue Sketches*. Avon, 1982.
Reik, Theodor. *Jewish Wit*. Gamut Press, 1962.
Richman, Jacob. *Laughs from Jewish Lore*. Funk and Wagnalls, 1926.
Spalding, Henry D. *Encyclopedia of Jewish Humor*. Jonathan David, 1969.
Wilde, Larry. *The Ultimate Jewish Joke Book*. Bantam, 1986.

FICTION

Aleichem, Sholem. *Some Laughter, Some Tears*. Putnam, 1968.
Bogardus, Mary. *Crisis in the Catskills*. Vantage, 1960.
Boris, Martin. *Woodridge, 1946*. Ace, 1980.
Jacobs, Harvey. *Summer on a Mountain of Spices*. Harper & Row, 1975.
Kennedy, William. *Legs*. Penguin, 1985.
Kober, Arthur. *Thunder Over the Bronx*. Simon & Schuster, 1935.
Ober, Norman. *Bungalow Nine*. Walker, 1962.
Offit, Sidney. *He Had It Made*. Crown, 1959.
Ornitz, Samuel. *Haunch, Paunch and Jowl*. Wiener, 1985.
Wallenrod, Reuben. *Dusk in the Catskills*. The Reconstructionist Press, 1957.
Wouk, Herman. *Marjorie Morningstar*. Pocket Books, 1955.

LABOR

Hurwitz, Maximilian. *History of the Workmen's Circle*. Workmen's Circle, 1960.
Shapiro, Judah H. *The Friendly Society*. Media Judaica, 1970.

ACKNOWLEDGMENTS

The Catskill Mountains resist agriculture and historians. Town and hotel records are scattered, old newspapers reside in attics, forgotten files, and college libraries. A few determined amateurs and academics are all that have kept the rich history of the Jews in the Mountains from disappearing.

I am grateful to all of them, but I must single out a few for special consideration. Dorothy Shapiro of Liberty, N.Y., was unfailingly intelligent and generous with her time and memory. Without her papers and references, this book could not have been written. Without the work of her colleague Michael Gold, many of its illustrations would not have come to light.

Alf Evers of Shady, N.Y., the premier historian of the Catskills, encouraged me at the beginning, and provided the initial impetus. He remains a model for any writer on the region.

Dr. Saul Gladstone contributed detailed ancedotes about his early days tummling alone and with Danny Kaye.

At the top I must also thank two who ingeniously ransacked institutional and private collections to produce the evidence I needed, and who were intrepid and efficient from the earliest stages to the last. During the progress of *A Summer World*, Emily Mitchell (a.k.a. Pearl Blau) became a writer and in the process the world lost one of its wittiest and most sensitive researchers. Susan Lukas, who does not know the meaning of fatigue, was able to unearth material thought to be lost or destroyed, both in New York City and in Greene and Sullivan Counties. She, too, is a writer, and it is characteristic of her selflessness that she put aside some of her own projects to help on this one.

John Weiner, whose family owned White Roe, supplied camp newspapers, memorabilia, and total recollections. Boris Thomashevsky's sons, Harry and Teddy, both men of advanced age but undiminished vigor, offered clear recollections of a time that now seems as remote as the Pleistocene Era. So did the kindly Ann Chester of Chesters' and George Gilbert of the Raleigh, both of whom, I am sorry to say, died while *A Summer World* was in preparation. Paul Glasser made many of the initial translations from ancient copies of *The Forward*. Frank Scioscia, owner of the Riverrun Book Store in Hastings-on-Hudson, N.Y., proved once again that no printed material is beyond his reach. Dr. Kenneth Libo of the National Museum of American Jewish History in Philadelphia, and Dr. Nathan Kaganoff of the Jewish Historical Society in Waltham, Mass., graciously furnished information and leads. The Catskill Art Society, the librarians at YIVO in New York City, at SUNY in New Paltz, N.Y., and in the towns of Liberty and Monticello, N.Y., were particularly helpful. A

Acknowledgments

few individuals, when they agreed to discuss Murder, Inc. or the basketball fixes, requested anonymity and I have of course honored their wishes. All others should be recognized and if I have overlooked any of them, apologies are extended along with a promise to make restitution in future editions. My gratitude to: Gordon Winarick, Milton Kutsher, Murray Posner, Tania Grossinger, Johnny Pransky, Bernard Seligman, Irving Shapiro, Lazarus Levine, Stuart Oderman, Bob Lazar, Michael Gold, Bea and Max Brender, David Gold, Rabbi Zvi H. Eisner, Max Lerner, Howard Fast, Pauline Winkler, Mal Z. Lawrence, Mac Roberts, Alan King, Henny Youngman, Jackie Mason, Peter Davis, Danny Vaccaro, Josh Greenfeld, Martin Silvestri, Paul Tush, Marty Reisman, Nat Perrin, Ira Wallach, Davey Karr, Larry Kelem, Howard Rapp, Arnold Graham, Sam Rosenshein, Mac Weiner, Lynn Weiner, Seymour Rexcite, Jerry Barondess, Sylvia Lescher, Cissy Blumberg, Barry Shoot, Dave Levenson, Manny Azenburg, Sylvia Herscher, Henry Stern, Janet Coleman, Sally Coleman, Steven Schlussel, Dave Pollack, Paul Maslansky, Bert Feldman, Barbara Wakefield Purcell, Richard Diamond, Lou Goldstein, Martin Stern, Carrie Fisher, Harvey Jacobs, Mordecai Richler, Suzanne P. Macht, Nina Lockwood, Donald K. Freedman, Miriam Burmeister, Sue Weber, Naomi K. Mandlebaum, Leslie Michaels, Danny Vaccaro, Louis Auster, David Falk, Selma G. Trautvetter, Daniel J. Tick, Patricia B. Roker, Simeon Baron, Paul Orseck, Robert M. Delson, Arnold Lapiner, Robert Lasson, Gloria Rosenthal, Abe Pincus, Fanny K. Caslen, Milton Horowitz, William R. Howell, Rose P. Collier, Harold Eiberson, Helen C. Sandford, Leslie Ben-Zvi, Margo Jones, Leon Wieseltier, Bob Rosenberg, Louis Sirroco, Robin M. Stein, Lorraine and Ed Fox, C. Budd, Leah Lipton.

Special thanks to the forbearing and thoughtful Linda Healey, in whose fertile brain this book first took shape, to her assistant Amy Peck, to designer Cynthia Krupat, and, finally and foremost, to May, to Lili and Nate and Andy, for more reasons than there are pages.

INDEX

Index

Index

Index

gambling, 41, 103, 118–19, 123, 210–20, 237–39

Gard, Eddie, 211–17

Gedymin, 35

Gelb, Alan, 289–90

"Gentile and Jew" (Beecher), 40

Gentleman's Agreement, 200–1

Gentle People, The (Shaw), 156

German Jews, 20–21, 26, 27, 32, 37–38, 77, 94, 170–72, 283

Germany, 12, 13, 22, 26, 170–72, 173, 252

Gerow, Ben R., 121

Gersh, Harry, 126–28

Gershwin, George, 95, 129

Gershwin, Ira, 162

Gerson, John, 47

ghetto life, 36–37, 44–46, 50–52, 56–60, 62–63, 64, 115, 133, 155, 157, 173, 180, 285

Gilbert, George, 275

Gilford, Jack, 189

Gimbel, Adam, 27

Gladstone, Saul, 141, 161–62

Glass, Irma, 261

Gleason, Jackie, 150

Glickburg, Selma, 275

Gold, Joseph, 84

Gold, Michael, 153

Gold, Nathan, 33

Golden Boy (Odets), 156

Goldsmith, Jack, 211–12

Goldstein, Jonah, 174

Goldstein, Lou, 5, 249

Goldwasser, Bill, 278

Goldwyn, Samuel, 156, 157, 166

Gompers, Samuel, 81

Gordin, Jacob, 56

Gordon, Waxey, 121

Gorin, Igor, 192

Gould, Jay, 33–34

Grand Hotel, 42

Grand Island, N.Y., 19–20, 21

Grand Union Hotel, 40

Grand View Hotel, 148

Grandview House, 47

Great Gatsby, The (Fitzgerald), 111

Great Metropolis, The (Moss), 44–46

Green Acres, 279, 280

Greenburg, David, 269

Greene, Graham, 112–13

Greenwald, Dennis, 294

Griesinger, Theodor, 29–30

Grossheim, Schreiber & Co., 27

Grossinger, Harry, 246, 263

Grossinger, Jennie, 75–76, 145, 174, 176, 207, 234, 237, 246; business management of, 149–53, 166; character and personality of, 7, 146, 147, 243, 261–63, 278; death of, 8, 261, 263

Grossinger, Malke, 7, 75, 144–45, 146–47, 152, 261, 263

Grossinger, N.Y., 7, 153

Grossinger, Paul, 237, 262

Grossinger, Selig, 7, 75–76, 146–47, 263–273

Grossinger, Tania, 207, 208–9, 210–11

Grossinger's Hotel and Country Club, 5–9, 75–78, 84, 128, 129, 235, 242–43, 249–50, 258; airstrip at, 204–5; decline and demolition of, 6, 8–9, 153, 277–79; expansion and growth of, 144–47, 166, 167, 234; founding and early development of, 7–8; golf course at, 146–47, 167, 277; "guest days" at, 145–46; hospitality at, 144–45, 147, 169, 278; playhouse at, 6, 150, 207, 209, 261, 266, 277; promotion of, 150–53, 206–9; sale and redevelopment of, 6, 8–9, 277–79; sports at, 152–53, 210–11; sumptuous meals at, 6, 147, 151

Guardarramas, Pedro, 272–73

Hackett, Buddy, 221, 225, 234

Haganah, 194, 204

Hajak, Frank, 145, 146

Index

Index

Index

Index

Index

Polan, Jerry, 119–20

Poland, 22, 38, 65, 77, 193

Polish Jews, 21, 38, 45, 77, 170, 282–83

Pomerantz, Joel, 152–53

Poole, Ernest, 52

"Poor Man's Shangri-la" (Gersh), 126–28

Poppo, Angelina, 293

Posner, Leonard, 189

Posner, Murray, 204, 241

Pransky, Johnny, 122, 169–70

Pransky's Troubadours, 169

President Hotel, 184

Pressburger, Shmuel, 281

Price, George, 51

"Prizefight Sketch, The," 161–62

Prohibition, 86–88, 96, 103, 116, 121, 123

Protocols of the Elders of Zion, 94–95

quarries, 32, 34, 54

Quintanilla, Luis, 172

"Race Prejudice at Summer Resorts" (Rhine), 42–43

Raleigh Hotel, 6, 110, 131, 235, 255, 275

Rankin, John, 202

Rapfogel, William, 284

Rapp, Charlie, 183–84, 234

Ray, Richard, 31

Reed, Lou, 159

Reik, Theodor, 107–9, 226–27

Reinhardt, Max, 61

Reise, Gretchen, 268

Resnik, Joseph, 248

resorts: competition among, 123–24, 149, 152, 166–70, 247–48; conventions at, 266–68; decline and closing of, 9–10, 148–49, 153, 257–61, 263–73, 275–79; myths and legends of, 158–59, 166, 205; organized activity at, 5, 99–105, 110–11, 129, 145; ro-

mance and courtship at, 8, 28–29, 63–64, 69–70, 72, 102, 103–5, 133–43, 180–81, 182, 204, 249–52, 267–68; social ritual at, 63–64, 65–68, 103–5, 127–28, 190–91, 249–52; staffing of, 101–2, 103, 125, 137, 139–41, 144–45, 176, 181–82, 190, 206, 242, 268–70

Rexcite, Seymour, 118–19

Reynolds, Debbie, 9, 234, 264

Reynolds, Quentin, 262

Rhine, Alice H., 42–43

Rich, Frank, 292

Richler, Mordecai, 8, 241–46

Richman, Harry, 102, 247

Riis, Jacob, 51

riots, anti-Semitic, 49–50

"Rip Van Winkle" (Irving), 17–18, 55, 158

Rise of David Levinsky, The (Cahan), 66–68

Rivers, Joan, 229–32

Robbins, Mac, 9

Robeson, Paul, 189, 197–98, 208

Robinson, Jackie, 7, 262–63

Rockefeller, Nelson, 7, 246, 247–48, 261–62

Rock Hill Jewish Boarding House, 47–48

Rodman, Elias, 22, 23

Rodman, Esther, 22

Rolnik, Joseph, 52–53

Rome, Harold, 223–24

Roosevelt, Franklin Delano, 154, 174–75, 205

Rosen, Charles, 212, 218

Rosenfeld, Morris, 36–37, 69–70

Roshi, Eido, 260

Ross, Barney, 152–53

Rosten, Leo, 4, 37–38, 86

Roth, Al "Fats," 213, 216–17

Roth, Philip, 245

Rothafel, Samuel L. "Roxie," 186

Index

Index

Index

PHOTOGRAPH CREDITS